COLLECTION MANAGEMENT

THE
CAT WHISPERER

THE
CAT WHISPERER

*Why Cats Do What They Do —
and How to Get Them to
Do What You Want*

Mieshelle Nagelschneider

BANTAM BOOKS

NEW YORK

Published in the United States by Bantam Books,
an imprint of The Random House Publishing Group,
a division of Random House, Inc., New York.

BANTAM BOOKS and the rooster colophon are registered
trademarks of Random House, Inc.

Library of Congress Cataloging-in-Publication Data

Nagelschneider, Mieshelle.
The cat whisperer : why cats do what they do—and how to get them to do
what you want / Mieshelle Nagelschneider.
p. cm.
Includes index.
ISBN 978-0-553-80785-1—ISBN 978-0-553-90723-0 (e-book)
1. Cats—Behavior.   2. Cats—Psychology.   I. Title.
SF446.5.N34 2011
636.8—dc22   2010038747

Printed in the United States of America on acid-free paper

636.8   www.bantamdell.com

2 4 6 8 9 7 5 3 1

First Edition

Book design by Jo Anne Metsch

For my late father, Blaine,
who by his example gave me the gift of giving
and experiencing unconditional love
among the animals

God made the cat
in order to give man the pleasure of
caressing the tiger.

—FERNAND MERY

Preface

by Dr. James R. Shultz Jr.

☙ 🐾 🐾 🐾 ☙

IT'S 6:15 ON A TUESDAY MORNING: I AWAKEN TO MY ALARM CLOCK radio and the weatherman announcing that today will be another rainy, gray, blustery day in Portland, Oregon. As I lie in bed, I can hear the raindrops crashing down upon the roof of my small house, and the sounds of Ferrari, my calico kitten, scurrying behind an unpacked box of clothes on the bedroom floor. I have been a veterinarian for barely four months at this point and have yet to find the time to unpack and get fully settled in the house. Heading to the kitchen for my early morning English muffin and coffee, I see Ferrari go flying down the hall dragging the now mostly empty sack of English muffins: "Hey! You come back here with that!" I try to scold her while laughing.

After breakfast, just as I am throwing my stuff in my truck to head off for the veterinary hospital, my pager goes off. I grab my phone and call the hospital. As a new graduate, my mind races with thoughts of what might be going on—a poisoning? a traumatic injury? will it require surgery? Melanie, the office manager, answers my call. "Hey, Mr. Walker is here with Gum Drop and he wants to speak with you right away."

"Is Gum Drop okay?" I ask.

"He seems fine," she says, "but Mr. Walker is in a bad mood again."

I can hear her sigh through the phone. *Not* the exciting medical case I had been hoping for, I muse, as I pull out of the drive and head for the hospital. Mr. Walker has been in several times because of problems with his cat Gum Drop, who has been urinating outside the litter box.

I arrive at the hospital twenty minutes later and make a mad dash through the pouring rain to reach the back door of the clinic. Putting on my lab coat, I catch a glimpse of Mr. Walker pacing back and forth in the waiting room. As the receptionist escorts Mr. Walker into one of the exam rooms, I can see that he seems upset, but I pop into the room with the exuberance and optimism only a new grad can possess. "Hi, Mr. Walker," I begin. "How is Gum Drop?"

With his gaze fixed squarely on the floor, he states, "I would like you to put him to sleep."

At this point, all eighteen pounds of Gum Drop are rubbing up against me on the exam table while he purrs away. Totally taken aback I reply, "What, why, is he sick, is something wrong?"

Gum Drop turns out to be the one patient they forgot to tell us about in veterinary school. He actually isn't sick at all, quite the opposite, in fact. Gum Drop is a beautiful, healthy four-year-old Ragdoll with quite the personality.

"Ya!" Mr. Walker states with an angry look on his face. "There is definitely something wrong. Gum Drop peed on my brand-new laptop computer last night and it's ruined. Three thousand dollars down the drain."

I tell him I am very sorry about his new laptop, but that euthanizing a totally healthy cat is not the answer. I add that it's likely that he sprayed or urinated on the computer because he saw how much time Mr. Walker spent at the computer and he just wanted to get some of that attention for himself.

"Dr. Shultz, you have run all your tests, even tried some medications, and you can't find anything wrong with Gum Drop, correct?"

"That's true," I reply, but . . . "It's behavioral," I blurt out, sounding more like a defense attorney than a veterinarian.

"Well, can you fix it?" Mr. Walker asks.

I explain, again, that behavioral problems are more complicated and take time. We could try a different medication. Perhaps Xanax or Prozac might help. As I keep talking more about medications and what little I have been taught about feline behavior in school, Mr. Walker calmly scoops up Gum Drop and puts him in his carrier. On his way out the door, he looks back at me and says, "Look, Doctor, you did your job, this cat's just crazy. If you won't put him to sleep, I will just have to drop him off in the woods somewhere. Then he can pee on whatever he likes." That was the last time I ever saw Mr. Walker or Gum Drop.

Tragically, Gum Drop's story is far from isolated. Depending on the source, four to nine million cats are euthanized each year in the United States. As I have seen firsthand, a disproportionate number of those lives are lost due not to medical issues, but to behavioral ones. When you have a cat who is destroying your new furniture or urinating around the home or attacking your other cats and you can't identify the reason, it can become exceedingly frustrating. And our responses to these problems can make things even worse because, from the cat's perspective, they are very stressful and therefore likely to lead to further problems. As a result, many clients feel there is no hope, and that they just can't continue living with these sometimes very destructive and damaging behaviors. Out of desperation they will end up releasing the cat to fend for itself, relinquishing it to a shelter, or in some cases even electing euthanasia. Only by first understanding feline behavior can we truly hope to change our cat's behaviors in the future—which is where Mieshelle comes in.

My experience with Gum Drop occurred in 1998, and it would be another five and a half years before I would have the pleasure of meeting Mieshelle Nagelschneider. At the time, there were many studies and programs designed to address the training and behavioral issues surrounding dogs, but far fewer studies focused on cats, and that remains true even today. Historically, dogs have been trained and utilized by humans to perform tasks, from pulling sleds to locating persons after disasters strike. Cats, on the other hand, have been viewed by many as too difficult to train and almost impossible to deal with when it comes to modifying their behavior patterns. In a nutshell, we understand the rule to be: *Dogs want to please, and cats will do as they please.*

Mieshelle, however, has taught me that many of our ideas about cats are wrong. To be totally honest, I was initially a bit skeptical of her. She would come to see me for veterinary care with one or more of her many animals in tow, and we would inevitably end up talking about cat behavior and the complex social structure woven into every multicat household. She would offer to help with behavioral cases and though I thought her ideas were interesting, I would respectfully decline. After several such visits with Mieshelle, however, I found myself, and members of my staff, asking her advice about some of our feline behavioral cases—advice that turned out to be very helpful. And soon I began referring clients with cats who had behavioral issues to her. She demonstrated time and again that she possesses the unique ability to communicate with cats on their level. To achieve this, one has to actually get inside the mind of these animals and see the world as they see it. One needs to literally learn to think like a cat.

Over the course of many years, Mieshelle has developed and refined her unique ability to think like a cat. You will be introduced to this concept in Chapter 1. On numerous occasions I have witnessed the life-changing benefits Mieshelle's techniques can bring to cats and their sometimes very frustrated owners.

The positive effects are multiplied when her behavioral advice is part of a program that is developed in consultation with a veterinarian. In Chapter 6, Mieshelle emphasizes the importance of frequent visits to the veterinarian and the need to rule out any possible underlying medical causes of undesirable behaviors in your cat. From bad teeth and mouth pain to urinary tract infections, many behavioral issues *do* have a medical explanation. Your veterinarian is the person who can best help you determine if your cat is in good health. Once you and your veterinarian have determined that your pet is medically healthy and the issue is behavioral, you can begin to employ one or more of the techniques Mieshelle outlines in this book to start the behavior modification process. From the basics, such as out-of-the-box urination and defecation, to the more complicated issues, like overgrooming, and aggressive and destructive behaviors, Mieshelle can help you and your cat navigate through these distressing problems and emerge with a happier, more rewarding relationship.

I am so excited that Mieshelle has written this book, and I was honored when she asked me to contribute the preface. I am confident this book will add immeasurably to the understanding of feline behavior, and enhance not only the lives of cats but the lives of their owners. If resources such as this book had been available in 1998, perhaps Gum Drop and his owner could have utilized some of the methods outlined in this book to resolve their issues, and continue to coexist harmoniously. As the owner of Meridian Park Veterinary Hospital, I will be recommending this book to *all* of my cat clients. Mieshelle, thank you!

Foreword

by Gwen Cooper

I ALWAYS SAY THAT IF A GENIE WERE TO POP OUT OF A BOTTLE and grant me a single wish, it would be that each of my three cats would be able to talk for just twenty-four hours. In nearly fifteen years of living with cats, I've found them to be charming, loving, insanely funny, surprisingly sweet and sensitive—when they want to be—but not easy to understand. "Why do you love licking plastic bags so much?" I would ask Scarlett, my eldest. Vashti, my "middle child," I would ask, "How come you only want to drink water from *my* glass, even though the water in my glass and the water in your bowl come from the same tap?" My youngest, Homer, taught himself to use the toilet a few years back but alternates—based upon seemingly random whims—between the toilet and his litter box. Why today? I sometimes want to ask when he comes in to use the toilet while I'm applying makeup. Why now?

As a writer, I'm inclined to believe that mystery and beauty are close cousins. We go through life liking and even loving any number of things that we can clearly explain (I love these sweatpants because they're so comfortable!). But our great, life-changing loves—everything from food to paintings to people—always carry a tinge of the unknowable. Relationships between humans and cats are grounded in just this kind of mystery. I often think that the reason there are "cat lady" stereotypes and no real corresponding "dog guy" stereotypes is that dogs are relatively simple to figure out. Dogs, like humans, are pack animals, and when dogs or humans are left on their own, they form small social groups remarkably similar to each other's. But cats are not pack animals, and so the relationships between cats and their humans are not as easy to put in a nutshell. Cats don't necessarily place pleasing us—simply for the sake of making us happy—high on their list of priorities. A cat who snuggles with pure, purring contentment on the pillow next to us at night is a lovely thing to behold, to hear, and to touch—but he's there for his own pleasure, not for ours. Cats will do many things that make us delighted to be in their presence, and the only thing that's clear is that they're *not* doing them just to delight us. Most of the time, not knowing exactly how they think, we're left to take our best guess or else simply accept their love and companionship without asking *why*.

Not knowing the why is the element of mystery in human/feline relationships, and in that mystery there is beauty—that of the improbable and inexplicable.

It's all well and good for me as a writer to wax poetic about things like mystery, beauty, and love. But sometimes that mysteriousness interferes with our day-to-day living situations. Sometimes cats engage in behavior that just is not charmingly mystifying but annoying, destructive, or downright threatening to us, our property, and the other humans and animals we live with. In not fully understanding why they do these things, we can find it difficult to know how to put an end to such behaviors without losing our temper or inadvertently harming the cat in the process.

This was a lesson I learned about a decade into living with cats, at a point in my life where mystery and love overlapped. In short, I fell in love with a man, decided to marry him, and moved into his home with my three cats. My husband-to-be, Laurence, had never lived with cats before. But I assured him—with the utter sincerity of ten happy years of cat parenting behind me—that everything would be okay. In fact, I may have even said something like, "You'll hardly even know they're here."

Is there a patron saint of the accidental lies that lovers tell each other? If not, that patron saint should probably be a cat.

As far as one cat went, the transition was simple. Vashti, a long-haired and green-eyed white beauty who always looks as if she's just stepped out of an ad for high-end cat food, fell in love with Laurence at first sight. From Laurence's perspective, there was something so flattering in having this exotic creature take to him so quickly and firmly that he was equally smitten in return.

But there were two other cats in my brood, and their transition into life with a new human was far more problematic. Scarlett is a gray tabby, quintessentially catlike in both her appearance and her temperament. She is the cat that people who don't like cats imagine — regal, moody, independent, and often aloof. She's incredibly loving and gentle with me, but many a hapless visitor has attempted to pet her and pulled back a bloody arm for his trouble. (For help with aggressive cats, see Chapter 7.)

If Scarlett was sure of one thing in life, it was that this stranger she was suddenly forced to live with had no right to touch her, approach her, or even share living space with her. Scarlett, an imperious little cat used to getting her own way, enforced this code with Laurence the same way she did with my other two cats — anytime Laurence approached her, walked past her, or otherwise got what she deemed to be too close to her, she hissed and raked him angrily with her claws. Sometimes she even did this in the middle of the night when Laurence was walking to the bathroom, which made the experience doubly nerve-racking for him.

And then there was Homer, my baby. Homer has been blind all his life. Being blind, he was more apt than the other two to pick up on emotional cues as a determiner of his own moods, and the tension between Laurence and Scarlett, and between Laurence and me when he would angrily demand to know why I was doing nothing to discipline Scarlett for her infractions, was palpable.

The tenser our home was, the tenser Homer became. And the

tenser Homer became, the more he was inclined to pursue Scarlett—one of the sources of the tension—in ways that were more aggressive than playful. And the more aggressive Homer was, the more tense Scarlett became, and the more likely she was to try to feel secure by slashing out at Laurence.

Scientists refer to a cycle like this—a series of events where one reaction creates another, which creates yet another and so on until it circles back to the original reaction—as a positive feedback loop.

Laurence and I simply called it "bad."

We went around and around like this for a few months, until one day I read an article on the website Salon.com about Mieshelle Nagelschneider. The article referred to her as the "cat whisperer," and told amazing stories of seemingly hopeless cases where Mieshelle, a cat behavior expert with decades of experience, had stepped in and helped patient owners correct everything from their cat's urination in inappropriate places (on a sleeping owner's face in one case, if I'm remembering correctly) to aggression against other cats, or even against their owners.

Desperate for anything that might work, I found Mieshelle's website and arranged for a consultation. The first thing to do, Mieshelle instructed me, was to spray a synthetic pheromone product strategically around our home, because certain pheromones have a calming effect on cats, making them feel more relaxed and less aggressive. Even if this didn't solve all of Scarlett's problems with Laurence, it might at least help resolve some of the problems that had sprung up between Scarlett and Homer.

Mieshelle's second recommendation for reducing the tension between the cats was one that I'd never come across before and haven't since. She called it "facilitated allogrooming," and she patiently explained that I was going to learn to be the "social facilitator" for my cats, creating a "group scent" that would make the cats feel more comfortable with one another and reduce their hostility. She then gave precise instructions—replicated in the book you are holding—about how I should go about applying what her own clients call the "Nagelschneider Method."

Mieshelle's third major recommendation, in order to make peace between Laurence and the cats, was that Laurence begin participating in the feeding of the cats. If Laurence fed them once or twice a day, it might help Scarlett distinguish between Humans Who Are a Threat (all humans except me, in Scarlett's opinion) and Humans Who Are a Food Source. The idea was to remove Laurence from the Threat list and add him to the Food Source list, not in the hope that Laurence and Scarlett would become friends per se, but in the hope that Scarlett would at least respect and trust him enough not to slash him with her claws every time their paths crossed.

At the time, some of Mieshelle's many prescriptions (for she offered more than three) seemed simple enough that I couldn't believe I hadn't thought of them myself. But of course, I was thinking about things from the perspective of a frustrated human. Mieshelle was the one who came into our situation and thought about it like a cat.

And lo and behold, within only a few short weeks the interventions she suggested worked! Scarlett doesn't exactly *like* Laurence these days, but she's come to tolerate and grudgingly respect him (and from a cat like Scarlett, that's a big concession!). She sits and sleeps untroubled when Laurence happens to walk past her, and even rubs affectionately around his ankles when he comes home at night.

And Homer, once the tension in our home eased dramatically, resumed playing happily with Scarlett and dropped his aggressive behavior. Our cats are calm and happy, and Laurence and I are calm and happy as well. We were married over a year ago, and it was Laurence who made huge poster-sized photos of each of the cats to display at our wedding, in order to "introduce" our guests to the three newest loves of his life.

For all that, though cats remain seductive enigmas to most of us — always tantalizingly beyond the reach of complete understanding — a few humans are blessed with an almost preternatural gift for answering the riddles of the feline mind. Mieshelle is one such person. Had I been lucky enough to have this book you're holding now, when I first moved in with Laurence, I could have saved my husband and my cats (and myself) months of frustration and tension.

Love is born of mystery, and our cats are mysterious and loved in equal measure. But sometimes the greatest blessing of all is a bit of light thrown into a dark place. Mieshelle Nagelschneider holds that light. Allow her to share it with you.

—GWEN COOPER
Author, Homer's Odyssey: A Fearless Feline Tale, or
How I Learned About Love and Life with a
Blind Wonder Cat

Contents

Contents

THE
CAT WHISPERER

Introduction:
On Cats and How I Learned to See
Through Their Eyes

[Mowgli] grew up with the cubs . . . and Father Wolf taught him his business, and the meaning of things in the jungle, till every rustle in the grass, every breath of the warm night air, every note of the owls above his head, every scratch of a bat's claws as it roosted for a while in a tree and every splash of every little fish jumping in a pool, meant just as much to him as the work of his office means to a business man.

— RUDYARD KIPLING, The Jungle Book

YOU MAY BE READING THIS BOOK JUST BECAUSE YOU LOVE CATS and have an interest in them. Or maybe you're at your wit's end with your cat, who just sprayed your partner's expensive new shoes, or has been urinating outside the box, or destroying your brand-new couch. You've tried everything. You feel guilty. Have you been shouting at your cat? Even spanked or thrown things at your cat? You may worry that you've mistreated your cat, that she will never learn to behave, that you will have to give up your partner or even the love of your life (that is to say, your cat). But I'm going to help you understand your cat, why she does what she does, and, in most cases, what you have been doing to cause or exacerbate the problem behavior, so that you and your cat—or cats—and the members of your household can live happily together. I'll give you the same easy-to-implement solutions that I've been giving my own consulting clients for twenty years.

The changes I recommend will help you, your cat, and the people in your life to coexist peacefully. If you have more than one cat, I will show you how to help them live more happily with one another. Cats who have never groomed another cat will lick away at their buddies—and grow all the closer. Cats who have slept apart will curl up next to one another. Your cats will blossom into the creatures they were meant to be—more confident and gregarious, more relaxed and secure—more catlike. My clients tell me that the cats I first met or heard about during their consultation with me are, as a result of it, not the same cats they have now. When I do a follow-up visit, I can see that it's true. In place of a battlefield, I walk into a feline Eden. The cats are either lounging in their separate time-shared locations or are curled up next to one another. There's no hissing, fighting, or attacking.

I'm also going to show you that there is a behavioral cure for nearly all cat behavior problems, that medication is rarely necessary, and that euthanasia, too often resorted to, should be reserved for the rarest of cases. In short, I am here to tell you that in most cases, help for your cat can be highly effective, natural, humane, and lasting. Oh, and on average, change takes about thirty days, which means that sometimes it may take longer than a month and sometimes less. Ready?

Let's begin with the case of Susan and Nada.

Nada was a small, silver tabby cat who had licked a deep wound into one of her legs. She lived in a mansion in a wealthy suburb of Seattle—a sprawling modernist building painted a glossy off-white, and perched on the highest hill around. When Susan opened the door for me, I saw that the minimalist aesthetic continued indoors: vaulted ceilings, huge and nearly empty white-walled rooms, and carpet in a grassy green color. There was a couch in the giant living room, and nothing else. Even before I saw Nada, I knew that she was probably one very understimulated cat.

Like all supposedly "domesticated" cats, she was, as I'll explain, still essentially a wild animal, and yet she was now a kind of prop in the minimalist vision of an owner with clear ideas about how some humans, at least, might like to live. I was reminded of the Tom and Jerry cartoon called "The Push-Button Cat," in which a manufactured Mechanocat is advertised this way: "No feeding, no fussing, no fur." That is, no *cat*. The only human being who could understand Nada fully would be one who had done time in solitary confinement.

When Nada finally padded in, she was dwarfed by the cavernous space. Nada was a little shy at first, but soon warmed up enough to approach me and rub against my shins. I knew what she was doing: *I'm going to place my scent on you (and hold on to some of yours) so I'll feel more comfortable. If I didn't trust you as much as I already do, I'd be rubbing that chair leg over there instead, to soothe myself.*

I reached down to pet Nada's cheeks. "Thanks, Nada," I said.

We watched as Nada walked to a far suburb of the living room. Susan and I made small talk. When I looked at Nada again, she had plopped down to lick her hairless, inflamed leg. Susan looked at me and shrugged. On the phone, she had described Nada's damaged leg as "raw meat," and she wasn't exaggerating. Nada, with her sandpapery cat tongue, had licked a four-inch spot on her thigh into an open wound. Susan had taken Nada to a vet who had told her that the problem was not a medical issue—there was no food or skin allergy involved. The problem was behavioral. Poor Nada was exhibiting a classic compulsive behavior, overgrooming.

Cats frequently overgroom themselves (or chew or pull out their hair) in an exaggeration of the self-washing that cats will perform in order to feel better in stressful situations. It's one of several kinds of compulsive behaviors engaged in by cats who experience repeated or continuous stress from frustration (*I want to but I can't*) or internal conflict (*I want two mutually exclusive things*). Like humans, who overeat or indulge in other forms of addiction, cats tend to displace their anxiety into activities that temporarily relieve that anxiety. Most of the time overgrooming creates an area that's nearly bald or covered with peach fuzz—sometimes a small area, sometimes the cat's entire chest and stomach—but only rarely an actual lesion or wound, like Nada's. Hers was the worst case I had ever seen. And now it was up to me to figure out why Nada was so stressed, and to deal with it before she did permanent damage to her leg. I just needed to apply what I knew about cats—what you'll soon know, too—to the environmental triggers that Nada was responding to and help to direct her attention away from the overgrooming behavior.

Surveying the Zenlike home, I began to collect clues. I noticed that there was not one cat toy in sight. (There was almost *nothing* in sight.) In general, the house appeared to have been set up without any of a cat's interests in mind. Also, as Nada sat down to lick her leg, Susan cooed at her and went over to pet her soothingly. When I asked Susan to play with Nada so that I could see how the two of them interacted, I realized she didn't understand how to properly play with a cat. Using a wand, she snapped the feather at the end back and forth at dizzying speeds, always out of Nada's reach. (To learn how to properly conduct the all-important prey sequence, see Chapter 5.) Perhaps the most significant clue came when I learned that Nada's overgrooming had begun *after* the family adopted another cat. He and Nada hadn't gotten along, so the two cats were now kept on separate floors.

Each clue to the source of Nada's problem gave me information about what had to be changed—not by Nada but by Susan. Because the tense relationship between the two cats was surely causing Nada a lot of stress, Susan needed to help the cats learn how to get along with each other. To keep Nada's mind and body occupied, give her ways to relieve her stress, and build her self-confidence, Susan would definitely need to deal with the near-total lack of environmental stimulation available to Nada, and change the frustrating way she played with her cat. Susan also had to stop giving Nada attention whenever she saw Nada licking herself.

Luckily, I was able to show Susan how to see the world through her cat's eyes. Once Susan became aware of how she had contributed to Nada's problems, she scrupulously followed my three-part C.A.T. Plan for behavior change, creating a more stimulating and entertaining environment for Nada and the other cat, and playing with them in more effective ways. Susan also followed the reintroduction plan along with the important group-scent technique I explain in Chapter 4, which is designed to bring two unfriendly cats back together so they can have a fresh start at becoming good friends. Within weeks Nada had become a much happier cat, and within a few more weeks her terrible skin lesion began to heal properly, until it healed completely a short time later. I was able to do the work I had done with Nada, from diagnosis to behavioral treatment, because I had learned to see a cat's life through its eyes—which you can do, too.

For me the process began very early on, at around the time I began to speak.

My Animal Family

I come from a family steeped in animal life. My uncles and grandfather on my mother's side were cattle ranchers and trophy-snagging rodeo riders in the Jordan Valley of eastern Oregon. My great aunt and uncle on my father's side were both horse-stunt riders, like their parents before them. They all loved their horses. Their grandson and my cousin, Tad Griffith, now works closely with animals as the owner of a stunt and production company in California.

In my hometown of Redmond, Oregon, my aunt Vicki has long raised Toggenburg goats, the oldest known breed of dairy goat, which hails from the Swiss valley of the same name. Aunt Vicki also had real pet cats, the kind that lived in the house. While the goats thrilled me, the cats—*indoors, for Bastet's sake!*—made me bitter with envy. Every Sunday our family would visit Aunt Vicki's house and I would spend the entire time playing with the cats. One of her cats, Elsie, didn't like to be stroked or held. My older cousin Samantha would remind me, "That Elsie's a biter, Mieshelle." But I found that you could indeed pet Elsie—just not for very long. You had to pay attention and watch for certain responses that indicated she had had enough. So I would pet her for a while, but stop *before* I saw her ears go back or her tail flick. Samantha bragged to everyone that I had the magic touch with Elsie, but I knew I was just petting her in the way she liked, and stopping before she got agitated. It was my first lesson, at the age of five, that you can't *make* a cat do what you want, but you can change your own behavior slightly to get a result that will make both of you happy.

On the Farm

I always felt a little introverted and shy around other children. But luckily I was let loose to run with the animals on the farm our family lived on, in the high desert of Central Oregon, and they became my companions. I found the animals a lot more interesting and easy to get along with than my much older brothers or the other children around me. And how many people have a wild hummingbird for a friend?

Yes, I really did! I first remember being aware of it when I was about four and I kept hearing a fluttering in my ear, like a vibration, as I walked around outdoors. The first time I saw it, I thought it was a bug or a bee, but others told me the creature, iridescent and green, was a hummingbird. It would fly over me and in front of me and hover for a bit like it was trying to tell me something. After a while, it would zip off, only to return again, making that odd sensation in my ear. My dad used to tease me because a hummingbird followed me around, which embarrassed me because I was sure he thought it was ridiculous. But one day I heard him bragging about me and the hummingbird to some visiting relatives, and I realized that there was something special about what had happened.

My father was a gruff, hardworking man. The only time I saw him show emotion, no, *melt*, was in the presence of animals. Maybe that's partly why I came to love animals, too. Dad kept all the kinds of animals that you'd expect to find on a family farm, and when I say he *kept* them, I mean he could not bring himself to put any of them on our dinner table. He and my mother had both grown up on cattle ranches, where raising animals for meat was simply what you did, but he grew too attached to the calves on our farm to turn them into tabletop beefsteak, even though he'd bought them for that purpose. So ten calves grew into ten cows, and those cows simply became among the largest of my pets. What we really had was not a working farm, like the one our next-door neighbors had, but a large petting zoo.

Of course we also had horses, Missouri Foxtrotters. I learned to love horses, and to ride at a young age. We had a Rocky Mountain horse named Sinbad who'd been given to my father because he was supposedly "no good." He had an injury to his hoof, so it was uncomfortable for him to run. Dad decided that that made him safe for me. A horse is a fantastic introduction to the world of animals. As any horse person knows, the big animals have a special, palpable sort of consciousness. I can stand next to a horse and feel the energy of a sentient heart and soul.

We had two sheep—I organized picnics with them—and many different types of fowl as well. The geese and the ducks and I sat in the dog house together, and I swam with them in their dirty pond (much to my mother's distress). The chickens needed me to spend time with them, too, and I climbed on the roof to crow with the rooster.

Then there was the enormous bull in a corral next to the house. No one could even go near him without being charged. My parents warned me many times to stay away. Even the dogs were terrified of him. But I felt sorry for him. So I hatched a plan: I would hop hop hop into his corral like a bunny. And he wouldn't be afraid or bothered at all. We had bunnies in our barn, after all, and he'd seen them, and I knew no one could be afraid of or angry at a *bunny*.

It wasn't so much that I was a lunatic. I was four.

First I took some paper and drew two bunny ears, which I colored pink as the inside of a bunny's ears. Then I cut them out and asked my mother to tape them on. "I need to be a bunny," I said, already savvy enough to speak to my mother only on a need-to-know basis. "How sweet," she said, and taped the bunny ears to my hair. I also knew I had to be a white bunny, like the ones in our barn, so I mashed several handfuls of cotton balls into a tail and attached it to my white ballet leotard.

It was a nice, warm summer's dusk when I crawled through the bars of the bull's corral. Careful not to look directly at him, I stayed low and hopped around the perimeter, as bunnylike as I could be, while he regarded me warily. Just going about my rabbity business. And then he stood up and walked over to me. I stopped hopping. His massive head blocked out the sun. His big nose reached down to me. His giant, light pink wet nostrils flared and pinched, flared and pinched. He snorted into the dust. And then I reached up and patted the fur at the top of his nose.

It was utterly exhilarating.

When my parents found me, I was sitting in the dirt at the animal's feet, stroking his head and caressing his neck and throat. The family lore of "Mieshelle and that bull" would echo in my ears throughout my childhood, instilling in me my first sense that I had a special gift and passion. Of course my parents were horrified. But why did I have to play with a big old dangerous smelly bull? Because my parents wouldn't get me a cat.

Unfortunately, the animals on whom I most wanted to deploy my special gift were cats—the one pet animal we didn't have on our farm. That's why, when I was four, I used to sneak across the street to a house where our neighbor ran a daycare service for children who were around the same age I was. I wasn't going there to play with the other children; I went to play with our neighbor's Siamese cat. Eventually the daycare owner told my mother that I could no longer come and play with the cat for free; my mother would have to pay for my being there, just like the rest of the parents did. But my stay-at-home mom didn't think it made much sense to pay for me to be allowed to pet the kitty across the street, so she told me that I was no longer allowed to go to the daycare lady's house.

So I began camping out in the woman's driveway. Sometimes the willowy Siamese would see me through the window and come outside to receive my petting. I used to bring a brush that belonged to my Barbie doll (which I'd quickly abandoned as uninteresting) and the cat would purr and knead on me until finally I was not allowed to sit on the driveway anymore either.

One night, when I was four-and-a-half, my mother said, "Come here to the phone, Mieshelle. It's Santa Claus."

Standing in my nightgown, I took the phone from her.

"What do you want for Christmas?" a voice said.

"I want a cat." I clarified that. "A *real* cat."

"You want a *real* cat?" said the voice, amused. This was already annoying.

"Yeah. A real one."

"Oh," he said, "I think you want a *stuffed* animal cat."

"I don't want any more stuffed cats. I want a cat that purrs and eats milk."

"I don't think your mother would want a real cat in the house."

"I want a real cat."

It went on like that for some time. Then, seeing no progress, I hung up on Santa.

For Christmas I got a large, pink, stuffed cat, a sad product of a misbegotten union between a domestic shorthair and the Pink Panther.

Not at all what I wanted, but now that my dad is gone, I wish I had kept that stuffed cat.

My campaign for a real cat continued for several years, and remained fruitless. One year, after my mother had enrolled me in the Blue Birds, the little-girl wing of the Camp Fire Girls, we were all given blank autobiographical scrapbooks we had to fill in.

There was one page called All About Me. My page read:

My best friend is: *My cat*

What I love to do the most is: *Play with my cat*

The first thing I do when I get home from school is: *Brush my cat*

If I could be anything I would: *Be a cat*

I'm not making that up. But I still didn't *have* a cat, a very sore point for me. I would soon, however, embark on a secret cat-taming project involving the feral cats in the canyon behind our house.

Cheshires in the Canyon

Like a lot of little girls, when I was a child I wanted to be Snow White. But not because of the prince. I wanted to talk to the animals. Lucky for me, our house sat at the edge of a shallow canyon, lush and green, with a nearly level floor, and that canyon was my haven to explore. The canyon was teeming with wildlife—deer, coyote, rabbits, butterflies, and hummingbirds—and, of course, our own pets—dogs, horses, rabbits, sheep, and calves—wandered there, too. The neighbor's white peacocks visited daily. They were all my friends.

Occasionally, I saw cats in the canyon. For me it was like spotting a unicorn—something rare, rarely seen, and unpossessable. These feral cats were really what drew me to the canyon. They popped their heads out from behind rocks and trees, and then, like the Cheshire Cat in the *Alice in Wonderland* coloring book that my father and I colored in together, they vanished just as quickly. And like the Cheshire Cat when he was invisible, they watched me from the dark places.

One day, I got an idea. I'd throw a tea party like the one in the Alice story, and I would invite the Cheshires of the canyon. So early one June morning, just after my fifth birthday, I gathered up all my plastic teacups and plates, a tablecloth, my stuffed animals, and a stack of peanut-butter-and-jelly sandwiches and descended into the canyon, where I sat atop a flattish volcanic rock by a small stream. On each of my plastic plates I put a morsel of PB and J that I cut with a pink plastic knife, and then the stuffed animals and I sat there, looking at one another, waiting for something to happen. Nothing did.

I ran back up to the house to get some milk. Maybe that would be the draw. As I was heading back down the trail to my rock, I saw a buff-colored shorthaired cat sitting at one of the plates, eating some of the peanut butter and jelly. A cat! As soon as he spotted me, he bolted and ran away.

But I knew I was onto something. Over the weeks that followed, I learned I could get closer to some of these flighty tea party guests— the ones who were more relaxed—if I remained at a distance until they gradually got used to me. But I also learned that some cats are more reactive than others and I couldn't get closer to them without their running off. In time, as they got used to my presence, even the highly reactive cats would not run as far and would return more quickly.

Looking back now, I'm sure that together we were discovering the behavior modification techniques of counterconditioning and de-sensitization. Counterconditioning pairs something attractive, such as food, with a negative stimulus (such as the presence of a little girl) in order to change an animal's negative feelings about the stimulus into something more positive. As the weeks went by, I learned that tuna fish sandwiches were the sandwich of choice; that milk bested Kool-Aid in all taste tests; and that as long as I made no sudden moves, I could sit and dine with my striped and whiskered friends with rela-tive ease and the happy certainty that no one would run off. After some time had gone by, I even managed to get some of them to let me pet them.

A year later we moved away from the canyon to a new house in the country. I missed my Cheshires and I renewed my campaign for a cat of my own. "What about all those cats in the barn?" my father grumbled one day. They were feral, almost as wild as the canyon cats, but after what I had learned from the Cheshires, I decided that I could make even better friends with the barn cats, if I just paid at-tention to what they liked. This was the beginning of several years of close observation. I copied their behavior; I tried to put myself into their heads and see the world through their eyes; and soon I felt that the barn Cheshires were becoming my family. If I got to the feral kit-tens early enough and played with them, I could make some of them quite friendly. I was about eight years old when neighbors noticed how friendly my barn cats were, and started asking me if they could adopt one or two as a pet. I even caught my dad cuddling one of the cats I had socialized.

The Egyptian word for cat is *mau*, which means "to see." Egyptians were fascinated by cats' eyes, most likely because they believed that cats could see into the human soul.

One morning, I saw a young, gray tabby cat crawl into a ten-inch irrigation pipe in our yard. I knew I had a small window of time be-fore water would surge through those pipes, as it did daily. Crisis! I called, whispered, dangled a leaf, patted the ground—I tried everything to lure the little cat out, hoping to save its life. Nothing seemed to work. Then, without really thinking about it, I made eye contact with her, closed my eyes briefly, wishing for her to come out, and then opened my eyes again.

And the cat blinked back at me, slowly.

I blinked again, slowly, and immediately the little cat came tumbling out of the pipe. She allowed me to move her to safety, and only a few minutes later the water came rushing through the pipes.

My parents saw how happy I was and, to my amazement, they let me keep her. I named her Curly, for her curious little spiral of a stump tail. Many years later, I heard the experts say that slowly blinking and then looking away is a powerful form of cat communication, but by that time I had long known that a cat that blinks slowly at another is feeling content and relaxed. The blinked-at cat, in turn, interprets this as meaning she is not in harm's way. Blinking can immediately reassure a cat and relax a tense situation. I still use this technique today, when a client's cat won't come out from under the bed.

The Vet Assistant Years

I was in seventh grade when I got my first glimpse of a world in which you could be with animals all day and even get paid to do it. My friend Jamie asked me to help her take her cat to the vet. Once there, a woman came into the exam room to take Shadow's temperature. She was very impressive. "How long did it take you to go to vet school?" I asked her. "I'm not a vet," she said. "I'm a vet tech." A vet tech, or veterinary technician, would become for me a kind of ideal profession, but from my vantage point of twelve years of age, it sounded impossibly far away.

The years passed quickly, however, and when I was nineteen, studying psychology at a college in Portland, Oregon, I got my first job at a veterinary clinic. Though all the vet techs were more experienced, it soon became apparent that the animals were somehow more responsive to me. When no one else could get a cat out of its cage, or hold it still while its blood was being drawn, the vet would call me. By touching a cat's body or just reading its body language, I could feel how a cat was feeling and sense what he was communicating—and I adjusted my touch accordingly. The clients as well as the vets began to ask for me to be in the exam room with their cats. I was able to calm cats who would not let anyone else close enough to inject them with vaccine or trim their nails. Clients also began to ask if I would pet-sit their cats when they were out of town.

For the next several years, I learned to do surgical prep, assist during surgeries, take X-rays, trim nails, give vaccinations, administer subcutaneous fluids, perform dentals, draw blood and run tests, and fill prescriptions. At the two clinics where I went next, I was named Head Vet Tech, and my responsibilities grew to include veterinary hospital administration and training new vet techs.

Over time, more and more of the clients asked me to watch their pets while they were on vacation. I would eventually make many thousands of house calls for cats with special needs. Then came the day that started me on my true path.

That day I happened to answer a call that came in to the vet's office. It was from a woman, in obvious distress, who was driving in circles around the parking lot of the local Humane Society. "My cat's in a crate," she said. "I have to give him up." She began to cry.

"Why do you think you have to give him up?" I asked.

"He's been urinating in the house for over eight years," she said. "My husband said either he or Bagel would have to go. I've been to every vet around, they ran tests on Bagel, I did what they told me to do."

"Can you do something for me?" I said. "Can you park and let Bagel out of his crate?"

She pulled over and let Bagel out of his crate. Soon he was purring so loudly I could hear him through the phone.

"Now he's curled up in my lap purring and kneading my leg," she said. I could easily imagine it. Kneading is soothing to cats. It's a behavior that begins in nursing, when a kitten rhythmically pushes and pulls its forepaws against the mother's teat, both to push the queen's skin away from the kitten's nose and to help stimulate milk flow. Cats ever after associate kneading with happy feelings. And cats purr not just when they're content, but when they are under stress and want to soothe themselves.

Now that she could clearly see and feel what was at stake, I asked her what she had done to stop the problem. She said she had followed her vet's advice: She'd added another litter box. Where had she put it? Right next to the original. Were there any other cats in the house? Yes, there was Arnold. Had she noticed Arnold sitting on any of the pathways to the litter boxes? Yes, in fact: He often sat in the hall right outside the mud room where the cat boxes were located.

Bingo. Adding litter boxes hadn't addressed the real issue, which was Arnold's territorial competition with Bagel. I suggested she spread the litter boxes out, have three, not just two, and ideally put them in separate rooms. I strongly recommended that she clean the smell from the areas where Bagel had been urinating, and told her the best way to do that. And I offered her a number of other suggestions that we will discuss in the following chapters. The woman thanked me and hung up the phone. A week later she called back to say that for the first time in eight years, Bagel was using the litter boxes. A few months later, the woman stopped by the vet's office and asked for "the girl who saved my cat and my marriage." When the vet techs looked at me, she ran over and hugged me, telling me that Bagel was completely reformed and that Bagel and Arnold were even getting along wonderfully for the first time.

That's when I knew it was time to choose between my job at the vet's office, and the work I was doing on the side, caring for cats in my clients' homes. I was spending so much time fielding clients' questions and tending to their cats, I felt like I was working two full-time jobs. And the second job was something nobody else I knew was doing. So, in my early twenties, I quit my "real" job and began to work for myself. I never again worked for anyone without four legs and the ability to purr.

The Cat Behaviorist: Filling a Void in Feline Behavior Expertise

I was able to help Bagel's owner because of what I had learned caring for the cats in my clients' homes. It was my habit to visit the homes once or even twice a day. Sometimes when I showed up on the first day, I would find the litter box packed high with feces and urine clumps, and I would immediately clean it out, and keep cleaning it every time I visited. When the clients returned, they'd thank me for cleaning the box, thinking, I guess, that I had saved them only some labor. But a few days later they'd call to report, "Hey, my cat stopped pooping outside the box!" That's how I learned how important a clean box is.

I learned a lot of other things during my pet-sitting days, often by trial and error. Ever since I was young I'd been unable to watch a cat without asking myself, *If I was a cat, why would I have done that?* If a cat was urinating outside the box, I'd ask, *Why would she want to do that? Poor access? Too obese to get into the box? Intimidation?*

I watched and made connections.

I also got to be very good at reading cats' body language. I could immediately tell if they were stressed, and began to understand whether they were upset about something in their environment, another cat or both. While I was nominally providing in-home cat care, I became something of an interior decorator. I made minor changes to each client's house to suit the needs of the cats (I made even more changes when a client left on an extended trip). And the cats stopped exhibiting behavior issues. When the owners came home, and saw, to their surprise, the positive changes in their cat's behavior, they became fiercely loyal to me. Over the years, I had in effect conducted a longitudinal study of thousands of cats, keeping track of which changes in their environments affected which behaviors.

Take the Maine coons that had defecated outside the box for over a year. Despite my suggestion, the owner had refused to separate the cats' litter boxes from their food. "They really like their food in the bathroom with the litter boxes," he insisted. My instinct told me otherwise. I also recommended that he give his big cats more and bigger litter boxes, but he never got around to it. Then he went away for three weeks. In the feline utopia I set up for his cats, not once did anyone eliminate outside of the box.

"What did you *do*?" he asked on his return.

"I followed my advice." After that, he did, too.

I didn't always understand exactly *what* may have initially caused the cat's problem. But I nearly always proved that it was largely environmental. Change the environment, change the cat's behavior.

Many of my clients reported that their cats were aggressive, nipping them or chasing other cats. Others reported that their cats hid, were shy or timid. But when I got a chance to rearrange the cats' environments, as I'm going to teach you to do here, they were calm, happy, and utterly friendly toward people and other cats.

"I don't know what you did," they'd call me up to say, a few hours after they returned home. "This is not the same cat I left here. She's so *confident* and so *friendly*, so affectionate and loving. What did you *do*?"

I even got cats to play. A shocking number of clients solemnly informed me that their cats didn't play, and some people would even illustrate—by *wiggling the cat's toy in its face.* But cats seem to have evolved to view anything that hurls itself into a predator's face as inedible, so in order to get a cat to play, you have to make the toy appear to be fleeing the cat.

Then there were the clients who would instruct me, "They all eat off the same plate." But I'd ignore the instruction and feed them separately as a matter of basic cat psychology, especially if the cats were *visibly* competing or looked uncomfortable eating from the same food bowl. When the owners returned, they'd always ask, "Why are the cats sleeping together? They've never done that before. And what did you do to make them stop fighting?" By eliminating the competition between them, I'd resolved the hostility, too.

I've now spent nearly two decades making house and phone calls to solve cats' behavior issues, affording me invaluable experiential information. In the last twenty years, not counting my observations of feral cat colonies in childhood or of my own cats, I've logged over

33,000 hours observing cats and investigating clients' reports of their cats' behaviors. If a psychologist worked over a twenty-two-year period while listening to patients' self-reports (as opposed to the more useful witnessing of their behavior) for a prodigious thirty clients per week, fifty weeks a year, she would reach a similar number. I have written this book to bring this knowledge to you and your cats.

The Cat Behavior Clinic

For the last twelve years, I've run The Cat Behavior Clinic, which is devoted to researching and solving cat behavior problems in person or by phone. Since I opened the clinic, I have worked with thousands of clients and vets from all over the world. My success rate on behavior issues—success meaning total or partial improvement—naturally depends greatly on whether my clients follow my instructions, but when they do, it's near 100 percent for most behavior issues, and well over 90 percent for even the most difficult problems.

The vets I've had the pleasure to work with are fantastic, dedicated people. But behavior issues aren't their specialty. Going to a non-behaviorist vet with a cat behavior problem is like getting psychiatric advice from your general practitioner. In fact, I'm often sought out by vets who have behavior issues with their own cats. The first piece of information they invariably give me arrives apologetically: "I didn't get much training in animal behavior, you know." Few, if any, veterinary schools even offer a course specifically on feline behavior. I'm amazed at this state of affairs. The instincts and behavior of the world's most popular pet remain a mystery to the caregivers who could make the biggest difference in the lives of cats and their owners.

Cat owners live in an informational vacuum. The fact is in North America there are only several dozen people trained in feline behavior. The good news is that while the field of cat behavior is relatively young, it is, finally, here.

I'm now privileged to help clients all over the world with their cat behavior issues, and I love my work, because I still have a fierce love for animals and I know from experience that most behavior issues can be easily solved. Today I have nine animals (some rescues), including six well-behaved cats (Jasper Moo Foo, Rhapsody in Blue, Clawde, Barthelme, Lady Josephine, and Farsi Noir), their playmate Piccolo (a Teacup Chihuahua), a soulful Great Dane named Jazzy, and a Monitor Lizard. The pure hearts of all these animals bring me to my next subject.

What "Good Death"? The Crisis of Feline Euthanasia

It would be so nice if something made sense for a change.
—Alice, *Alice in Wonderland*, LEWIS CARROLL

A behavior problem, in a cat, is all too often tantamount to the pet having a terminal disease. The most common drug-based solution for behavior problems in cats surrendered to animal shelters is the drug used for euthanasia.[1] "Euthanasia" is Greek for "good death" or "dying well." I can think of few more ironic and tragic misuses of language. No death due to easily prevented behavior problems can be considered a "good death." I'm passionate about showing cat owners how to prevent, or even stop causing, behavior problems that often lead to euthanasia.

Cats are more often killed for unwanted behavior than for any other reason. Imagine if the number one killer of human beings was not disease but behavioral problems. We'd view that as a mental health epidemic. But every sixty seconds in the United States, between four and nine cats are given the "good death." Since you began reading this section half a minute ago, between six and thirteen more cats were killed. That's at least 4 million, and perhaps as many as 9 million, cats killed every year.[2]

The Shelter and Abandonment Crisis

About 10 million pet cats are surrendered to shelters in the United States every year, or about one out of every eight. Only one out of four of the cats sent to shelters will find a home, while the other three will face the "good death." Euthanasia in shelters is the leading cause of death among American cats. Studies suggest that one-fifth to one-third are killed because the owners cannot cure or tolerate unwanted behaviors like out-of-the-box elimination or spraying, the top two issues I deal with at The Cat Behavior Clinic. Here's the really tragic part: Most behaviors are easily treated, especially these two.

At the time of this writing, in the United States there are 88 million pet cats (compared to about 35 million in France, Germany, Italy, and the U.K.), and there are another 40 to 70 million homeless or feral cats.[3] By contrast, there are 75 million dogs in U.S. households, but relatively few homeless or stray dogs.[4] The truth is, though cats now outnumber dogs in many countries, they are still not as highly valued as dogs. There are several reasons for the difference in treatment between cats and dogs. Primary among them is that during the course of over ten thousand years of domestication, dogs have learned to watch and react to every smile and scowl on a human's face, so arriving at a mutual understanding with dogs is relatively easier than with cats. The behavior of pack animals just seems more natural to group-oriented animals like ourselves, who are also highly responsive to the body language and expressions of those around us. Both humans and dogs "live in extended family groups," veterinary behaviorist Dr. Karen Overall points out, "provide extensive parental care, share care of young with both related and nonrelated group members, give birth to altricial [immobile] young that require large amounts of early care and sustained amounts of later social interaction, nurse for an extended period before weaning to semisolid food (dogs do this by regurgitation; humans use baby food . . .), have extensive vocal and nonvocal communication . . . and have a sexual maturity that precedes social maturity."[5]

Cats, who are not pack animals, are less emotionally dependent on us, and may therefore sometimes seem less responsive to us, and so less personlike. Most owners simply lack awareness about why cats behave the way they do and how to change their behavior when necessary.[6] Overcoming this lack of understanding is one of my major concerns in writing this book.

According to the American Humane Society, cat owners are less likely than dog owners to tag or microchip their pets with identification, so shelters are unable to return found cats to their owners. Whatever the reasons for the high rate of abandonment of cats at shelters, cats are more often euthanized, given up for adoption, and thrown out of the house than dogs, and far more likely for *behavioral* problems than are dogs. (As an aside, people also take their dogs to vets for medical care at considerably higher rates than they take their cats, which might be one reason that behavioral issues related to medical problems get habituated, instead of being nipped in the bud.) There are no lucky rendered cats: Even those sent to no-kill shelters don't live happily-ever-after. Shelters don't solve behavior problems, and spraying and unwanted elimination are such turnoffs for the adopting humans that "problem" cats just get recycled through one shelter and home after another.

But that's not the only horror facing our cat population. Hundreds of thousands or even millions more each year are thrown out of houses to become strays, and, often, to die prematurely. These outdoor cats, even those still fed by their owners, may have a very difficult time adjusting emotionally and physically to outside life. They will not live as long or as healthy a life as an indoor cat. In most cases, this decision is inhumane, not to mention avoidable. It's a terrible life for them.

It's time for a change. Cat owners must take responsibility for their cats and for themselves. People who choose to own cats should use all means available to remedy their cat's behavior issues. This is particularly true when you consider that the unwanted behavior is often a result of something the *owner* has done or is still doing—a major topic of the next chapter. Many owners surrender their pet to the shelter before even seeking behavior help.

Why I Wrote This Book

So why this book; why now? Quite simply, I have not been able to find a book on cat behavior that provides the information about behavioral and environmental change that cat owners need to know—one packed with information that's complete, accurate, and up-to-date—and not accidentally designed to cause more problems than it solves. The book I wrote is the one I always wanted to read.

This book is for all the cat owners I've seen who were hungry for information. My own clients have been crying out for years that there is "nothing out there" for cat owners. They have even admitted to having tried dog obedience techniques (old-school, inhumane dog techniques at that) on their cats! (I debunk the usefulness of an alpha dog-training model for cats in Chapter 3.)

I hope that the book you hold in your hands will be your cat be-havior bible—the one reference book you will read and reread, dog-ear (so to speak), give to your friends, and use with all the cats that you will know over the years. In the vacuum of veterinary knowledge about the behavior issues of household cats, the invaluable experi-ential knowledge of the dedicated feline behaviorist is a critical re-source. And while most of the academic studies that have been written about cats have been about ferals, the cats I have observed, helped to retrain, and written about here are household cats. More-over, most cat studies involve only a very small sample size of two dozen cats or fewer, over limited periods of time. My thousands of cat encounters, including many that took place with the same cats over many years—what researchers call a longitudinal study, and all but absent from the feline behavior literature—will add a good deal to this fragmentary picture. So in this book, I'll combine my own ex-perience with the latest in the scholarly literature. Where I disagree with certain experts or with urban myths about cats, I'll point it out in a Conventional Advice Alert. For the curious who want to consult sources, I have included selected endnotes.

In the rest of this book, I will explain how my three-part C.A.T. Plans can give cat lovers real solutions to the seven major behavior problems—litter box issues, spraying, multiple-cat tension, aggres-sion, yowling, destructive and otherwise unwelcome behaviors, and compulsive behaviors. I'll also tell you how to keep behavior issues from recurring. My approach is holistic, in the sense that it is dedicated to dealing with the whole picture. I'll show you how to consider not only the behavior issue at hand, but other aspects of the cat's life that may have caused or may be exacerbating the behavior.

By reading about real-life examples from my decades of experience, you will learn how to look at your cat's environment through its eyes, and then see what is wrong. I will then teach you how to change your cat's environment and your own behavior so that the two (or more) of you can live together in complete harmony. Soon you will fall in love with even the "problem cats" all over again.

ONE

Mind-Throwing:
Inside the *Being* of the Cat

"Curiouser and curiouser!" cried Alice.
—Alice in Wonderland

WHAT IF OUR ANCESTORS SURVIVED AND EVOLVED ACCORDING TO how well they were able to put themselves into the minds of the animals they relied on for survival? What if those who did so best were our first scientists? Some anthropologists are now proposing just that. Louis Liebenberg, an expert on the tracking techniques of the Kalahari (or San) Bushmen of Africa and an expert tracker himself, suggests that "it is in the art of [animal] tracking that we may find the wellsprings of the scientific quest"[1]—of man applying the scientific method far earlier than previously imagined. The renowned Italian historian Carlo Ginzburg concludes, "we perceive what may be the oldest act in the intellectual history of the human race: the hunter squatting on the ground, studying the tracks of his quarry."

Liebenberg proposes three stages of tracking. The first is simple tracking: following visible tracks in ideal conditions. Next is systematic tracking, which uses the same analytical process to interpret many types of spoor evidence under difficult conditions.

The third kind of tracking is a lost art, known today to only a handful of people in the world: one term for it is speculative tracking. Here the tracker views the last visible evidence of spoor and adds to it his knowledge and instincts about the animal's behavior, habits, and instincts, its terrain, the season, weather, soil type, and more. Instantly weighing these "complex, dynamic, and ever-changing variables," the tracker attempts to put himself into the mind of the animal in order to "see" its motivations and actions. One writer notes that "[a]nthropologists who have worked closely among the hunters of the Kalahari and elsewhere have found that hunting is not simply an instinctual practice but also involves considerable and occasionally great learning and intellectual insight"[2]—comparable to the methods we now use in history, psychology, and quantum physics.[3] As Liebenberg explains, "The modern [Kalahari] tracker creates imaginative reconstructions to explain what the animals were doing [at the time they laid down the last spoor sighted], and on this basis makes novel predictions"[4] of what they will do next—and where they will go next. This imaginative, intuitive act involves executing "complex mental operations with lightning speed."[5]

In fact, speculative tracking involves precisely the kinds of mental acts described by Malcolm Gladwell, in *Blink: The Power of Thinking Without Thinking*, as "thin-slicing"—the rapid and largely unconscious sifting of enormous amounts of information to reach a conclusion invisible to the less experienced. It wasn't until I read *Blink* (which says thin-slicing expertise arrives in a mere ten thousand hours of practice) that I saw there might be an explanation for how I developed my intuitions on cat behavior after thousands of hours of practice.

The hunters themselves have another name for speculative tracking: "mind-throwing." The hunter *throws* his mind ahead of himself, into that of the animal, in an attempt to become one with it. Imagine—science midwifed by man's attempts to see through the eyes of the animals. Animals that, we should remind ourselves, men and women of antiquity often viewed as sacred. Let me be clear: I'm not a proponent of hunting in the modern world. But could hunting-related empathy with animals be part of our own naturally selected abilities? The anthropologist Claude Lévi-Strauss famously said that human societies revered animals not because they were good eating but because animals "are good for thinking." He was referring to how humans understand the world around them, and their places in it, through their knowledge of animals.

Unfortunately, we've forgotten a great deal of that lore, or obscured it from our awareness. And cats in particular are now hard for us to read. Among the clouds obscuring our view of cats' minds is the common belief that cats behave and are motivated just like dogs. I'll discuss this further in "Forget the Alpha Model: Dogs are From Mars, Cats are From Venus" (Chapter 3). Another is imagining that they think and feel like humans. We call this anthropomorphism. The third is the belief that cats are just inexplicable—that they are so quirky and eccentric that no one could possibly understand them. (For example, nearly everyone who heard of the writing of this book actually expressed shock that there could be such a thing as modification of cat behavior—everyone but the clients and the vets I work with, that is.) Finally, many people believe it is the cat who is responsible for its behavior, and who must be trained to change its behavior. None of these beliefs is accurate. Cats are not like dogs, or like us; but they are hardly inexplicable. And it is relatively easy to change most of their behaviors—but doing so almost always requires changing our own behaviors and the environment we have created for the cat. Do that, and the cat will respond naturally with the behaviors we want to encourage.

Anthropomorphism and Its Pleasures—and Pitfalls

I always enjoy the anonymous "Excerpts from a Cat's Diary" that frequently makes its way around the Internet. It begins with the "Dog's Diary," which simply lists a dozen things like "Wagged my tail!" and "Milk bones!" each followed by the refrain, "My favorite thing!" The more cunning cat's diary is an amusing example of thoughts and motives attributed to a cat:

> Day 983 of my captivity. My captors continue to taunt me with bizarre little dangling objects. They dine lavishly on fresh meat, while the other inmates and I are fed some sort of dry nuggets.
>
> The dog receives special privileges. He is regularly released— and seems to be more than willing to return. He is obviously retarded. The bird has got to be an informant. I observe him communicate with the guards regularly. I am certain that he reports my every move. My captors have arranged protective custody for him in an elevated cell, so he is safe. For now . . .

If you're a cat lover, you nod and smile as you read this, remembering, re-experiencing your own cats past and present; you feel the pleasure of recognition. How true, you think to yourself! And yet . . . it's not.

I understand that it's hard not to think of animals as being personlike, with personlike feelings and, especially, *thoughts*. It's fun and touching to imagine that my cat Josephine (on the cover of the North American edition of this book) is *my little girl* who is *so sweet* and *such a good little girl*, who is *nice*, who *loves me* and *wants to express her love to me*, who *really feels my love*. I'm especially moved when I imagine she's lonely without me and needs my love. And there are definite benefits to such anthropomorphism, for the pets as well as their owners. One is simply that when we feel empathy for an animal's suffering and feelings, we become curiously more human, and more happy. The feeling of connection seems to be a source of well-being for us, with animal owners in general showing better psychological health than nonowners. Imagining that our cats feel and think as we do helps us feel closer to them and contributes to our taking better care of them.

However, we must be modest in our anthropomorphism. Why? The first reason is that since cats are *quite* different from humans, we're often wrong in our projections. Readers who prefer to enjoy the fantasy that their cats are just like them may wish they could skip what I am about to say, but I aim at a higher target: I want to restore to cats their catness. Rather than trying to imagine cats as micropeople, I insist that we let cats be cats, allow them their otherness. What dog trainers say about dogs is equally true for cats: They are not small people. All domestic animals remain profoundly other—but the only partly domesticated cat is especially so. The cat, as Rudyard Kipling said, "walks by himself."

Is your cat sweet? I have a hard time thinking of mine in any other way. Why else would something be so cute, so charming, so endearing and affectionate to us, other than because it is, and intends to be, sweet? But guess who the sprayers in your house often are. Give up? The sweetest ones. Anxious cats find ways to soothe themselves and increase their confidence. One way is to spray. Another is to always be near and rub up against the human who gives the affection and food, and has the soothing voice—that is, to be sweet toward the human. So the most cuddly cat may also be the most intractable sprayer. The original breeder of Ragdoll cats claimed, in the 1960s, that the queen cat who founded the breed was especially affectionate by nature. But that cat had become unusually attached to her owners only after experiencing the great trauma of surviving serious injury in an automobile accident. Socialization of a cat is faster "if the kitten encounters stress [or] has a strong emotional experience such as hunger, pain, or loneliness,"[6] agrees veterinary behaviorist Dr. Bonnie Beaver, author of a highly regarded guide to cat behavior for veterinarians. Is that sweet, or anxious? Affectionate, or needful of reassurance? Some people conclude that Siamese are more friendly than other breeds—but at least some of that friendliness may be because they have thin coats and seek human heat.

A few years ago, Jeffrey Masson, a former psychoanalyst and the author of several popular books on the emotions of animals, turned his close powers of observation to the emotional lives of cats. Early on in his book *The Nine Emotional Lives of Cats*, I thrilled to his statement of his mission: "Too many people tend to see cats as uncomplicated creatures with few emotions, at least none worth thinking about in any depth. I am convinced that, on the contrary, cats are almost pure emotion."[7] He's absolutely right. In the last decade, research on many animals has shown they lead rich emotional lives. Beyond mere fear and anxiety, they are capable of grieving the loss of their human or animal companions; they can become depressed; they can experience anticipation and pleasure. And as you'll see in the rest of this book, they experience dramatic emotional responses to changes in their environment. Cats share with humans the same brain neurochemistry that allows us to feel.

But cat emotions are at once far less complicated and far more foreign to us than most people—including, I think, Masson—often make them out to be. For example, Masson writes that a cat newly brought into the home sits endearingly atop his chest as a calculated and "cunning ploy," a "decision" the cat made in its "cunning little feline heart," and that the cat ceases the behavior the moment he "knows" he will be allowed to stay in the home. Masson also remarks that one of his cats does not like to play while others watch. Why? Because, he says, she views play as "undignified." While Masson understands that cats feel no guilt, remorse, shame, or sheepishness, he believes a cat can be "embarrassed" or "humiliated" by missing a jump—as evidenced, in Masson's view, by the cat's subsequent licking of its paws. Masson believes that a cat that visits its absent owner's room and meows (or "raises her head and gives a small, hopeless cry"), then travels through the house (or "wanders the apartment restlessly") until returning to that room, is showing powerful "evidence" of "love." And he says that cats stare "out of affection."

In reality, cats do not think about us, at least not in our sense of thinking, because they lack the cognitive framework necessary to such thinking. They certainly cannot process the thought, *I'm going to get back at you*, or *I know you hate this, but I do it to spite you*, or *Here is yet another act of mine that, yes, you* should *take personally*. Like a Zen master in meditation, the cat merely regards us, without thought or judgment at all. "I have lived with several Zen masters," Eckhart Tolle has said, "all of them cats." That we cannot often identify with this state of being is unfortunate, but that doesn't make it any less true. Cats do not design and plan cunning ploys, nor calculatedly manipulate us with aforethought. If they miss a jump, they are startled, frightened, perhaps even hurt, and they lick themselves afterwards because washing is a form of self-soothing. They are not embarrassed. That is what *humans* feel when they fall before others. Cats cannot feel humiliated any more than a gerbil or a fern can. Cats just *are*. The patron saints of cats are not Freud but Buddha or Lao Tsu, not Dr. Phil but, yes, Eckhart Tolle.

> *A cat may look at a king. I've read that in some book,*
> *but I don't remember where.*
>
> —*Alice,* Alice in Wonderland

As for staring, when a cat stares at another cat, the act is both intended and received as assertive, even threatening; it never signals affection. The staring cat means to intimidate. While cats often look at humans with harmless intent, a cat who feels aggressive may well stare at a human threateningly as well. In any event, there's no reason to believe that a cat, which is pure instinct, would somehow modify its wiring to stare at humans with *affection*. Moreover, what we imagine as the cat staring at us may not even be the case, since a cat's field of vision is quite wide. While apparently staring at us, the cat may actually be taking in an entire room, or focusing on a point somewhere between himself and us. The misunderstanding about what staring— and being stared at—means to a cat is in fact responsible for yet another of the many mistaken ideas about cats. How many times have you heard it said (or said it yourself) that cats invariably find the one guest in the room who doesn't like cats in order to jump into that person's lap—just because they are so perverse? What's actually going on in those situations is that the person who doesn't like cats or isn't interested in them has probably not bothered to make eye contact, and has therefore not been perceived as being hostile or threatening.

Finally, what about feline love? While it is happily impossible even for me not to believe that my cats "love" me, I know that if I use a meaningful rather than casual definition of *love*,* I cannot say that Josephine's meowing at my absence or the expression in her eyes when I pet her is evidence of love rather than, respectively, anxiety over food or the loss of a companionship to which she's attached, and simple animal pleasure. But as any human over the age of twenty-something knows, the difference between love and pleasure is all the difference in the world.†

If typical descriptions about cat cognition referred instead to badgers or cows, or the very intelligent pig, we could see the absurdity of them—and we'd see, too, that statements like Masson's "the cat is happy to be himself" apply to any animal, not just a lionized cat. It's only because cats live so intimately with us that we come inevitably to project our own cognition onto them. The writer Stephen Budiansky states it well: "Cats are not so much pets as fellow travelers, and we impose our hopes and expectations and wishes upon them to our peril." And to their peril too, I would add.

Animal owners have better health and live longer lives. Anytime we can find reasons to express love, we are happier, and healthier.

In short, anthropomorphizing may be good for you. It's certainly fun. It feels good to feel, or imagine, that connection. I know I will continue to "feel the love" from my cats and, even better, give them

---

* I have in mind, among others, M. Scott Peck's definition in *The Road Less Traveled*, where "Love is the will to extend one's self for the purpose of nurturing one's own or another's spiritual growth."

† I think we are more animal-like than we think; a good part of our own feelings of "love" also derives from survival instincts playing out in the brain's chemistry. Almost all cat behaviors are related to survival, and many humans' behaviors fall into that category as well.

back my love. And I wouldn't suggest that you stop. But it's the dark side of anthropomorphism that I want to talk about most. I call it the Anthropomorphic Trap.

The Anthropomorphic Trap

Being among animals is greatly simplified when we imagine they are just like us. As I grew up, it was hard for me to be aware of my own anthropomorphism. After all, as a little girl I thought even my stuffed animals had real feelings and thoughts. But when we imagine that cats feel the same kind of love we do, that they are happy in the way we are happy, that they are *trying* to be sweet or adorable, or are embarrassed, it's a very short step to giving them other, less-attractive human intentions like spitefulness or vengefulness, stubbornness or intransigence.

And then we do things that harm them.

As veterinary and shelter staff know too well, we punish cats when we think their problem behaviors are somehow directed at us or are done when the cats supposedly know not to. We scold them. *You know very well you're not supposed to be on that counter!* We hit them. *You peed on that to get back at me. Take that!* (A great deal of child abuse also happens over toilet training.) We throw them out of the house. *If you can't stop scratching you'll have to stay outdoors!* We abandon them. *You just keep spraying and spraying, no matter how many times I tell you not to.* We give them the "good death." But it's wrong to think that cats understand the connection between our abuse—for that's what it is—and their behavior. And it's certainly misguided to project rebellious or spiteful intent. Cats are motivated purely by survival. Spite, like any other higher-order human emotion or intention, doesn't serve the cat's survival. Urine and feces are not used as ways to get back at humans. As Sigmund Freud might have said if he had been a cat behaviorist, *Sometimes poop in ze shoe is just poop in ze shoe.*

I believe it's possible to have a real emotional or spiritual connection with an animal. When I look into my Josephine's or Jasper's eyes, I believe I sense a sentience there, a consciousness that is aware of me in some meaningful way that I can't properly describe. My life's work has been not to project my feelings onto them, but to try to understand their feelings. I invite you to do the same. Charles Darwin's father, Erasmus, put it well when he said: "To respect a cat is the beginning of aesthetic sense."

Falling into the Anthropomorphic Trap can be an especially bad idea when you react with punishment and reprimands, which:

- are ineffective—they usually won't stop the behavior
- are often counterproductive—they may increase that behavior or begin another problematic behavior
- can ruin your bond with your cat
- are inhumane
- don't reflect well on the intelligence of our species

Stick with positive anthropomorphism ("He's sweet") and stay away from the negative ("He knows he shouldn't do that, and wants to annoy me"). Better yet, learn how to meet your cat on his own turf.

TWO

Meet Your Cat on His Territory: Using the Three-Part C.A.T. Plan to Change Your Cat's Behavior

Of all God's creatures there is only one that cannot be made the slave of the lash. That one is the cat. If man could be crossed with the cat it would improve man, but it would deteriorate the cat.

—MARK TWAIN, *Notebook*, 1894

No Punishment, No Reprimand

I suppose I should not be anymore, but I'm continually surprised by the number of clients who tell me they've rubbed a cat's nose in a puddle of urine, hit the cat's nose when she bit them, or kicked the cat when she attacked the owner's leg. Some clients tell me they have read you should flick or tap the cat firmly on the nose, or to grab the cat by the scruff of the neck. I'll never forget the woman I met at a social function who proudly told me how she believed she had solved her cat's habit of jumping on the counter: She scooped up kitty and threw her across the room and into a wall. But her punishment surely made things worse. Hitting, kicking, or shouting at your cat may make her see you as a potential aggressor, causing the fight-or-flight response. She may start attacking you because you are now associated with something negative. These practices are ineffective and inhumane. Animals don't have the kind of brains that can connect (1) the spot they soiled (often hours before), (2) your anger and punishment, and (3) what they are supposed to do instead. There is simply no behavioral basis for punishing or reprimanding animals.

I recall a Canadian client, Adele, whose breeder told her to swat her Ragdoll kitten, Bianca, on the nose or rear when she playfully attacked Adele's hands, and Adele did. By the time Bianca was five months old, she no longer just playfully attacked, but became fearful whenever Adele came near, and attacked out of fear. Bianca's pupils would dilate like saucers, her ears would flatten, and Adele could not get anywhere near Bianca without receiving serious puncture wounds to her hands, legs, and face. One attack required a hospital stay. To protect herself from further wounds, Adele placed Bianca in a bedroom. She couldn't easily enter the room to clean the litter box; she had to quickly slide new bowls of food through a crack in the door before Bianca hurled herself at it. Happily, using the behavior techniques in Chapter 7, we were able to rehabilitate Bianca in about eight weeks. Today, Adele and Bianca coexist peacefully.

To get a cat to stop doing something, say, to stay off a counter, I hear the following advice a lot: "Just tell it 'no' *very* firmly." This makes me smile. You may as well scold a squirrel. When in doubt about the effectiveness of reprimands, imagine your cat is as domesticated as a squirrel or raccoon. A squirrel will quickly deduce that you are someone to be associated with harm, and will learn to avoid you; a raccoon might defend himself or attack you.

Even in dogs, recent research suggests that confrontational or aversive methods, such as staring them down, striking or intimidating them, and other elements of a so-called alpha relationship, are ineffective and can elicit more aggression.[1] A dog *may* change his behavior to avoid the unpleasant sounds coming from you. But a cat? Cats, motivated by their survival instincts, and without regard for your strategy of playing alpha-cat, will just avoid or attack you—or they may perform the behavior again to get attention.

Finally, punishment or reprimand may teach your cat a local, rather than generalized, lesson, and she'll develop what's called an owner-absent behavior. Even if your cat could learn to stay off the counter when you yelled "No," she will associate *you* with that unpleasantness, not the counter itself. Because the unpleasantness was with you, the cat will simply wait until you're not around and then jump on the counter. Or say you punish or reprimand your cat after she has sprayed urine and she runs away looking scared and upset. You think you've gotten your point across. Congratulations on a very small victory: You may have just taught her to spray when you're not around—or even made her spray more often because you have further elevated her anxiety, and spraying is one of the ways cats soothe anxiety. Bad idea. You need a much subtler approach, a silken-glove response worthy of these feline masters of nuance.

What Works: Withdraw Your Attention and Even Your Presence

I'm not out of reasons why you should avoid punishment and reprimands. Like a child with a parent, most cats crave any form of attention from the owner—even if it's negative attention. For some cats, a firm "No" can actually be a reward. Instead of scolding your cat when he exhibits problem behaviors, try leaving the room immediately. This technique has a good pedigree: Mother cats teach their kittens what not to do precisely by withdrawing attention from them. Over time a cat will learn that when he meows excessively or playfully attacks you, you, much to the dismay of the cat, leave the room. Later in this chapter I'll also explain how to distract and deter your cat from his problem behaviors.

You Have the Power to Solve Your Cats' Behavior Issues

There are so many misunderstandings about cats, and they are particularly prevalent among the very people who are likely to give up their cats to shelters—or to the "good death." These cat owners are often unaware of their cat's estrous cycle; mistakenly think that females should have a litter before being spayed; believe that cats act out of spite; misinterpret the meaning of normal play behaviors; and are unaware that the number of behavior problems goes up with the number of cats in a household.

The idea that cats themselves have behavior issues or problems is itself a kind of misnomer: In almost all cases in which the issue is behavioral, as opposed to medical, in origin, the behavior that most needs to be changed is the owner's. I am a cat behaviorist, but the first behavior I modify is always *human*.

Cats just are. This is why we love them. Lacking our kind of cognition, lacking ideas about how things ought to be, cats simply observe or respond, with no verbalized thought in between. They respond reliably, dependably, to what we call love and affection, which they feel in their cat bodies as good energy and pleasant touch. They respond to our generosity in setting down a bowl of food, not with gratitude but with relief from hunger and from anxiety about being hungry. They respond to what we do just as nature has conditioned them to. They respond to their environment in ways that would have maximized their survival strategies in the wild. There's no good or bad about it. Most of the time, we adore their natural response: giving and getting warmth, purring, playing, resting serenely.

Sometimes, however, their response to their environment is not so pleasing. But that is often because *we* have acted in ways alien to, or at least challenging to, their nature. There are many reasons that cats stop using the box, for example, but once you can rule out medical problems, in almost every case the behavior is triggered by owner error. (And that's good news.) It's one thing to expect cats to walk into an unnatural structure and eliminate in a plastic box with fake or processed sand. It's quite another to expect them to use a filthy box, or to trustingly enter one with a towering toddler, or an aggressive cat, standing nearby. We enjoy cats who play gently, but we grow angry if they respond according to their conditioning by *us* and bite or scratch too hard.

Cats don't have a sense of ethics, or morals, and they can't plan ahead to consider your feelings. Don't project complicated intent onto your cat. Whatever he's doing, it's not out of sheer cussedness. Thinking that your cat is doing something to get back at you is as silly as thinking your cat is furious with you for refusing to get him a smartphone. Cats don't take things personally, and so can't respond personally. That's what we humans do.

So we arrive at three key points.

1. Your cat responds according to its nature (its genes) and its conditioning (its rearing). Its responses are normal, not thought-out, malicious, wrong, or otherwise bad.
2. You, as the owner of a cat, must willingly shoulder the responsibility for whatever conditioning your cat had prior to your ownership, and you have direct responsibility for any conditioned responses (including those arising from its environment) the cat developed after becoming yours.
3. There is no one in the world, human or cat, who has as much power and control—and thus responsibility—over the conditioned responses of your cat as you do. The answers lie in you. You will be doing the work I set out here, not your cat; your cat will simply respond, naturally. The good news? That's what makes it so easy.

THE SEVEN CLASSES OF
BEHAVIOR PROBLEMS IN CATS

I define a behavior problem as any action that causes distress for someone, including the cat in question. If you are a heavy sleeper and your cat's four A.M meowing doesn't wake you up, then it may not be a behavior problem for you. But once your significant other moves in to the apartment and you find that he's a light sleeper, the meowing may become a problem. (It may also be a problem for your cat, if your cat is doing it because she's stressed.) There are many different ways cats express their anxiety, and even more causes, but in my decades of working with them professionally I've come to categorize feline behavior problems into seven basic classes.

1. Cat-to-Cat Tension

You bring home a new cat, and the resident cat runs away and hides — and won't come out. Or cats in the home suddenly start hissing and posturing every day to the point that you have to divide up your home to give them separate living arrangements. (See Chapters 2, 5, and 7.)

2. Aggression

There are different forms of aggression — many triggered by fear. You can see an extreme form of feline aggression in the cat that scratches or bites humans or other animals. These cats can raise the most serious and challenging of all behavior issues, especially if you have small children.

The typical advice includes: "Set boundaries and tell him 'No.'" "Interrupt them by clapping." "Put them on anti-anxiety medication." "Feed your cats near each other." "Separate them." "Use a squirt gun." "Re-home your cat." Some of these techniques are counterproductive and will make the situation worse — and some may have *caused* it! (See Chapter 7.)

3. Litter Box Issues

One day your cat decides the litter box isn't good enough anymore — she prefers your sheets. Or your desk. Or your shoe. Urination or defecation (I'll refer to both as elimination) outside of the litter box is the most common behavior issue I see.

The typical advice includes: "Add more litter boxes." "Change litters." "Clean the area with a good enzyme cleaner." "Scoop more often." "Go to a vet to see if there's a medical cause." All good suggestions. If only these things are done, however, improvement may be nonexistent or temporary. The habituated unwanted behavior is still a *habit*. It must be undone. In Chapter 8, I'll show you a complete treatment plan.

4. Spraying

You're noticing a peculiar odor in some of the corners of your home, or you've caught your cat squatting to urine mark or backing up to a wall to release a spray. Often the advice for this is to either put up with it, or get rid of the cat, because "spraying is the one cat behavior you can't stop." No. Spraying is *easily* solvable. No need to euthanize or abandon a sprayer, and most of the time no need even to give him drugs. It's critical to understand *why* your cat does it—e.g., anxiety—and then either eliminate the stressors or help your cat view them in a less negative way. The stressor is usually something in the cat's environment (and I can help you figure out what that might be) or social tension with another cat inside the home. (See Chapter 9.)

5. Excessive Meowing

You're trying to watch TV and your cat keeps calling from the other room—and he's not asking you to change the channel. In fact, he doesn't seem to have a reason at all. Or, it's four in the morning and your cat wants to be a leopard stalking a gazelle, or he sits in the shower and sings into the great acoustics for hours. There are different reasons why a cat may be meowing excessively, and I'll tell you what those reasons are, and help you change the behavior. (See Chapter 10.)

6. Destructive and Unwanted Behaviors

Your couch is shredded. The cats won't stay off the counters. These things drive you *insane*. The typical advice includes: "When she's on the counter, tell her 'No!' " "Smack her!" "Squirt her with a squirt gun!" The first two will make the situation worse, and the third solves the wrong problem. All of them can cause owner-absent behavior. Help is on the way in Chapter 11.

7. Compulsive Behaviors

Excessive chewing or eating of nonfood items, overgrooming, and sucking at carpets or fur can be compulsive behaviors. You may have been advised either to yell at the cat, or to pet and talk soothingly to her to make her feel better. These acts can reinforce the behavior. Learn to stop it in Chapter 12.

When you have an urgent problem and you're in a hurry to find some answers, this book is designed to allow you to go directly to the chapter that will give you the tools to stop your cat's specific behavior problem. But I hope that cat owners will read the entire book—all of my methodology is designed to optimize cats' happiness, and a loving cat owner can never understand too much about her cat's mind. No matter what your cat's issue is, be sure to read Chapter 5, Purrtopia, on cats' critical territorial needs.

Except in the most extreme cases, every cat owner dealing with nonmedical feline behavior issues should be able to use this book to put together a plan of action that in most cases will be 100 percent effective and is completely *natural* or *drug-free, durable,* and *humane.*

The Elements of an Effective **C.A.T.** Plan

There are three ways to remedy animal behavior problems: by changing their physical environment, by performing behavior modification techniques, and through pharmacology. I will mention medication only occasionally. To remedy most unwanted cat behaviors, I have developed and refined a comprehensive, holistic three-part treatment plan—two parts behavior techniques and one part environmental change. It's as easy as C.A.T.

1. Cease the unwanted cat behavior—behavior modification and other techniques to eliminate the cause of a behavior or make the behavior or its location unattractive
2. Attract the cat to a desirable behavior or location—behavior modification with a lot of positive reinforcement to make an alternative behavior more attractive

3. Transform the territory—change the physical environment

Don't even think of abandoning a C.A.T. Plan before you've implemented it *in its entirety* for thirty days—and sometimes sixty! Cat owners who set their expectations accordingly are far more successful than those who don't.

For reasons of convenience, I will refer to these actions as steps, and I'll present them in the easy-to-remember C.A.T. order, but with some obvious exceptions, you should carry out the techniques *simultaneously*—for at least thirty days!

CEASE the Unwanted Cat Behavior

You can get your cat to stop unwanted behaviors by making the behavior or the locations it's performed in less attractive. There are a variety of ways to do this. To break a cycle of unwanted behavior, you can do some combination of distracting the cat and giving her a negative or conflicting association with the *location* of the undesirable behavior. At times you'll use several techniques at once. Let me focus on some techniques that work . . .

What Works: Mastering the Act of God, and the Art of Distraction

Ideally, every time little Antonio tried to jump on the counter or scratch a stereo speaker, he would hear, in the distance, rumbling thunder and lightning. When such a mysterious event is mildly aversive or unpleasant, I'll call it an Act of God. When it's not unpleasant but merely distracting, well, that's a distraction. Unless you're able to make the weather, or are a ventriloquist who can make thunderous sounds appear to come from somewhere else, your options for creating an Act of God are limited, for example, to surreptitiously squirting water from a gun or air from a can (the kind you use for cleaning a computer keyboard or camera).

I call it an Act of God because it seems to the cat to come from nowhere, as though some invisible presence is monitoring his behavior. What's critical is that *you* not be seen to have created the slightly aversive outcome; otherwise you risk damaging the human-cat bond, causing the cat to develop owner-absent behavior, or even encouraging the problem behavior with your attention. If you squirt your cat and he looks at you suspiciously, you've got to have plausible deniability. *Who, me? No way!* Acts of God can work for two reasons: They're unpleasant to the cat, and they interrupt the cat's behavior before it can be further rehearsed. Striking a cat is not an appropriate Act of God.

The most effective time to interrupt an animal is within the first few seconds. (If more time than that has passed, the cat won't have a clue that there is any connection between his behavior and the mildly unpleasant event that occurred in response.) Acts of God should not be disturbing or prolonged enough to be considered a form of punishment, and they should *never* be used in highly tense situations, such as when cats are staring each other down or fighting. They're a way of creating something that's basically a nuisance for the cat. Even so, they are to be used sparingly. Think LIMA: least invasive, minimally aversive. Every cat is different, however, so please respect your own cat's level of sensitivity. One cat might be terrified of air-in-a-can, where another cat could walk up and sniff the can, waiting for the blast of air to hit his nose.

If you are not around to perform an Act of God *and* you are trying to deter an activity in a particular location, you can delegate the Act of God to a **remote deterrent** you set up in the location in question. Remote deterrents include motion-detecting compressed-air sprayers, carpet runners with the points facing up, and double-sided sticky tape. The idea is to make the location an unattractive place to visit. We'll cover remote deterrents in detail in Chapter 7.

Another important technique is that of **distraction**, sometimes combined with redirection of the cat's attention. Unlike Acts of God, distractions are *not* aversive and they *must* be delivered *before* the cat engages in the undesirable activity. Distractions work better than Acts of God when your cats are tense and would react strongly and negatively to something aversive. When I say to use a distraction, I mean to use Ping-Pong balls, wadded-up paper, or other light, tossed objects that do not hit the cat, or to do something that redirects the cat into play. You would use a distraction *before* most other misbehaviors, such as when your cat is walking toward the counter, eyeing the food on it, staring at another cat, or approaching an object he commonly scratches or marks with urine.

Let's say you see your cat heading toward the speakers he likes to scratch. If, by some apparent miracle, before he gets there you use the stereo remote to cause an eruption of music—loud enough to startle, but not painfully loud—he will learn to leave the speaker alone without associating you with the Act of God. You could also toss a Ping-Pong ball to distract him.

ATTRACT the Cat to a Desirable Behavior, Location, or Time

After you've deterred your cat from the unwanted behavior— clawing your speakers, for example—you'll move on to the Attract step. Here you will show your cat what *to do* or where to do it or both. Using play therapy in particular, you'll *redirect* clawing behavior to an activity and a place that will be acceptable to both you and your cat (e.g., a sisal cat scratcher or scratching post). Attraction methods work on all kinds of unwanted behaviors, like urine spraying, clawing, aggression, going outside the litter box, and more.

Of course, we can't forget praising and giving the cat loads of attention when he performs the desired behavior! Clicker training (see Appendix A) is a great way to accentuate the positive. If the unwanted behavior is motivated by a natural instinct such as hunting, which can cause cats to yowl or race around late at night or very early in the morning, then we will just retrain the cat to express its natural instinct at acceptable times.

TRANSFORM the Territory

You're not done yet! Most cat behavior advice tells you how to show your cat what you don't want him to do (Cease). If the advice stops there, it rarely works. Sometimes you are also advised to redirect his behavior into what you do want him to do (Attract). This works more often. But long-lasting behavioral change usually means making specific changes to his territory. Otherwise, *he may quickly be conditioned back to his old ways.* There is almost always a cause for your cat's behavior—anxiety, boredom, fear, territorial tension, instinct—that must be addressed in his territory to ensure the short- and long-term success of any behavior plan. I'll discuss cats' territorial needs and instincts in more detail in the next three crucial chapters.

THREE

Life on the Wild Side—
Where Even the Tamest Cats Live

*"Well, then," the Cat went on, "you see a dog growls when it's angry,
and wags its tail when it's pleased. Now I growl when I'm pleased,
and wag my tail when I'm angry. Therefore I'm mad."*
"I call it purring, not growling," said Alice.
"Call it what you like," said the Cat.

—Alice in Wonderland

THE FUNDAMENTAL CAUSES OF MANY UNWANTED CAT BEHAVIORS
go back much further in time than the immediate triggers you
may see—straight to the cat's instinctual make-up. I'll focus in this
chapter on three key causes of problem behaviors, both primal and
present day. They are:

- super-territoriality (which comes into full flower upon a cat's
  entrance into social maturity)

- incomplete domestication
- inadequate socialization

There is no animal quite like a cat. That's why we must expect them to act like nothing other than themselves, and treat them only as their nature dictates. Cats are unique in two ways that I'll stress here. First, most cat species are by nature self-reliant and very, very territorial, a fact that brings with it a host of natural behaviors that can be challenging to human sensibilities. Second, even house cats are not fully domesticated (and some seem to retain more of their wild-cat ancestors' instincts than others). For behavioral purposes, it's better to think of them as half wild. Welcome to a new way of thinking.

There are rural wildcat sanctuaries all over the United States that take in all kinds of wildcats — lions, tigers, lynxes, bobcats, African servals, caracles. People love the idea of owning these beautiful cats while they're kittens, but as the cats grow and their natural behaviors become more pronounced (resulting in destruction of the owners' homes), their owners surrender them to these zoolike animal sanctuaries. What are the behaviors that make their original owners give up? Destructive clawing, aggression, and urine marking.

Sound familiar?

Cats: Self-Reliant, Highly Territorial, Champion Survivors

All other domesticated animals began in the wild as group-oriented animals, and they remain so. Horses, pigs, sheep, cattle, donkeys, ducks, chickens, goats, and dogs (like wolves) all live, by instinct, in groups. The evolutionary rationale for being part of a group or pack has to do with survival: When food resources are inconsistent and distributed over a large territory, it makes sense for animals to band together for protection or cooperative hunting. The very size of some predators' prey, like that of wolves, also requires the predators to hunt in groups.

Most of these now-domesticated animals were in deep trouble, having difficulty surviving as a species, until man intervened. By now their wild counterparts are either extinct or nearly so. The wild Przewalski's horse, the forebear of the modern horse, survives only in zoos and human-managed herds. All wild sheep species are endangered. You haven't heard of the wild ancestor of the cow because the aurochs is long extinct. Wolves? There are only 150,000 in all the world. Domestication was often the only reason that some of these species continue to live today. But as Stephen Budiansky points out in his priceless *The Character of Cats*, "Cats were *not* in evolutionary trouble in the wild; they did *not* need to throw in their lot with man to survive; they did *not* undergo the rapid and automatic genetic transformation that broke down the barriers between the wild and the tame in the case of other wild beasts that became malleable and accommodating partners of man. Primitive man succeeded in taming the ancestors of dogs, cattle, sheep, and other true domesticates largely because these species had the inherent genetic potential to tame themselves genetically once people appeared in their environment." But the ancestors of cats? "Cats refused to play this game."[1]

The ancestor of the domestic cat (and the feral cat) is the African wildcat. Although most of the other thirty-six feline species in the world are endangered or threatened (though often not because of their competition with nature but with man's incursions), wildcats have spread across the world. There are 40 to 70 million feral cats in the United States alone. Of all of man's animal friends, cats are, as Budiansky puts it, "the least tamed and the most successful." He adds, "Cats have spread over the world in the company of man faster than man himself ever did, all the while keeping one foot in the jungle." Here is the only place where I might disagree with him slightly: Our cats have at least two, and probably three, feet still in the jungle.

So cats didn't need our help. Many still don't, a fact some people cite as evidence of their incomplete domestication.[2] Moreover, the cats of most species don't rely on each other for purposes of survival, either. Like the human and the shark, the crocodile and the cockroach, they are evolutionary champions. What helped them survive? Well, exactly the same natural traits that make them behave in ways you may not like, including their self-reliant nature and their many territorial behaviors. In other words, it's what makes them cats.

Why do our cats act as they do? "By the process of Darwinian evolution, cats behave in a way that is well adapted to the type of social and physical environment in which their ancestors lived."[3] So who were their ancestors, and how did they live? The answers vary, depending on which cat species we are talking about, some of them being more social than others. Unlike social felines like lions, and, according to recent speculation, even sabertooth cats,[4] the domestic cat's ancestor, the still-extant African wildcat, is generally solitary. African wildcats have large territories and live far from each other, so they don't need a tight social structure and don't go in for all the appeasement behaviors you see in dogs. Unlike lions, which hunt cooperatively, both wild and domestic cats always hunt alone. Wildcats interact with each other harmoniously only during mating (males and females) and the first few months of kitten rearing (mother and kittens). That doesn't mean such cats can't become socialized, however. Under certain circumstances, they do.

Cats Can Make Friends, Too

Let's be clear: Domestic cats have recently been proven to be quite "social" in the sense that they like to be with other cats as well as with humans and other special friends. They mutually groom one another and bond, they have preferred associates, females midwife and cooperatively rear one another's kittens. Indeed, cats have twice as many vocalizations as dogs and many ways of communicating through scent, touch, and posture that would not exist if they weren't social beings. Even when cats aren't in close proximity, they are always communicating—by means of scent and visual markings.

Even domestic house cats don't have the tight social hierarchy that dogs do. And while dogs love to go anywhere as long as they're with the group, wild and domestic cats are relative homebodies, guarding and feeling more secure in the territory they know so well. Nonethe-

SOCIAL GATHERINGS

Cats have occasionally cobbled together intricate social networks for reasons known only to themselves. Consider the cats, all strangers, who some years ago were seen every evening coming to the borders of their territories—near a small square on the outskirts of Paris—to hang out in a group for varying periods of time. They sat close to each other, grooming and observing one another, with surprisingly few displays of hostility. Sometimes, said observers, the tomcats "paraded" before the group. Then by midnight they all dispersed, back to their respective territories.

less, I do know a few cats, namely some of mine, that love a car ride, especially if I'm there with them—evidence not so much of their love of travel but of the bond they feel with me. Most of my cats come running when I walk in the door or call them, and our cat Barthelme follows my son and me around so much, lifting a paw or standing on his hind legs for a petting, that we've nicknamed him Puppycat. So I want to make clear that cats can form social bonds and appear very doglike socially. It's a myth that they are purely solitary and antisocial creatures.

But absent a pathological separation anxiety, cats don't badly *need* to be social in quite the same way humans and dogs do. (Thus the occasional "aloof" house cat.) Cats' more self-reliant nature is linked to an extreme territoriality you won't find in other animals. That territoriality, far greater than in dogs, gives us the champion-survivor behaviors that most people fail to see are natural aspects of *catness*: their suspicion, their dislike of novelty, their single-minded predatory behavior, their spraying and claw marking, and their aggression, especially toward newcomers. Their territoriality can even cause compulsive behaviors, and can also cause an intimidated cat's avoidance of litter box areas, which leads to elimination problems. It all starts here. I'll return to this territoriality again and again, but now let's look briefly at the psychology of the dog, because so many cat owners confuse their cat's psychology with that of dogs, and vainly try to modify their cat's behavior accordingly.

THE DOG/CAT DIFFERENCE

Wild Dog crawled into the Cave and laid his head on the Woman's lap, and said, "O my Friend and Wife of my Friend, I will help Your Man to hunt through the day, and at night I will guard your Cave."

"Ah!" said the Cat, listening. "That is a very foolish Dog." And he went back through the Wet Wild Woods waving his wild tail, and walking by his wild lone.

— RUDYARD KIPLING, *Just So Stories*
"The Cat That Walked by Himself"

Dogs: *Always Eager to Please*

Witness the dog. See Spot run—back to the pack every time. Dogs are quintessential pack animals. The mere act of *being in the pack* satisfies a real survival craving. A dog, alone, is a most miserable beast. It's not part of healthy dog social life for a dog to be or feel alone. That's why it's normal for your dog to follow you (the alpha of the pack) around, to be desperate to go on a walk *with you*, or to sleep *with you*, or to listen and respond to *your* commands. For a dog, pleasing other pack members, especially those of higher rank, which includes you, is paramount. Humans have a long, close history with dogs: at least ten thousand years of avid domestication, even symbiosis. No other animal has been so bred and selected to hang on to our every change in tone of voice or facial expression. "To his dog," Aldous Huxley once wrote, "every man is Napoleon."

Dogs do better at reading cues from humans than do other animals in part because we spent millennia breeding them to have an instinctively powerful desire to look at us and respond (a desire and ability completely absent in wolves).[5] At the same time, humans have bred in dogs a facial musculature that gives rise to a rich vocabulary of apparent expressions, which humans choose to interpret as if they were coming from another human: sad, forlorn, happy, guilty, embarrassed, curious, etc. My Great Dane, Jazzy, seeks out the expressions on my face as if they were signs from heaven. If she could think in words, they might be: Approov? disaproov? Hapy? Stay in pack? R u luking at treat cubbard? My cats—not so interested. (On the other hand, maybe cats *can* read our facial expressions, but just can't think of a good enough reason to pay attention.)

Cats: *Always Eager to Be Pleased*

As many people who are not fond of cats have found, cats have no intrinsic desire to please us. Some people resent this autonomy; others prize it. As the joke goes, a dog looks at all the things we provide for it and thinks, *You must be God.* A cat looks at all the things we provide for it and thinks, *I must be God.* Here's another favorite: "Dogs have masters; cats have staff."

Cats: Forever Wild

Besides not living in groups, the other primary way that cats are unique among domesticates is that their domestication is only partial—and relatively recent. Dogs were first domesticated—separated from wolves—at least fifteen thousand years ago (and according to recent findings, perhaps as long as 33,000 years ago), sheep and goats about nine thousand years ago, cattle seven thousand, and horses six thousand. While archeologists in Cyprus have discovered a cat skeleton, likely an African wildcat, that had been interred alongside a human's as far back as ninety-five hundred years ago, cats don't show up routinely in domestic settings alongside man until about thirty-six hundred years ago, in Egypt, when they were brought into human establishments first to control rodents and later for religious reasons. They still weren't domesticated, even then. Horses, dogs, sheep, goats, and camels all have walk-on roles in the

Bible. The cat, still wild in most of the world at the time and living with humans only in Egypt, is absent.

It seems that you can take the cat out of the jungle, but you can't take the jungle out of the cat. All other domesticated animals have been bred and selected, over and over again, for domestic traits, with the wild traits bred out. But for most of our shared history, humans did not selectively breed cats for domestication features at all.* Even today cats are bred primarily for physical traits.

Our lack of control over cats' genes is obvious: While cats have been breeding in our midst for many years, house cats and their African wildcat ancestors are still the same species—*Felis silvestris* (though sometimes domestic cats are denoted as the subspecies *Felis silvestris catus* for clarity). The genetic differences among and between African wildcats, European wildcats, and domestic cats are no larger than the difference between, say, any two domestic cats. Genetic studies have proven that domestic cats differ from their wildcat cousins almost solely in . . . their hair color—and, in some breeds, a few other superficial physical differences brought about through breeding.

While it's convenient to refer to house cats as domesticated animals, they're actually closer to what we call man's exploited captives, like deer, camels, and Asian elephants, or human symbionts like the rat or house sparrow. We don't consider these animals tame. Cats are otherworldly precisely because from a behavioral perspective they are still inherently wild in so many ways.

True, house cats' ancestors had to be minimally tamable, capable of and even desirous of socialization. We probably wouldn't have pet cats at all if the African wildcat had not existed. By contrast, the European wildcat is so unfriendly that it could turn the most committed cat fanatics into dog lovers. Even being around one of the kittens of a European wildcat is, in the words of one zoologist, "eerie." Another

---

* The first recorded breeding program was undertaken, in around A.D. 999 in the Imperial Palace of Japan. The Japanese ultimately tried to control cat matings to such an extent that cats were not permitted outdoors. When mice nearly wiped out the silkworm industry, cats were let back outside.

observer said their four-week-old kittens "looked right through you as if you were not there." They are impassive in the face of encouragement to play or to interact with humans. It would be humbling to any cat owner to face such implacable indifference. As they reach sexual maturity, European wildcats become, in the words of another zoologist, "proud and bold." They act like they're as big as leopards. They routinely intimidate large, ferocious dogs. Even when hand-reared, they are "fierce and intractable."

Split from their European sisters only twenty thousand years ago, African wildcats are much friendlier and more intrinsically tamable than the northern cats, giving them the genetic head start that made the human-cat bond possible. European naturalists in Africa in the 1800s described how easily the indigenous peoples caught and kept African wildcat kittens, "reconciling them to life about their huts and enclosures, where they grow up and wage their natural warfare against the rats."[6] Another European, writing from Rhodesia (today, Zimbabwe) in 1968, found that while the wildcat kittens were initially difficult to handle, soon enough they grew unnervingly affectionate:

> These cats never do anything by halves; for instance, when returning home after their day out they are inclined to become super-affectionate. When this happens, one might as well give up on what one is doing, for they will walk all over the paper you are writing on, rubbing themselves against your face or hands; or they will jump up on your shoulder and insinuate themselves between your face and the book you are reading, roll on it, purring and stretching themselves, sometimes falling off in their enthusiasm and, in general, demanding your undivided attention.[7]

Sound familiar?

However, people who have been befriended by African wildcats report that while they are indeed "superaffectionate" toward humans, they are even less likely to put up with human punishments than domestic cats. They are also highly territorial, and may prey on other animals in the household. Now consider that our cats split from the

African wildcats only four thousand years ago—a blink in genetic time. (Compare their 4,000 years of divergence to the 1 million years separating the lion and leopard.[8]) No wonder we still see so much of the wild in them. Real aficionados of "domestic" cats appreciate them precisely because they feel a sense of awe, feel honored, that these essentially wild beings choose to live and be with us.

HISTORY OF THE HOUSE CAT

Wildcats likely began to associate with humans about eleven to ten thousand years ago, when agricultural societies arose in the Fertile Crescent. Grain stocks would have attracted mice, and humans would have quickly grasped that cats excelled at disposing of them. And they are indeed formidable hunters, even today, and even when provided with food. One cat was recorded as having killed 22,000 mice in twenty-three years, or about 80 a month, every month. A kitten managed to kill four hundred rats in four weeks, all before six months of age.[9]

Cats leapt into Britain between AD 300 and 500, courtesy of merchant ships and soldiers. In Asia, the spread of Mi-Ke (calico) cats was facilitated by the belief that they could predict storms at sea. Cats have always been well-regarded in Islamic countries, even put under protection of scripture, because they were Mohammed's favorite animal.

Christian countries, however, have had a more tortured history with the cat. When cats were first brought into Europe, they were believed to have appeared in Jesus' stable to protect him from the Devil. But a variety of other events, such as the cat's association with the pagan moon goddess Diana, led Christians to associate the cat with the Devil and witchcraft. In Europe they were exterminated, even burned, throughout the Middle Ages. So were the people, especially women, who showed excessive interest in them. Cats were nearly exterminated in Europe, a victory for vermin and the plague they carried, the Black Death, which wiped out between one-third and one-fourth of the population.

But the cat's usefulness ultimately overrode the superstitions: When the Crusaders returned to Europe with an infestation of the brown rat and the plague, the world's most effective rodent controller was again tolerated. Serving the same purpose, cats came to the Americas aboard British ships in the 1600s. In monasteries, cats were allowed to protect precious manuscripts from rodents; monks preferred cats of a certain color and coat, and thus were the Korat and Chartreux breeds introduced. And when microbes, or germs, were discovered in the 1800s by Pasteur, the cat's relative cleanliness brought it even closer to favor. This was all long before the mountains of evidence demonstrating the significant health benefits to humans of pet companionship.

Taming the Wild: The Socialization Process

Since cats aren't genetically tame, the only way to make them friendly—to other cats, and to people—is to socialize them. This process must occur during a very sensitive five-week period after birth. The kitten's mother, other kittens, and humans all have a role to play in the socialization process, and if it is to be successful, it has to take place between the ages of two and seven weeks. How well your cat was socialized to other cats as a kitten plays a huge role in how well your cat will get along with other cats now and in the future. The same holds true for a cat's relationships with people. If kittens do not interact with people during this "sensitive period" between two and seven weeks, and do not have the instructive example of seeing their mother interacting with people, then it may be very hard to socialize them to human contact later. Thus kittens born to feral cats can be socialized to people if the mother allows them to be handled by people, but, conversely, even a house-born kitten can quickly revert to feral (unsocialized) behavior if the people in the household have not made an effort to socialize it. Cats are always just one step away from being wild.

Socialization attempts by humans before two weeks make little or no difference, and after seven weeks are much less likely to succeed. Chances are high that a cat not socialized during the sensitive period won't relate well to people, to the family dog, and possibly not to the other cats in the family, either. Such an animal is "handicapped" in normal social situations and undergoes "a great deal of stress if forced into" one, says Dr. Bonnie Beaver.[10] Millions of cats' lives would be saved each year if humans properly socialized kittens. It is also absolutely crucial that young kittens remain with their littermates and mother until they are twelve weeks old. Otherwise, you are likely to see more behavior issues, such as increased aggression and random activity. Kittens separated too early will be more excitable and slower to calm down, and they won't learn appropriate play behavior (see Play Aggression in Chapter 7), which is something their mother and, secondarily, their littermates are meant to teach them.

Responsible breeders and cat shelters will make sure to gently and safely expose kittens to a wide range of people and possibly to other species (like dogs), so that when they go to their new homes, they are properly socialized. Being handled by people has many positive effects on development, such as the age at which kittens open their eyes, become weaned from and less dependent on Mom, explore more, or, in the case of Siamese, develop their distinctive coloring.[11]

You can socialize a kitten very well with as little as fifteen minutes a day of daily handling during the sensitive period. An hour is probably ideal, and, according to studies, more probably won't help,[12] but you'll probably want to play with your precious ball of fur for longer, because it's so much fun. Kittens can become *very* attached to whatever they are socialized to. If you've seen pictures of cats sleeping with dogs, playing nice with ducks or mice, or snuggling with gorillas, you have seen the power of early socialization.

THE WELL-FED KITTEN

Good nutrition is also critical to socialization (and other aspects of growing up). As with human children, kittens who are malnourished for any reason — because their mother is, or because they have been separated from their mother — may experience poor brain development, under-developed learning abilities, and delayed physical maturation. They are more reactive to stimuli and less responsive to other cats. Males show more play aggression and females may climb more or less than usual. Both sexes show increased vocalization and difficulty bonding with the all-important queen. They have more accidents in play. Mild or brief malnutrition may be undone with a proper diet; in cases of severe malnutrition, learning disabilities are more likely to be permanent. Kittens raised without their mothers or whose mothers were fed a low-protein diet within a month before or after birth show retarded or overly gregarious social behaviors.

Kittens are also highly imitative. Dr. Beaver writes of a kitten raised with dogs that learned to raise its leg on a tree after watching its companions.[13] I knew of a kitten that saw my client use toilet paper to pick up an errant kitty stool. After the kitten's next deposit, she sought out some toilet paper, brought it back to the stool, and gently tucked it in. I've heard of a cat who watched a fox dive into a molehill over and over, catching moles, after which the cat developed a habit of doing the same.

Unfortunately, if a kitten was not properly socialized, you cannot entirely reverse the consequences. Owners of feral cats especially have to manage their expectations. In one study, nearly half of feral kittens who had not been handled by humans before seven weeks of age could not be held by their owners for one minute. However, the owners said they were still happy with their untamed little pets. Expectations are everything. And even if these cats would rather not be touched a lot or not sit in a lap, they may follow their owners around, giving and seeking attention and affection in other ways, and forming very close bonds with their caretakers.

While you can't go back and socialize your cat, you can introduce cats, and even reintroduce poorly socialized cats, to one another in ways that promote harmony. I discuss the crucial art of the introduction in the next chapter.

Territoriality, Conflict, and Social Maturity

To understand your cat's propensity toward unwanted behaviors, you need to understand feline territoriality. A cat's social behaviors (or "problems") are closely linked to his tolerance for sharing his home range, which, indoors and out, overlaps with other cats'. In the wild, male cats travel throughout a home range of about 153 acres; females about 42. A territory, which is the area a cat defends against other cats, is usually smaller than a home range, but cats' territories in the wild are still considerably larger than our houses. And the closer one cat gets to another's core territory, the more aggressive the defender will be.

Fortunately for us, domestic cats may be not only inherently less shy and more sociable than African wildcats, but more willing to live in social groups that share territory, especially if they grew up in a group. Even feral females, usually under the watchful eye of a dominant matriarch, will set up a kind of Ministry of Mutual Defense and Welfare. The girls share duties of defense, kitten training—jointly rearing and even suckling the kittens—and hunting or bringing back delicacies from the garbage dump or someone's backyard birdhouse. (Males are far less likely to join a colony or to participate in rearing than they are to try to *eat* the young.) A queen who gives birth may be aided by a female who quietly cuts the umbilical cords (with her teeth), helpfully eats the placentas, and licks clean the kittens' perianal areas. (You think *you've* got good girlfriends?) And like domestic cats, feral cats curl up and sleep together, and groom one another in ways that we find touching. In fact, feral cats fight each other less frequently than do our house cats.

Why would house cats fight more than feral cats? When a feral cat feels threatened, he can simply melt away into the extra space that the outdoors provides, but indoor cats, forced to live within four walls and to share more crowded resources, have to delineate territory in a pressure cooker. Consider that in a 10-room house, indoor males will try to claim a territory of 4 to 5 rooms, and females 3 to 3.6. Then consider that in the United States and several European countries, there are more cats per household than ever before (and most of us are certainly not fortunate enough to live in ten-room houses, either). We're crowding our cats. Think of five toddlers in a room, with two toys.

For cats, issues of rank and territory are inextricably entwined, so cats look for ways to move up in rank in order to get more territory and vice versa. The dominance hierarchy is relative; social ranks depend on particular locations or circumstances. One cat may be the higher-ranking cat in the morning and be found sitting at the top of the cat tree, but later in the day he may defer to another cat in that location. Similarly, a higher-ranking cat may defer to a lower-ranking cat in the latter's sleeping area. Often it can be just a matter of time before they work things out between them. Cat hierarchy is so interconnected with issues of territory—who gets what space at what time—that cat behaviorists have a term to describe the time-sharing arrangements: the spatio-temporal hierarchy.

Cats who get along well will usually share the same space or path-ways to and from important resources, even during the same times of day. But cats who are feeling fearful or territorial (and some cats are more territorial than others) may change their intended paths. Like teenagers staking out their own space, territorial cats spend more time in their own rooms or far away from one another. Sometimes the only time you will see these cats together in one area is when they're with you on your bed or couch. (The bed can truly signify contentment and security. Your cats may view it as a safe zone.)

However, such jockeying may not always be peaceful. It can involve various forms of inter-cat aggression, and with aggression comes stress—hence spraying. The increase in multicat households sharply increases the odds of unwanted behaviors. In single-cat homes, the

FORGET THE ALPHA MODEL:
DOGS ARE FROM MARS,
CATS ARE FROM VENUS

If there is a Mars and Venus among domesticated animals, it would be the dog and the cat. In fact, the difference between the psychology of dogs and cats may be even greater than that between human males and females. Yet many cat owners who are familiar with dogs suffer from an irresistible temptation to project the dog mind onto the cat, which usually involves borrowing the alpha model concept of behavior from dogs. This is a big mistake. Regardless of the validity of the alpha model for dogs—a model that many dog experts dispute,* most alpha research having been done on the very different wolf, whose line diverged from the dog over ten thousand years, and four thousand generations of breeding, ago—dog and cat instincts and languages are quite different, and the alpha model definitely does not apply to cats. It has no relevance to the way they relate to you, or to the way they relate to each other when they have to share a territory—for insofar as cats have a hierarchical relationship to one another, it has to do with territory.

While cat colonies may have an alpha male in the sense that there may be one cat who simply has taken over more territory, cats do not behave like alpha wolves, and any feline group will lack a clear linear hierarchy. A cat's social system is very loosely knit; there may be some hierarchy, but it is much more fluid and subtle, and can change with the time of day and location, cats being experts at time sharing.

---

*In the wolf world, an alpha is basically a good leader of the moving nursery that is the wolf pack, perhaps because he is the parent, the oldest, or has been around the longest and is a good leader—but not because he is the most aggressive. Aggression from the alpha is commonly reserved for intruders from *outside* the pack.

While cats' brains are of course similar to dogs' and they learn in similar ways, many of the approaches used with dogs will not translate to cats (a notable exception is clicker training; see Appendix A).

chances of the cat being sent to a shelter for behavior problems are 28 percent. Add a second cat and it's about 70 percent.[14] The likelihood of a cat spraying in a one-cat household is about 25 percent, but by the time you shoehorn ten cats into a house, the probability has increased to just about 100 percent.

What you may also see are the hisses or spats—the external evidence of competition. Cats have a less exacting social hierarchy than dogs, so conflict is even more likely if you have cats of similar assertiveness who are unwilling to back down or defer to another cat. It's the cats closest in rank that usually do the most fighting. The probability of your cat seeing or otherwise sensing the existence of a strange cat outside your house is also higher than ever. That leads to even more behavior issues, as you'll see.

Luckily for us, domestic cats have developed an ingenious solution to the problem of limited household territory and resources: the time-share arrangement mentioned above. Even before humans had invented the beach condo and ski villa time-share, cats had figured out how to share the same space at different times. Through trial and error, scent marking to communicate information (see Chapter 9), and the performance of a finely nuanced dance, they often make it work.

But not always. Many, many behavior problems begin when cats reach social maturity, and we see just how territorial the cats really are. Sometimes even cats who were very well socialized as kittens can become hostile to their fellow cats because of territorial issues. While kittens are not born territorial, social maturity, which they enter between the ages of two and four, eventually drives them to it. (Sexual maturity is different from social maturity; it may happen as early as five months of age so don't underestimate those kittens!) Upon social maturity they say good-bye to the carefree days of kittenhood and begin to look at their environment through a serious territorial lens. The survival instinct prompts them to focus on protecting themselves by securing territory and makes them possessive of resources—at which point the troubles in your household may begin.

Cats who were the best of friends may suddenly, on the occasion of their second birthdays, log into Facebook to unfriend each other. In extreme cases, former friends can't even be left alone without your coming home to find tufts of fur on the floor or having to take one or both to the vet to have wounds treated. If problems between your cats began or got worse between the ages of about two and four, you now know at least one of the likely—and, quite natural—reasons.

The situation is not hopeless, however, no matter what you may have been told. You can help your cats negotiate a peace between themselves. Yes, believe it or not, you can play a major role in the ability of cats to get along with each other—those cats who are meeting each other for the first time, and those cats who were once old pals but now seem estranged or even hostile to each other. It's better not to leave this to chance, because you may be living with the consequences for many years to come, unless of course you simply give up and keep the cats separate, or get rid of one or more of them. This is such an important subject, because it can have a long-term impact on the quality of life for both you and your cats, that I have devoted the entire next chapter to teaching you how to introduce two (or more) cats to each other for the first time, or reintroduce cats who used to get along but are now behaving like enemies.

FOUR

Cat Etiquette:
The Art of Introducing, or
Reintroducing, Cats to Each Other

"Who are you talking to?" said the King.

"It's a friend of mine—a Cheshire-Cat," said Alice: "allow me to introduce it."

"I don't like the look of it at all," said the King: "however, it may kiss my hand, if it likes."

"I'd rather not," the Cat remarked.

—Alice in Wonderland

IT'S SO EXCITING TO ADOPT A NEW KITTEN OR CAT. YOU LOOK forward to watching the new cat and your resident cat become friends, chasing each other around the house, grooming each other, curling up together to sleep, doing all the delightful, charming, hilarious things that cats who adore each other do. You probably think they'll just do what comes naturally. However, because of the territorial and survival instincts of the cat, such amicable behavior may not be natural at all, but something that can be achieved only with a lot of help from outside — mainly you. Yes, it's up to *you* to shape the cats' initial encounters with each other so that they become the friends you want them to be.

Each cat you bring into your household who is unfamiliar with the resident cats will have to be very carefully introduced to all the resident cats, using the process I describe in this chapter. Introducing cats too fast or incorrectly is one of the biggest reasons for an array of inter-cat social issues. I've seen many clients try to rush their cats into familiarity in a few days, with severe consequences (which, happily, may be undone with my *reintroduction* technique). After a bad introduction, two cats may not be able to be in the same room for more than five seconds before one makes a beeline toward the other and attacks. After a *very* bad introduction, many clients feel they have no choice but to keep the cats separate forever, or to give one up for adoption. A first impression can last for the life of your cats (and a big chunk of yours), and is a big cause of cat abandonment, so correct introductions are of the utmost importance. How well you introduce your cats in the beginning will make all the difference in how well they get along in the future. Will they be enemies, merely coexist, or become closely bonded housemates? You can do a lot to make this last scenario come true.

The instructions I give for introducing cats are very detailed. I believe they are the most comprehensive you'll find on cat introductions anywhere (and as of this writing, they may be the *only* instructions on reintroductions). Accordingly, if you are not planning to bring a new cat home soon, and the cats who currently live with you are getting along just fine, you may wish to skip this chapter for now. If, however, you are about to adopt a new cat, or the cats already in your home are currently having problems with each other, you should read both this chapter and Chapter 7, on aggression.

Introductions

In the instructions to follow, I'll show you how to introduce your new cat, Newcat, to your resident cats. Because you won't introduce all of the residents at once, I'll refer to the first resident to be introduced as Homecat. Note what we won't do: We won't walk in with Newcat and drop him into Homecat's terrain unannounced. Instead, we will (1) prevent any contact between the two at first and (2) very gradually build up in each cat positive associations with the other cat, one sense at a time. We'll do this by providing the cats with rewards, affection, and fun, while slooooowly desensitizing them to one another. And, using our knowledge of how feline communication works, we'll be taking particular advantage of their primary sense language—scent.

Reintroductions

If your existing cats are in an intractable pattern of aggression, you'll need to perform a reintroduction, along with the rest of the C.A.T. Plan from Chapter 7. Just follow the instructions for introducing Newcat and Homecat—with a few differences. Reintroductions, unlike first-time introductions, will almost always take place between only two cats. If it's clear that one cat has been the aggressor and the other the victim, then I recommend that you give the victim cat more of the preferred areas of the home, for more of the time, than you give the aggressor. As I'll explain in Chapter 5, cats with preferred territory will feel more confident, and that will prove very useful in the reintroduction. In reintroductions, unless you know that one cat's scent alone makes the other one aggressive, you won't be likely to need a robe or change of clothes. Finally, reintroductions will always feature a see-through barrier you'll place between the unfriendly cats; first-time introductions will not include a barrier unless one or both of your cats prove to have persistent difficulty relaxing around each other.

First Impressions: Desensitization, Habituation, and Counterconditioning

The process of **desensitization** will involve slowly and gradually exposing each cat to the sight, sound, and, especially, smell of the other cat—always making sure that the stimulus presented is below the cat's fear threshold.

Habituation will happen when each cat becomes acclimated to the once-novel stimulus of the other and they appear either enthusiastic about each other, or indifferent to or bored by each other. At the end of the introduction or reintroduction process, your cats may get along famously. But if, during or after the desensitization and habituation, your cats seem like they could not care less about one another, you will still have achieved wild success — and that may be just the beginning of the good news.

We'll also use **counterconditioning** on the cats by pairing desirable activities, such as playing or eating, with the smell, sound, or sight of the other cat. Play will be a very important tool in this process. Keeping a cat in an animated state of play prevents him from feeling fear, for cats simply cannot engage in play behaviors and feel fear at the same time. Food and treats given outside of normal feeding times will also play a big role. Be sure to break any treats up into smaller pieces so that you don't treat your cats so much as to interfere with their normal nutrition.

In an attempt to capture at least some of the many permutations of events that could occur during an introduction, these instructions are highly detailed. Most owners will not require all the detail. But for some owners, there may not be enough detail. If you are in that minority — your cats are reacting negatively or not getting along no matter which suggestions you try, and you can't figure out what to do next — it may be time to go to thecatbehaviorclinic.com or your nearest search engine and look up an experienced cat behaviorist to walk you through the process dynamically, by phone or in person.

STEP 1: SETTING THE STAGE BEFORE
NEWCAT COMES HOME: THE SAFE ROOM
AND PHEROMONES

Two weeks before bringing Newcat home — if you can plan that far in advance — install pheromone plug-ins in the parts of the home where the resident cats spend most of their time. Also, install a pheromone plug-in in a room that will be the designated safe room for Newcat when he first arrives.

CAT'S-EYE VIEW: PHEROMONES

As far as we know, cats have five facial pheromones, which they release by rubbing their sebaceous glands on other animals or objects. Cats have sebaceous glands in their paws and pads, cheeks, flanks, tail, forehead, lips, chin, ear canals, perianal areas, and on the base of the tail, and cats love to rub and have them rubbed. Indeed, simply rubbing your cats' facial areas can help to greatly relax them.

Cats naturally rub one facial pheromone, called F3, along with their own distinctive scents, on objects around the home (and humans) when they feel calm and safe. You can make a cat even calmer if you apply that same facial pheromone (F3) to the cat's surroundings. In days of yore, veterinary researchers did this by swabbing a cat's face with a cloth and dashing about the lab to distribute the scent. Fortunately for you, there's now an easier way.

Synthetic versions of facial-marking pheromone come in both a spray and plug-in form and are sold in pet supply stores and online.* I'll refer to them collectively as pheromones.

---

*See catwhispererproducts.com.

The safe room for Newcat should be one that you can close off and devote solely to him. If possible, it should be a room the residents have not spent much time in and don't consider highly desirable. A properly set up safe room should contain *two* litter boxes (see below), as well as bowls for food and water, new toys, and unscented (or new) perching, resting, and scratching areas. The litter boxes, food, and water bowls should all be as far away as possible from one another. The safe room should have a hiding place, such as a bed, or other piece of furniture, or one or more of the following: a large empty box turned on its side, a cat tunnel, a paper bag with the handles removed and the cuff rolled down to keep it open, or a cat tree complete with a cubby hole. Make the room cat-safe from any hazards such as items that could easily be ingested (string, plastic bags) or dangling cords. Put child guards on the electrical outlets, and if the room is a bathroom, put the toilet seat down. Place a heavy object over part of any heating vent covers. I know of frightened cats who have pulled up the covers and escaped into the duct system. (See Chapter 5 for more on how to expertly set up a cat territory.)

On the day you bring Newcat home, use a handheld pheromone sprayer at cat-nose height (about eight inches from the floor) to spritz surfaces on and near *both sides* of the safe room door, and on several other locations inside the safe room with which the cat is likely to come in contact. Never spray pheromones or place pheromone plug-ins near litter boxes, or eating and drinking areas (and never ever spray them directly on a cat). If possible, put a pheromone diffuser plug-in on the residents' side of the door, too. Place in the safe room a robe or a set of clothes you can change into, and if there is a gap under the door to the room, block it with a rolled-up towel. Fill the water bowl, and have food and treats ready to be opened when Newcat arrives. The two litter boxes should also be filled. If Newcat is used to one kind of litter, and you use something else for the Homecats, you can take this opportunity to start transitioning him to the house litter as follows: Set out one box with Newcat's accustomed litter, and put a good maintenance litter (see Chapter 5) in the second box. Now you are ready for Newcat.

Immediately before Newcat's arrival, put the resident cats in a room you can close off, as far as possible from the path you will be taking from the front door to Newcat's safe room. Make sure the residents aren't stressed out (if they are, play with them for a few minutes), then walk calmly away and shut the door. You can let them back out once Newcat is in his safe room.

Bring Newcat, still in his carrier, into his safe room. Once there, play some soothing music, and change into either your robe or your other set of clothes, hanging the clothes you were wearing in a place where they will not come into any contact with Newcat. Open the carrier and allow Newcat to leave it in his own time. After a while, if Newcat appears stressed and doesn't want to come out of the carrier, put some food or treats just outside the carrier or maneuver a toy to help relax him, and lure him out. Allow him to explore his room and be sure to spend an ample amount of time with him, petting and talking to him.

Before you leave the safe room, change back into your other clothes or take off your robe. Then shut the door behind you and go directly to a sink and wash your hands and arms (your face, too, if you got face-to-face with Newcat). The reason for the change of clothes and the washing is to avoid upsetting your resident cats by allowing them to smell Newcat too soon, especially on the scarce resource of *you*.

For the first few days, keep Newcat in his safe room and spend as much time as you can with him, playing with him and giving him attention. Keep playing with the resident cats, too, of course.

STEP 2: MAKING THE FIRST SCENT INTRODUCTION: THE SCENT SOCK

Newcat Once Newcat has become comfortable in his new surroundings, and shows no signs of stress (he's eating, playing, and so on), and the resident cats are all relatively calm, it's time to start the scent introduction process. Put your hand into a clean sock—not a new one, and not a dirty one, but a clean sock of your own, which will still have your scent on it. (Make sure it's free of bleach or other strong scents.) A thin, smooth sock usually works best. Gently pet Newcat's face with your socked hand, concentrating on his whiskers and cheeks, the corners of his mouth, the area between his eyes at the top of his nose, and his temples. What's in these places? His calming facial-marking pheromones are. The petting and swabbing should take only a matter of seconds, but cut it short if he seems in any way distressed by it. After petting Newcat with the sock, spray one short spritz of pheromones on it.

If Newcat does not want to be petted with the sock, then just leave the sock in his bed for a few days.

Once you have managed in one way or another to get Newcat's scent on the sock, place it in a very prominent location, such as the middle of the room, in the resident cats' area. Do not put the scent sock near important resources like the cats' regular food, water, or resting and perching areas. But once you have placed it, *do* put some treats or food next to Newcat's sock to facilitate in the resident cats a positive association with Newcat's scent.

Homecat Now, using another clean sock, you are going to perform the same sock-rubbing sequence with Homecat, so that you will have a face-scented sock to bring to Newcat's room. (If you have two or more resident cats, start with the residents who tend to be the most calm and nonreactive, using one sock for each, labeling them or choosing distinctive colors to keep straight whose sock belongs to whom.) Just as you did with the Newcat-scented sock, place the Homecat sock or socks in the safe room with Newcat, away from Newcat's critical resources. And, as you did with the other sock, place treats, or a second bowl of regular food, next to the socks to create a positive association with the Homecat smell.

Newcat and Homecat Once a day, refresh the scent on all the socks. Take Homecat's sock out of Newcat's room, let Homecat sniff it (in case the sock now has Newcat scent on it), and if Homecat doesn't react negatively, pet his face with it again. Then return it to Newcat's room. Do the same with Newcat's sock. Take it from the residents' area and, after presenting it to Newcat and making sure he doesn't react negatively to it, rub him with it to refresh the scent, before returning it to the residents. (If you get any negative reactions upon presenting a sock, remove the sock and start over with a fresh one.) Do this for at least a few days, or until none of the cats are reacting to the scented socks.

Now it's time to move to the mixing of scents, but you are still not going to allow the cats to actually see one another.

STEP 3: MIXING SCENTS LIKE A REAL SOCIAL FACILITATOR: ALLOGROOMING AND ALLORUBBING

Allogrooming and allorubbing are the feline kiss and hug, respectively. Allogrooming, or mutual grooming, occurs when one cat licks, or grooms, another: It's a natural affiliative behavior that helps cats build a group scent and engenders a familiarity that can help them get along better and even bond. Allorubbing, which occurs when one cat rubs up against another, or against you, can also help maintain the group scent. Allorubbing is often seen when one cat greets another. It is generally *not* mutual, or reciprocal: One cat is doing the rubbing, usually the lower-ranking cat. Feral cats allorub when another cat comes back from hunting—just as your house cats may rub their faces against your pants, shoes, or groceries when *you* come back from "hunting"; probably they are marking you and your items to ensure the continuity of the household's proper group scent. British veterinary behaviorists Jon Bowen and Sarah Heath go so far as to say, "Of all the feline social behaviours rubbing is the one with the most significance in the cat-owner relationship."[1]

Social Facilitation—Creating and Maintaining a Group Scent

When clients' cats are not getting along, avoid one another, or haven't yet met, I always recommend creating a group scent. Remember, cats rely primarily on scent for communication. Doing introductions and reintroductions requires you to fill the role of what cat behaviorists

call a "social facilitator." In your new job description as social facilitator, you will use a brush daily to create and maintain a group scent
for your cats.

In some multicat households there are cats who act as social facilitators. The social facilitator is the cat who offers and receives greet-
ings and engages in other affiliative behaviors with cats from different
cliques, or factions, within the home (and from outside as well). The
social facilitator routinely grooms (allogrooms) and rubs up against
(allorubs) one cat (or group of cats) and soon afterward does the same
with another cat (or group of cats). Thus the social facilitator carries
the scents from these encounters back and forth, applying them to
all the cats. By mixing the scents of all the cats, the social facilitator
is creating a group scent. A group scent helps cats feel affiliated and
more accepting of one another. There will in turn be reduced stress
and hostility among them. If the social facilitator is removed, dies, or
becomes ill, the group scent will be lost—and you can expect tension or aggression to surface among the other cats. Think of the facilitator as the cat-world version of a courier and diplomat rolled into
one.

Sometimes, even without thinking about it, cat owners act like social facilitators, such as when they pet, brush, or pick up one cat, and
then do the same to another cat, thus mixing all the scents into one
group scent.[2] And that's what you are going to do in this very important Step 3, using a single cat brush to combine your cats' scents. If
you were to follow the rest of the behavior plan and left out this one
technique, your cats would be far less likely to feel social and be relaxed around one another.

The scent introduction in Step 2 was just about putting one cat's
scent on each sock, but to create a group scent you'll go back and
forth to mix the scents of all of your cats. If you have more than one
resident cat to introduce to Newcat, start with the least reactive and
most friendly cats (though for simplicity I'll continue to refer to
Homecat in the singular). You'll be able to introduce any other residents later. Refer to Figure 1 for visual instructions on how to create
and maintain the group scent each day.

Take heart: After you create and maintain the group scent, your cats *will* feel affiliated with one another, more relaxed, and more accepting of one another. Each year I have hundreds of clients tell me that their cats enjoy the technique and do become accepting and friendly with one another. As one client put it, "Instead of hissing at Cooter and swatting at him when he walks by, now Oliver just licks Cooter's face."

Present Homecat's Scent to Newcat

Start this scent exchange with a soft cat brush. You'll begin with the friendliest part of the cat—the face—where the friendly pheromones are secreted. Gently brush the entire area of Homecat's face, head, and neck with several strokes (see Figure C1). Later on, when the cats have become comfortable with one another's facial scent, you will also brush the cat's shoulders and sides. Be sure to avoid the hindquarters of the cat (the least "friendly" of the scented parts of the cat). Now take that same brush—and some irresistible treats—back to Newcat and present the brush and treats to him. Let him sniff the brush (and eat the treats if he wants to). Make sure he's still not showing any negative reaction.

Watch His Response

- If Newcat seems okay about Homecat's scent on the brush, then gently brush Newcat's entire head, face, and neck with the brush (see Figure C2). This will put Newcat's scent onto the brush while also putting Homecat's scent on Newcat. You might think it's a bad sign if he sniffs the brush and does nothing, but no. Indifference is a very positive response.
- If Newcat gets upset when sniffing the brush, or when you try to brush him, *stop*. Do not force the brush on him. Leave the brush in his room, near some treats (but not near his *main* food source) in order to create a positive connection. There's no reason to feel discouraged by his response, but you'll need to take the introduction process more slowly. Go back to the previous step and keep presenting the scent brush for sniffing only, along with food or treats, until he shows no negative reaction. Not until then

should you try again to brush his face with the brush containing Homecat's scent (see Figure C2).

- If Newcat continues to react badly to the brush, it's possible that he just doesn't like having his face touched with the brush. You may want to try this entire technique with a sock on your hand instead. You could also try brushing anywhere *but* Newcat's face, concentrating on his neck, shoulders, and along his sides (again, staying away from his hindquarters). It can also help to keep the brushing sessions short or to brush while Newcat is distracted by playing with a toy or eating treats.

Present the Mixed-Scent Brush Back to Homecat

If Newcat reacted well or indifferently to the mixed-scent brush and you were able to brush him with it, take it back to Homecat and present it for sniffing. If Homecat doesn't react negatively to sniffing, then, in addition to brushing his head, face, and neck, brush his shoulders and sides. (See Figure C3). If Homecat does react negatively to sniffing the brush, follow the Watch His Response instructions beginning on page 75.

Now take the brush and repeat one more time with Newcat (see Figure C4).

Your goal is to brush each cat twice daily, for four to ten strokes total, on the cheeks, head, neck, chin, shoulders, and sides (leaving out the hindquarters and tails). You don't have to complete the entire technique at one sitting. You can brush one or two cats in the morning and then finish the technique when you get home from work, brushing them both once again.

Be sure to use the group-scent technique daily throughout introductions to help maintain the group scent. You can stop when the cats are finally integrated and coexisting peacefully, but if you later notice tension or fighting, I recommend you continue your social facilitator duties indefinitely. The majority of my clients tell me that eventually their cats begin to groom and rub up against one another and that is when my clients relieve themselves of their duties.

THE NAGELSCHNEIDER METHOD:
REINTRODUCTIONS USING THE
GROUP-SCENT TECHNIQUE

Based on the results of hundreds of cases where I have intervened, I've determined that with the modifications I outline in this chapter, the group-scent technique may be used as part of a plan to *reintroduce* cats, too—cats whose long-time familiarity has only bred contempt. (You'll learn exactly when to use the technique in Chapter 7). Many clients have told me that when they stopped the group-scent technique or began using it less, without making any other changes, their cats went from getting along well to fighting again. So it may be necessary to make this part of your daily schedule to ensure ongoing success, or until the cats begin to maintain the group scent on their own by grooming and rubbing up against each other. Veterinary behaviorists Jon Bowen and Sarah Heath report the same results when the group scent ceases: trouble.

Some cats may resist the group-scent technique at first, but I've made the process very gradual and without force, and you'll have already carefully created positive scent associations between your cats, so there is very little chance your cat will become aggressive toward you when you use the technique. In hundreds of cases where clients have followed my advice carefully, I have never heard of cats acting aggressively toward their owners. That said, it's always possible that your cat could send you signals that he just doesn't want to continue with this technique. Use your best judgment; if you have any questions, contact a cat behaviorist.

Note: It's a common misconception to think that if cats are living together, their scents will already be everywhere around the home and that is enough to help cats get along. Cats smelling alike, or having the group scent on them, is very different from finding another cat's scent on a dining room chair leg. Your cats must all be of one group scent and have that scent *on them*. Without it, trouble may begin (or resume).

SOCIAL FACILITATION

The Group-Scent Technique

See the accompanying illustrations for a clearer picture of what's involved in this process, which should actually take only a few minutes out of your day.

If after two weeks the cats feel comfortable with the group-scent technique, you will be ready to move to the next step of letting the cats see one another. Try to respect the reality that every cat and situation is unique. The goal, before moving forward in the introduction plan, is to have no negative reaction from either cat when they either smell or are groomed with the opposing cat's scent. If that takes longer than two weeks, give it whatever time is necessary. Also, please use your best judgment. Though it's rare, some cats may never like the idea of having another cat's scent placed on them. We need to respect that and not use this technique on those cats.

STEP 4: CREATING CONFIDENT
EXPLORERS: TRADING PLACES

All cats feel more confident in territory they have explored, which is why cats are so curious. Newcat needs to be allowed the chance to quench his curiosity and safely investigate his new home's sights, sounds, and, especially, smells. It's very important that Newcat start to feel like the rest of the home is part of his territory. A lack of confidence or even fear may translate into later aggression. At the same time, getting Newcat's scent into the rest of the home will help the resident cats get used to the idea that the new cat is also part of the territory and will eventually have access to the whole house.

Before you let Newcat out of his safe room for the first time, spray the pheromone spray at cat-nose height (about eight inches from the floor) throughout the home: on furniture, on door frames that lead into rooms he will be exploring, and in several locations along the paths he will take as he ventures into the rest of the home. The pheromones will encourage Newcat to do facial marking on those locations with his own pheromones, which will help him feel confident and safe in those locations.

Newcat in the House

At least once a day, when there's no other activity occurring in the house, you're going to give Newcat the run of the house—or at least that part of it where he won't run into any Homecats. In preparation for letting Newcat out, close the door on an area where you can confine the Homecats, making sure to leave them with adequate litter, food, and water. Now open the safe room door. Lure Newcat out by using a wanded toy or offering some treats. Do not force him. If Newcat resists coming out, simply leave his safe room door open so that he can see and smell the rest of the home, and use wanded toys and treats again to try to relax him. If he goes into the rest of the home, be sure to keep the safe room door open so he can dash to safety any time he wants. If he doesn't move around and rub himself on things very much, use a clean scent sock to pet his face and then transfer his facial pheromones to objects around the house.

During the first few sessions, Newcat may be interested in spending only a few minutes a day in the rest of the home, but his innate curiosity will ensure that he'll gradually work up to longer periods of time. Give him ample opportunity to explore and find all the good perching and resting places, as well as the escape routes and places to hide. Build up his confidence further by maneuvering a toy to trigger his prey drive. Drag the toy down the hallway, onto the couch, the cat tree, into the kitchen, and anywhere else you foresee him spending time in the future. Offer food or treats after the play time. Also feed Newcat in other parts of the home to build positive associations with areas outside of his safe room.

Homecats in the Safe Room

Once Newcat is able to explore comfortably, put him in a room other than the safe room, and, while he's safely behind closed doors, bring one or two of the friendliest residents into Newcat's safe room. (If you perceive any risk of one of the residents redirecting its fear as aggression onto the other, then bring only one at a time.) Offer the Homecats treats or initiate a play time to give the room, with Newcat's smell in it, a positive association.

Keep doing this at least once a day for several days, until all the cats are relaxed and able to explore the appropriate territory without negative reactions. If certain Homecats don't feel comfortable in the safe room, don't force them. It's more important that Newcat explores and feels as comfortable as possible in the main part of the home. Depending on the cats and your own execution, the exploration step can last anywhere from several days to a few weeks—during which period you will also continue using the brushing technique to maintain the group scent. We have to respect cats' comfort levels even as we work to increase those levels. By taking them through all these preparatory steps before their visual introductions, you help to ensure that Newcat and Homecat will already have developed an affiliation and familiarity with each other by means of the form of communication that they rely upon most—*scent*—coupled with the positive associations created by food, treats, and toys.

INSTANT GRATIFICATION?

It's common for cat owners to make the mistake of rushing through the introduction process. They want the cats to be friends and be friends fast! This is usually very counter-productive. If you force the cats together too soon, you'll push their panic buttons and they will have a very negative experience. You might not only have to reintroduce them, but it could take twice as long because they've already had negative interactions with one another. In the long run, taking the extra time will *save* time.

STEP 5: MAKING THE VISUAL INTRODUCTION—THE ART OF SMOOTH TRANSITIONS

Finally, your cats get to see each other for the first time! You probably won't be surprised to hear that the visual introduction will take place during meals, treat-time, or play—the ultimate feel-good times for cats.

For Reintroductions and Difficult First-Time Introductions

If you are reading this chapter because you are reintroducing familiar cats who have become hostile, or if you have been trying to introduce stranger cats and it hasn't been going well, you will now temporarily install a barrier such as a screen door, stacked baby gates, a plastic shield, or other see-through barrier in the safe room doorway. Spray synthetic pheromones onto both sides of the see-through barrier daily. Next to or over the see-through barrier you will place a temporary *opaque* barrier—an opaque door, piece of cardboard or towel—that will prevent the cats from seeing one another at first. Be sure to also spray pheromone on the opaque barrier daily. The rest of the instructions below apply to both introductions and reintroductions, except that for introductions the barriers are rarely required—just distance.

For Introductions and Reintroductions

If you normally have food available all day (as I advise for most cats; see Chapter 5), you will need to take the food away about three hours before the viewing sessions, to make sure that they will be eager to eat whatever you're going to offer them while they are catching their first glimpse of each other. You will offer either delectable treats that you know the cats like, or food, if it's about time for a wet-food feeding. Before you allow the cats to take their places on opposite sides of the barriers (or room), check their mood. If either one seems anxious, be sure to play with him using an interactive toy to relieve stress.

When you decide that the cats are ready, place the treats or food in bowls ten to twenty feet apart (even more if needed) on either side of the barrier or room. As they begin to eat, remove any opaque barrier, open the door, lift the cardboard, or remove the towel. Whether you have used an opaque barrier to begin with or not, they will be able to see each other, and the fact that their first sight of each other occurs while they're eating will give them a good feeling about what happens in each other's presence. Be sure to end the viewing session while things are going well by replacing the opaque barrier or, if the cats are in the same room, by removing one of them—by using a wanded toy to lure them out of the room. If you get any negative reactions, end the viewing session, and the next time you have one, position the food bowls at a greater distance. If a cat won't eat, do a prey sequence (Chapter 5) to help his mood and then offer him food.

CAT'S-EYE VIEW

Some Homecats are very territorial about their humans, so cuddling Newcat in front of Homecat can cause Homecat to feel threatened and give him a reason not to like Newcat. So until your cats are getting along, love and cuddle your Newcat privately and give Homecat more attention than usual, especially if he seems more needy.

In the beginning, your first viewing session should last only a few seconds. End the session by simply shutting the door or sliding a piece of cardboard in front of the see-through barrier so that the cats can no longer see each other. Wait a few moments and then start another viewing session for another few seconds. Repeat this as long as your cats stay interested in their food or treats and do not appear tense. It's critical to end the sessions well *before* either cat becomes agitated or does anything to trigger fear in the other. Each cat should remember that the last time he saw the other cat, he got to eat and nothing bad happened. This is how you can help them form a positive association with and tolerance for one another. If one cat keeps trying to approach the other cat (or the barrier), put a harness and leash on him or put him in a carrier or cat playpen during the viewing. If a cat won't readily eat his food, use automatic toys, or a wanded toy, to play with him. The cats should remain the appropriate distance apart. If you're using a barrier, do not let cats get close enough to sniff at each other through the barrier! Interrupt any intense staring with a distraction like a toy. If one cat does become fearful or aggressive, end the viewing session. Try again when they're calm.

So long as neither cat is upset, gradually increase the length of the viewing sessions and decrease the distance between the cats, all while still feeding them or engaging them in a play time. If the meetings have been at all tense or challenging, the cats should never see each other except under your supervision; when you're not feeding or playing with them during a viewing session, keep them in their respective territories with a solid door shut between them. You should also continue letting them explore each other's territories once a day and continue Newcat spending time in the main part of the home while the other cat is safely in another room. Depending on your cats, the viewing period can last a few days to a few weeks. Good progress will be evident when each cat is relaxed when he sees the other cat.

If you've been using a barrier, the next step will be to let the cats see each other without anything between them. If you think there's any chance that one cat will bound over to the other (even with friendly intent) and scare him, use a leash and harness. Keep a good distance between them, use treats or food and *separate, far-apart* wand-toy play to help keep things positive or to distract as necessary, supervise the sessions, and end them while things are going well. If anyone seems stressed, end the session right away. You may also find that a mix of sessions with the barrier and some without can provide a nice, gradual shift. Over time, you will be able to increase the length of the viewing sessions until Newcat and the fully introduced resident cats have the run of the house together. For a while, however, Newcat may continue to want the safe room to be available to him, closed door and all, and I recommend this when you're unable to supervise.

Pay attention, because when all of the cats are finally ready to roam freely together in the home, you will need to relocate or add feeding stations, litter boxes, cat beds, and perches throughout the home.

CHECKLIST OF THINGS TO REMEMBER DURING THE VISUAL INTRODUCTION PROCESS

* Be prepared to go very slowly, at the cats' preferred pace.
* Keep the cats far enough apart that they remain comfortable. For some cats this may mean twenty-five feet (or more) in the beginning. I do NOT recommend letting them view each other through a crack in a door—only inches away. Clients have tried this on their own and the result was *nuclear*.
* End each viewing session *before* the cats show any signs of agitation or anxiety. In other words, end the viewing while things are going well.
* Let the cats see each other only under your supervision, especially if the process has not been entirely smooth.
* Use food, treats, and toys to create positive associations and improve the cats' moods.
* Use toys as positive distractions to interrupt burgeoning misbehavior.
* Never punish or reprimand.
* Continue to maintain the group-scent daily.

If your cats hiss or growl at any time in the process, you have moved too quickly for them. They are either too close together or your viewing sessions are lasting too long, or both. Move forward with longer viewing sessions and increasing proximity to one another only when no one is showing signs of stress. If your cats hiss, growl, or show signs of stress (tails flicking, ears back, and other warning signs of aggression; see Chapter 7), you will need to go back a step and proceed very slowly, always pairing food and play time with viewing sessions to help the cats build up positive associations with one another. Your cats will let you know when you've moved too quickly.

If cats are posturing aggressively or showing other signs of being about to attack, see Chapter 7 for what to do when you see signs of imminent aggression, and also for tips on what to do if a fight actually breaks out and you need to separate them.

If you experience difficulty with the introduction or reintroduction, be sure you have given each step a few weeks' time. If you have been trying to introduce cats who were once strangers to each other and are having difficulty, let them see each other only through a barrier and follow the barrier-related instructions. If you did so and one cat is still highly reactive, or if you made a mistake that you fear began a negative dynamic, it could be time to consult a cat behaviorist or consider consulting with your vet about using temporary drug therapy to help calm an aggressive cat and enhance the confidence of a timid cat. For an advanced technique that adds a bit more complexity but further assures success, see Appendix A to read about clicker training as a way of rewarding good behavior.

FIVE

Purrtopia:
Transforming Your Cats' Territory

But the wildest of all the wild animals was the Cat.
He walked by himself, and all places were alike to him.
—"The Cat That Walked by Himself," *Just So Stories*

CATS ARE TERRITORIAL BY NATURE, PARTLY BECAUSE IN THE wild they don't have other members of a pack to rely on. A single cat *is* the pack, the whole organism—solely responsible for her own survival. Cats crave a territory rich with resources and they have a powerful drive to preserve and secure those resources for themselves, and only themselves (and, among mother cats, for their young). That craving can feel like a low level of background anxiety that is with them always, sort of like the constant anxiety of a person who is worried about resources—such as money, love, or attention—that she perceives to be in limited supply. Whenever a cat's anxiety about resources is revved up, for whatever reason, she feels best when she's *doing* something to secure those resources.

What she does is what humans call the problem.

The stress of worrying about scarce resources—and competition for them—may lead not only to behavior problems, but to lowered immunity and health problems.

ATTENTION!

This may be the most important chapter you read. Cats' innate territoriality is the least appreciated of the things you *must* understand about them. You will refer to this chapter again and again to remedy each and every unwanted behavior. The advice in this chapter is also powerfully preventative, and will last you throughout your relationships with all of your cats.

Understanding the ways in which your cat is hardwired for survival will help you create an environment that channels her instincts in ways acceptable to both you and her. With the exception of the mating instinct (which requires that you spay or neuter your cat in order to avoid the related problems), every major feline behavior problem either has its root in the cat's home environment or can be helped by a holistic approach to changing that environment. You must fix the environment, or territory, in one way or another, to maximize the effectiveness of any behavioral modification program. Let's look at an example of the subtle chain of environmental causality. Some of the most upsetting behavioral problems that people come to me about are those related to urination and defecation outside of the box. Why does this happen? Not because the cats are perverse, or bad, but because something in the environment in or around the litter box, or in the greater environment, has upset them. Cats often urinate or defecate outside the litter box because they have too few boxes, or the boxes are located contrary to the needs of both hazard-avoiding cats and territorial cats, or there's competition for *other* resources among the cats. People also frequently consult me because their cats are yowling, clawing, biting, or knocking things over. This can happen if cats are stressed, don't get enough attention, or if they're bored because they lack a stimulating environment with appropriate prey targets and other items that allow them to fulfill their instinctive drives and release pent-up energy or tension. A cat whose territory provides no outlets for releasing tension may also start eating holes in your furniture, among other destructive or annoying behaviors. All of these problem behaviors can be changed — by changing the environment.

In this chapter, I'll give you guidelines on setting up your cats' environment to make sure you have the healthiest, happiest — and least destructive — cats possible. Here's where you will find the most comprehensive explanation of how to Transform the Territory, the "T" part of the various C.A.T. Plans that appear in the chapters to come. While in each chapter I usually summarize the "T" step for the behavior issues discussed there, you'll always want to return to this chapter for the fullest description. The changes I recommend will help you adapt your cats' environment to their primal needs and instincts, which include the following:

- the mating instinct
- the need to feel safe: perching, resting, and hiding areas; friendly pheromones; and your deterring of outside cats away from the home
- the need to release pent-up energy, anxiety, or tension or mark territory with scratching posts, etc.
- the desire for a choice of safe pathways to resources
- the need for food and water — and in the right locations
- the need for prey targets and other environmental stimulation: toys, cat tunnels, novel feeding opportunities
- the desire for companionship and a group scent
- the need for attractive, safe places to eliminate

The Mating Instinct: Humane Sterilization Reduces Many Behavioral and Health Problems

In Chapter 7, I discuss in detail how failure to spay or neuter cats leads to many behavior problems. Unless you are a breeder, the first and most important step to take to adapt your cats to your home and the other animals in the home should be to neuter or spay them at the appropriate time. Aside from reducing the population explosion that results in so many unwanted, unhealthy, and miserable animals, sterilization has many other benefits — both for the cats and for you.

Neutered males
- are less likely to spray or to escape your home
- have less desire to fight and are less likely to suffer the resulting abscesses
- are less likely to contract diseases such as Feline Leukemia Virus (FeLV) and feline immunodeficiency virus (FIV)
- are not prone to testicular cancer
- are not likely to develop the "stud tail" caused by overactive tail glands
- cost less to feed, requiring about one-quarter fewer calories

Spayed females
- have a decreased risk of mammary cancer, especially if spayed before the first heat
- have no uterus and therefore no risk of ovarian or uterine cancer or pyometritis, a virulent and potentially fatal inflammation of the uterus that can afflict cats soon after estrus
- are less likely to try to escape the home

Before discussing the specifics of transforming the territory in order to change unwanted behaviors, let's talk first about what that territory consists of.

Should He Stay or Should He Go?

Whether your cat is an indoors-only cat or is sometimes allowed outside, his perceiving another cat outside — by direct encounter as well as by seeing, hearing, or smelling one through a window or door—is the single most common cause of spraying inside the home (see Chapter 8), and also a major cause of what's called redirected aggression (see Chapter 7), which can seriously damage many good cat relationships. However, those aren't the only considerations to be taken into account in deciding whether to let your cat outdoors or keep him inside. Let's look at the major pros and cons.

Go Outside

In North America, about a third of urban and suburban cats are let outside; in the United Kingdom the figure is considerably higher. The outdoors can enrich a cat's environment and break up monotonous days indoors. For *some* cats, that stimulation can actually prevent or diminish many behavior issues, including, possibly, spraying inside the house. Sometimes (but by no means always) having an opportunity to spray outside, often in response to seeing other outdoor cats or smelling their urine, *could* satisfy the urge to spray.

If you do want to let your cat outside, the watchwords are supervision and safe experimentation. See what works best for your cat. To be ultra-safe, take your cat out on a harness and leash or in a walking jacket, and watch him carefully. If you take him to your yard, it's best to do this when you're sure there is no scent from other cats in the yard—which you achieve mostly by having deterred outdoor cats from your property in the first place (see Chapter 9). On the other hand, if outside cats are staying away, your cat may no longer have an urge to go outside.

As a general rule, if your cat has never been outside, it's best not to start. In my view, you should let your cat outside only if you know the cat is safe—that is, because your cat is in a yard or cat enclosure that it can't escape, on a harness and leash with you, or in an area where there are no cars, predators, competitors, or anything else that might harm or stress your cat. Of course, even if he's in an enclosure or you're taking him out on a cat harness and leash, as long as he's outside and able to see and smell other cats, he may feel some stress. Also, because fleas and ticks can be an issue for cats allowed outside (even if just briefly), make sure your cat is protected with a cat flea and tick product.

If your cat isn't neutered or spayed, he or she should *never* be allowed outside.

Stay Inside

Though letting cats outside can sometimes decrease their spraying or urine-marking inside the home, it can also have the opposite effect. There's territory to be marked! If it's not being marked outside, a cat may feel anxious: Time to mark indoors. So if your cat is not spraying and you don't want him to start, don't let him outside. If he *is* spraying, it's a toss-up as to how going outside will affect the spraying problem.

The outdoors, great or suburban-style, poses many hazards that can injure your cat—sometimes fatally—or make him sick. Cats may be hunted by dogs or wild animals. (And there are also people out there who just don't like cats.) They can be hit by cars, contract parasites from drinking stagnant water, acquire feline diseases, and suffer extremes in weather and temperature. They may get into fights with other cats and be badly hurt. And cats in their turn threaten bird species throughout the world, including the songbirds in your back yard. (On the other hand, so do humans, as cat lovers never tire of reminding bird advocates: Human activity is fifty-six times more likely to kill birds than cats are.)[1] Once a cat has gotten a taste for the hunting life, it is very difficult to get him to stop.

Other than the safe outdoor alternatives I've already mentioned, my advice is generally to keep your cat indoors. He'll be safer, live longer than an outdoors-only cat (an average of twelve years versus three, according to some estimates), and feel less need to urine-mark his territory.

There are plenty of ways to make the inside of your home just as stimulating as the outdoors—which is what the rest of this chapter is about. Many unwanted behaviors can be remedied by mimicking aspects of a cat's natural environment. As awareness of cat behavior has grown, so have the number of useful and even very nearly magical tools that you can use to transport cats to a feline Eden—all while keeping him indoors, safe and happy.

NOTE ON RECOMMENDED BEHAVIOR TOOLS
AND PRODUCTS

The tools I recommend include toys such as preylike targets at the ends of easily manipulated wands, battery-operated toys, cat trees and tunnels; food puzzles and timed feeders; pheromone sprays and plug-ins that calm and soothe cats and help them get along; high-grade enzyme-based odor removers to help ensure that cats won't develop an association with the location of inappropriate elimination; and deterrents to the outdoor animals that can cause your cats anxiety and lead to all kinds of behavior problems.

Now, products and brand names may both come and go. Those that were once the best may suffer degraded quality control, be overtaken by a competitor, or have their names changed by new owners. (Indeed, as we were editing this book, one of my long-time favorite behavior-modification products was taken off the market.) Some product manufacturers may go out of business. And some may not be available in certain countries at all. Yet I want the advice in this book to remain as relevant and up-to-date as possible. So I have hit upon several solutions.

* When I refer to a behavior modification tool you will need to make or buy, I'll often use a generic term for it (e.g.: pheromones, wanded toy, etc.; see the full list in Appendix C).
* When I do recommend one brand of product over the others, I will provide the brand name of that product as available in early 2012 to online and offline shoppers in the United States.
* For my views on the latest and greatest behavior modification tools (increasingly to include, I hope, those available outside the United States), *always*

refer to the most up-to-date research and product
recommendations at catwhispererproducts.com.

Magical as some of these tools are, under no circumstances should you attempt to remedy your cats' unwanted
behaviors through the use of products alone. For maximum
effectiveness, they should be incorporated into my program
of behavior modification techniques, and used according to
my instructions—which will not always be the same as the
manufacturers' directions.

REAL ESTATE AND RESOURCES

Feelings of Safety: Cat Trees and Other Forms of Vertical Territory

Ever notice how your cat likes to climb up, jump up, or lie on top of
things? A big difference between you and your cats is that you never
walk into a room and look around for the highest, safest spot. This is
the spot—the top of the couch, the windowsill, the mantel, the coun-
tertop, the chair, the bed, or your lap—from which the cat could
safely observe a big dog, a dominant cat, or some other possible danger coming from any direction and from a long way off. Your cat likes
to have places from which he can get a good view of the carpet savan-
nah and wooden forest floor that is your home. He may contest these
safe, valuable spots with other cats in the household, especially if you
haven't provided enough of them. (Or, if you're lucky, he may develop
an amicable time-sharing schedule with the other cats.) Humans and
dogs don't need vertical territory, but cats' territory must encompass
three dimensions, especially if you have more than one cat.

The way to create vertical territory for your cats is by providing cat
trees and perches they can climb around and on top of, giving them a
feeling of safety while also stimulating their minds. The more cats you
crowd into your home's fixed territory, the greater the chance of con-

flict among them. Adding vertical territory with multiple levels can truly be life-altering for cats, because the increase in available territory will decrease territorial tensions. Cats were born to escape predators, carve out territory, and sleep on elevated surfaces. Support your cat's natural behaviors: to climb, to perch, and to stake out territory and elbow room. More than one cat, more than one tree level and more than one perching area. All cats should have a cat tree, window perches, and even cat walks—shelving mounted on walls in configurations that allow cats to perch at different levels. A cat can spend hours spiraling up and down a cat tree, now perching, now resting. Experiment with different locations until you've figured out which ones maximize your cats' use of the elevated places. Sunny spots are usually popular. Unused, far-off corners of the home may or may not work for your cat.

If your cats compete for an area like the back of the living room couch, try placing a cat tree nearby. One cat may decide to utilize the cat tree instead of the couch some of the time. Such time-sharing arrangements can help reduce the competition that can lead to hostility or outright fighting—which in turn can lead to many other seemingly unrelated behavior issues. Vertical territory helps timid cats to feel more confident and relaxed, and dominant cats to feel less of a need to be bullies.

CAT TERRITORY ON A BUDGET

To save money on cat trees and perches, clear off the top of an armoire or dresser or remove the picture frames or plants from a windowsill and you've just created more perching and resting areas for your cats.

Cats also don't care that the cardboard boxes they play in and scratch on cost nothing, or that the paper bags (with the handles removed and the cuffs rolled down to keep the bags open) they enjoy were free.

To create an inexpensive cat tunnel, turn an open, empty box on its side, toss a few toys and some catnip inside, and create a fun fort in which cats cavort.

Scratching Posts and Other Stimulating Gear

Cats need environmental stimulation to relieve stress and excess energy and, well, to enable them to act like cats. Environmental stimuli can take many forms: climbing frames, cat trees, cat tunnels, interactive playtimes, battery-operated toys, fish tanks, bird feeders, novel feeding opportunities like cat grasses, different feeding stations, and especially food puzzles, which require the cat to work at getting food or treats.

Scratching posts or pads answer several needs at once, and are particularly important. In addition to channeling the cat's need to scratch onto something more desirable (from your point of view) than furniture and other household items, scratching materials allow cats to get rid of old claw growth and keep their claws sharp, stretch their muscles, mark territory, and release emotional tension (even cats with amputated toes and claws will want to paw-mark, so they need scratching posts, too). To see what your cats prefer, experiment with horizontal and vertical surfaces (cats who like to *stretch* when they scratch may prefer a tall post), and pay attention to whether they like tree bark, wood, fabric, rope, cardboard, or carpet. Cats like to scratch-mark along their usual pathways, so put some scratching posts along those pathways. Cats will generally use cat scratchers more if they're closer to the core of the home instead of the outskirts. Make sure that you have at least one cat scratcher for each of your cats, and place them throughout the home in areas where your cats tend to spend a lot of time.

Cat tunnels and hiding places can keep cats busy and feeling safe. They're great for the fearful or timid cat who needs a safe place to hide or a way to covertly move about the home. You can also keep boredom at bay by mixing things up a bit: Move toys, boxes, or tunnels around every so often.

Bird and squirrel feeders are also entertaining for cats, and you can place them outside, near a window whose view your cats can watch like a big-screen TV. Or you can set up an indoor fish tank, making sure it has a tamperproof top. Many cats will also watch bird videos, though my own otherworldly cats prefer the fish from *Find-*

ing Nemo. When the fish swim off the edge of the television screen, my cats look for them behind the TV and even in other parts of the room.

Food puzzles are also great stimulants. Puzzles trigger your cat's prey drive and then allow him to sink his teeth into the treats or food he's able to work out of the puzzles. There are several great food puzzles on the market, but you can make your own food puzzle out of a shoe box or any plastic container in which you've cut a hole and placed food to be fished out. Food puzzles help to prolong feedings and reduce anxiety or tension. Visit catwhispererproducts.com to learn how to make food puzzles of your own or to see the products I recommend most highly.

In addition to pheromones (covered in Chapter 3), natural holistic remedies such as flower essences have been shown to have a profound effect on behavior issues in many cats, as well as to calm fearful cats. Many shelter staff members have reported to me that the effects of natural holistic remedies are sometimes the only reasons fearful or timid cats are able to get adopted. Of course, I recommend you incorporate such remedies into an overall behavior plan, but even used alone, the remedies may still have positive effects. Depending on the remedy, you may add them to your cat's food, water, or skin (to be absorbed transdermally), to help your cat become more relaxed, confident, and better able to deal with stressors. Visit catwhispererproducts.com to see recommended holistic remedies.

THINGS TO KNOW FOR BOARDING

Pheromones and other holistic remedies are so effective at calming and soothing cats that you should ask a key question of any cat boarding facility you are considering: "Do you use pheromone plug-ins around the cats' living quarters?"

DISPERSAL, TIME-SHARING, AND
CHOICE OF PATHS

In a multicat household, cats care about more than just the size or amount of a resource. They care about having multiple resource locations with multiple pathways to them. This will give them choices about which ones to visit, when to visit, and will make it easier for them to time-share those resources with one another. The easier it is to time-share, the less conflict and territorial behavior you will see and the greater the feeling of self-confidence for all the cats. For best results, you should apply this principle of abundance and dispersion to all your cat's resources, from litter boxes and toys to cat trees and perches. Let's start with food.

ADD AND MULTIPLY

Throughout the advice that's to follow, keep in mind that, for the best possible results, you will want to make available *several* feeding stations throughout the home, *several* water stations, *multiple* perching and resting areas, *multiple* litter box locations, *multiple* cat scratchers, and *multiple* prey targets, or toys, in different locations. Even if you think your cats are happy without such a land-o-plenty, I urge you to try it and see the results for yourself. I've had many clients tell me they didn't realize what a happy and confident cat was until they made these changes. Even my clients who live in small apartments in New York have noted that their cats get along much better or become less "aloof" or "stressed" after the addition of something as simple as another food bowl somewhere else in the apartment.

Food

In a multicat household, if you offer your cats one big communal cat food bowl or even several cat food bowls all within the same room, and feed them all at the same time, you will fail to address the cats' territorial needs. The existence of only one location for food and a limited number of pathways to it could be enough to create the kind of tension at mealtime that leads to fighting and bullying. Some cats may end up unhappily hungry as others bully them out of the way. Food abundance and dispersion are easy but critical ways to keep space between your cats, allow them to time-share more efficiently, and keep them happy.

Free-feeding, which consists of keeping food available to the cats at all hours of night and day, preferably in several locations throughout the home, is another way.

PLANT EATERS

No one really knows why cats like to eat plants, especially grass, but they do. While ingesting plants is probably normal—feral cats eat grass nearly every day, and one study showed that 36 percent of pet cats eat plants—it can be dangerous, as most houseplants are toxic to cats in small amounts and some are even deadly.

To get your cat to stop chewing plants, spray a bitter anti-chew product (see catwhispererproducts.com) on both the tops and undersides of the leaves. If your cats nibble at the plants, keep reapplying the solution. I recommend not having toxic plants accessible to your cat.

Offer your cat such alternatives as a stalk of celery, a leaf of Romaine lettuce, or cat grasses from your local pet store or farmer's market. You can even grow your own pesticide-free herbs, grasses, or catnip. Putting more vegetable matter in your cat's diet may be particularly effective if you're trying to prevent her from chewing or eating either houseplants or flowers.

Why free-feed? Cats have small stomachs that empty out in a couple of hours. An empty stomach is no fun, especially if it's empty for several hours. Cats in the wild and those allowed to set their own feeding schedules eat quite frequently—from nine to sixteen mouse-sized meals per day—and appear to have evolved to eat that way.[2] Not surprisingly, cats who are fed only twice a day, during scheduled feedings, can become agitated, and they can get even more cranky if the food isn't served on time. Their stomachs will be growling and their dinner conversations may be kind of grumpy (sometimes even hostile), causing them to take their unhappiness out on each other. Dominant cats will want to make sure everybody knows that they're in control and they are going to get the food first. Dominant cats who are concerned about a perceived scarcity of food resources may be so anxious about preserving their dominance that they intimidate lower-ranking cats not just at mealtimes but at other times of the day, too.

Even a cat who doesn't have to share food with other cats is happier when she can readily follow her body's natural rhythms. Anytime a cat eats, she's at her most content, with a more stable mood and emotional state. Many clients are totally unaware their cats are stressed about food until they see the difference in the cats' personalities after they begin either free-feeding the cats or providing them with more than two meals a day.

Cats fed on timed, human schedules tend to be less cooperative and more aggressive than cats allowed to eat on their own schedules. In most cases you don't need to worry that free-fed cats will gain weight. In fact, I've seen obese cats lose weight once food was made readily available, because once they realized that there would always be enough food and there was no need to gobble it up all at once, they stopped overeating. Free-feeding may also reduce some cats' tendency to bolt their food down and later regurgitate it.

If a cat is not able to regulate her food intake, however, I do not recommend free-feeding. You may create an obese cat. For these cats, a timed feeder that delivers food four or more times a day is ideal. You won't be increasing his calorie allotment—just how often he is fed. However, for cats who can regulate their intake and for whom obesity is not an issue (75 to 90 percent of cats), I would go as far as to say that feeding them only twice a day is inhumane.

Dispersal of food resources can have strikingly positive effects on the happiness and harmony of your feline household. Place food bowls in different locations throughout the home (not just in different areas of the kitchen or bathroom)—for both free-feeding and scheduled feedings. There should be as many feed bowls as there are cats. Feeding cats together is a surefire way to *start* a behavior problem. Experiment with placing bowls on different levels—some on the floor and some on tables or windowsills. A more timid cat may not feel comfortable eating on the floor.

Food puzzles (described earlier) are a great way to help prolong your cat's feeding so he doesn't gobble down all his food at once. Instead, he'll have to work to get the food out of the puzzle, which also gives him the mental stimulation that he needs. You might start out with using the food puzzle as a supplement to his regular feeding until you're sure he is actually able to get all the food out.

As for what to feed your cats—when in doubt, talk to your vet about your cat's diet.

CAT'S-EYE VIEW

Kittens should be exposed to various types of cat food flavors and textures. If they're not, they may later refuse to eat anything but what they were conditioned to eat as kittens. Cats can be finicky about food. They won't necessarily eat a healthy meal even if they're hungry. They've been known to starve to death (or eat their young) rather than eat an unpalatable meal. Compare your picky child to that!

Indeed, cats are so finicky that cat food manufacturers are forced to use humans to test cat food because cats themselves refuse to do it.*

---

* According to writer Marc Abrahams's review of a scholarly paper on human cat-food tasters, "[h]uman volunteers rated 13 different commercial pet food samples, concentrating on 18 so-called flavour attributes: sweet; sour/acid; tuna; herbal; spicy; soy; salty; cereal; caramel; chicken; methionine; vegetable; offaly; meaty; burnt flavour; prawn; rancid; and bitter. . . . The tasting protocols depended on

Water, Water, Everywhere

Water is as important to cats' health as it is to ours. Water helps to soften hard stools, digest and absorb nutrients from food, regulate body temperature, and flush waste. Cats can live for days without food, but bodily functions simply shut down if they lack sufficient water.

As with the food bowl, all it takes is one cat sitting next to the water bowl or on the pathway to it to intimidate another cat. So spread the water wealth.

Ever wonder why your cat prefers to drink out of your glass? Or from anywhere other than the water bowl next to his food? Instinctively, cats prefer to drink water that's located away from their dead prey which, in nature, may contaminate their water with bacteria. To honor this survival instinct, separate their "dead prey"—which in this case is their store-bought food—from their water. Both food and water should also be placed in an area separate from your cats' litter boxes. To make water appealing, keep it fresh—I refill my cats' water several times a day, and I recommend you do so, too, if your cat doesn't drink enough. A bowl should either be wide or filled to the brim with water. Why? Because cats' whiskers are very sensitive. They may use their paws to dip the water out, and spill it on your floor, rather than push their whiskers against a narrow-brimmed or less-than-full bowl to drink from it.

Cats are drawn to running water, so if your cat doesn't seem to be drinking from his bowl, try a fountain. Cats are notorious for not drinking enough water, and these simple prescriptions can make it more likely that they will get what they need.

the texture of what was being tasted. When munching on meat chunks people assessed the hardness, chewiness and grittiness ('sample chewed using molars until masticated to the point of being ready to swallow'). But they gauged gravy/gel glops for viscosity and grittiness ('sample placed in mouth and moved across tongue')." See Abrahams, "Pet projects: Can humans tell pâté from dog food?," *The Guardian* (May 26, 2009), www.guardian.co.uk/education/2009/may/26/improbable-research-pet-food.

Toys

Why are there so many different kinds of cat toys—often complicated, many seeming more like puzzles—compared to what's available for dogs? Because cats are more predatory than dogs. Cats need to strategize and hunt and chase and kill more than any other animal. Outdoor cats even kill prey animals they have no intention of eating (or even of offering to you).

There are several types of toys: **inanimate toys** (which I also call "dead prey"), **battery-operated toys**, and, best of all, **interactive toys** (the best of the prey targets). There's nothing wrong with dead prey, those little fake mice and glittery toy jingle balls, but a cat without an interactive toy may be a cat that doesn't play or never gets to express its catness by completing an entire prey sequence. When you maneuver an interactive toy in a prey sequence like the one described in the next section, your cat will come to life! Battery-operated toys act like interactive toys, but are useful for letting cats play and work out stress even when you're busy or not around. I recommend having plenty of all of these kinds of toys spread all over your home, like all feline resources, and kept out in the open (not all in a box or cupboard). Do rotate toys, however, keeping some of them hidden, so they can be brought out and appear new all over again. And there are some toys that you should put away after each use, such as toys with feather or string that your cat might ingest or get wound up in.

It's important to experiment with what kind of toys your cat enjoys. Does she like the ones that make noise? That roll or bounce? That have catnip in them? Some cats dislike sharing toys and will even want their own set of toys with only their scent on them.

I've spoken to many clients who've insisted their cat would never play with a toy under any circumstances. This is a sad and unhealthy situation. But not long after a consultation with me, in which I always discuss the "prey sequence," they call back to say their cat is literally leaping in the air after a toy. Some tell me they feel guilty that their kitty could indeed have played all these years. They go on to tell me that their cats are completely different cats and are so much happier now. A prey sequence completed means a happy, more confident, and satisfied cat. The key is in choosing the right toy and knowing how to make it look alive. Ready?

The Prey Sequence

Stalking and catching prey, or its bloodless equivalent, is crucial to your cat's happiness and to both remedying and preventing behavior issues. It's the same with humans: Exercise reduces our anxiety, irritability, and other behavior issues, and increases our mental alertness, our feel-good brain chemicals, and our longevity.

Cats are calmed and their confidence and mood are improved by completing one or two prey sequences consistently, every day, so set up a daily schedule and stick to it. Predictable playtimes let a cat know when it's time to be active and, at least as important for some owners, when it's time to rest. For an adult cat, try one to two playtimes daily, from ten to thirty minutes each. Maneuvering two toys far apart can enable you to save some time by playing with two cats at once—*if* they don't mind it. Automatic toys are also time-savers for humans and they can be just as important for cats so they don't become reliant on humans for all their physical exertion. For a kitten, I recommend as many as four playtimes per day, which mirrors kittens' natural preference. If your cat is easily bored, then first make sure you are conducting the play sequence properly, and if you feel confident that you are, give your cat a two- to five-minute break and then resume playtime.

I recommend performing prey sequences even if your cat isn't (yet) exhibiting a behavior problem. Your cats will be less likely to hunt at unwelcome times, intimidate other cats or people, or develop anxiety problems. Play is so important to a happy, well-functioning cat that for years the signature area in my emails to clients has said, "Have you completed a prey sequence with your cat today?" A prey sequence is also a redirection and reassociation technique that we'll use for several behavior problems (compulsive behavior, aggression, inappropriate elimination, and spraying), so I'll describe it in some detail.

You will play with one cat at a time, at least to start. Never create tension and competition for the prey target by using one toy to play with more than one cat at the same time. I've seen such competition be the reason two closely bonded cats became archenemies. If you must play with two cats at once, or you just want to, it's best to maneuver one wanded toy in each hand, far apart, so as to keep the cats as far apart as possible. If a particular cat feels uncomfortable playing while another cat watches intently, separate the cats so they can't see one another during the playtime. How do you know if your cat is uncomfortable? When he will not play or plays for only a short period of time.

STOP LOOKING AT ME!

Sometimes the only reason a cat will not play is because there are other cats in the room—a sure sign you probably have some intercat social stress within the home. Try taking the timid cat into a room with you and close the door. Then initiate a playtime with a wanded toy. You might be surprised by the outcome!

The Wand Toy Among interactive toys, wand toys are the best at allowing you to replicate a real hunt with the *unpredictable* movements of real prey—just the kind that your cat is programmed to notice. A wand toy has a long, thin wand that's attached to a string, which in turn is attached to a toy or a cluster of feathers. The best feathers make a *twirling* motion and fluttering sound that mimic a bird in flight. Play in terrain, such as a living room, with plenty of furniture, barriers, and hiding places. Cats don't like to hunt out in the open but in an area where they can ambush their prey.

When you maneuver the wand toy, doing your best to replicate real prey and a real hunt, your cat will generally display the following motor patterns, which are part of her instinctual hunting repertoire.

- staring at the prey (or toy)
- stalking and chasing

- grabbing, or pouncing and biting
- the kill bite (seen most clearly in outside cats who hunt for their food)

From Eye Stare to Kill Bite: The Complete Sequence *You* are essentially the life of the prey target. Wave or twitch the toy several feet away from your cat. How? Cats are irresistibly riveted by certain sounds like the pitter-patter of tiny feet, the sounds of crinkling, slithering, flopping around, and scurrying, and by motions that look like hopping, snaking, and flying, limping and fluttering—and dying, with one last gasp. Don't wiggle the toy in your cat's face or move it toward your cat. This won't make sense to your cat, and it might frighten her. Real prey moves *away*. Real prey hides. Your cat also needs the mental stimulation of strategizing how he's going to ambush that mouse behind the couch. It's not all about chasing and pouncing and biting. So be sure to hide the toy for a few moments behind a chair, sofa, or even an empty box (complete with scurrying or flopping sounds) before making it reappear. This will really help release those feel-good chemicals in your cat.

Your cat's menacing *stare* is the beginning of the sequence, as he orients himself to the toy. Watch him *stalk* or *chase* it. Some of the stalk may be invisible: The cat is strategizing. Then he may crouch near the ground or break into a slinking trot, now and then taking cover. The stalk or chase may be brief:* some cats like to launch themselves (the *pounce*) at the toy almost immediately and bite into it. Or your cat may wait and then, while planting his claws into the ground to pounce, make the telltale butt wiggle that signals an impending takeoff. Or he may just try to **Grab** and **Bite** the toy, perhaps as he sits atop his cat tree and strategizes how to grab the toy as it flies

---

*In some species, like cheetahs and pumas, the motor pattern is so tightly wired together that stalking and chasing is absolutely necessary. Amazingly, cheetahs can't even paw-slap or eat an animal that they haven't chased first, which is why wobbly newborn calves are safer from cheetahs than older calves that can run. For this fascinating observation I am indebted to Harvard instructor Raymond Coppinger and his wife, Lorna Coppinger, and their book, *Dogs: A New Understanding of Canine Origin, Behavior, and Evolution*, p. 207 (The University of Chicago Press, 2001).

over. Many cats will play with their "prey" and, by purposely releasing it, repeat the stalk-and-chase and grab-and-bite steps over and over again.

Make sure it's a game, neither too easy nor too challenging. Don't keep the toy away from your cat so that he never gets to catch it, and of course don't just hand it over, either. Your cat will decide how many repetitions of the prey sequence he needs, how many stalks, chases, grab-and-bites, and so on. So repeat the sequence several times so that he can catch the toy over and over again. If he doesn't seem to follow through with the entire sequence, don't worry. Just have fun with your cat! He will know what to do.

Eventually, cause the toy to slowly "die" as you put less and less energy and motion into it. This will bring your cat to the end of the prey sequence and calm him down. You may also witness something that looks like the **Kill Bite**: Your cat won't want to let go of the toy, and may even try to carry it off. Or he'll roll onto his side and kick against the toy with his back legs while biting into it. Letting your cat finish the kill can be very satisfying and rewarding to him. By contrast, I've seen cat owners stop far too soon, putting the toy away midhunt, when the cat is completely revved up to chase and grab over and over again, as a cat would in the course of weakening real prey.

The Happy Ending: Food! After your cat sinks his teeth into or

---

CAT'S-EYE VIEW: POWER DOWN
THE LASERS, JEDI

As fun as it can be to play with laser lights — "Look at that crazy cat, chasing a spot of nothing!" — laser lights can cause frustration in a cat because he never can catch or grab onto anything. If he feels unsatisfied, he may find ways to complete the hunt with something else he can sink his claws into — like another cat or your ankle.

If you do use the laser light, follow it up with a tangible toy he can "kill."

grabs the toy one last time, offer him treats or feed him his regular food. He clearly can't eat the toy (though some have been known to eat a feather or two—not good), but he *may* want to eat something, so you're substituting treat-prey for the toy-prey. It's the best kind of bait-and-switch. Offer food even if you think your cat is not hungry. Eating and hunting are independently controlled behaviors in cats, and cats will hunt even if they're already satiated. But if your cat's intention was to eat and he doesn't have a chance to do so, he may feel unsatisfied. Some cats will actually drag the toy over to the food bowl after playtime and start eating on their own! Food rewards will also teach your cat to love his prey target. If your cat doesn't eat the food or treat, that's okay, too.

Toys with strings and feathers can present hazards to your cat, so be sure to put them away when you're finished playing.

Companionship and Group Affiliation

You could call companionship a form of stimulation—so be sure to provide your cat with plenty of it. Most pet cats have been socialized to be around humans (or other cats or animals), and they form lasting bonds. Some cats may experience separation anxiety if their people leave on vacation or even for a few hours, or if one of their animal friends suddenly goes absent. Many cats, when left alone for long periods, may develop other behavior problems.

We owners are very important resources for cats. We feed them and boost their confidence and sense of security. So give your cat lots of attention. You'll not only stimulate her but reduce, and even eliminate, the stress and anxiety that can lead to behavior issues. One great way to give your cat a boost is to let her sleep in your bedroom, whether you're there or not. New kittens especially love the companionship of other cats.

Clean, Safe, Attractive Places to Eliminate

Even a poor litter box situation usually has something going for it. If there's something in the box that a cat can dig into, she may still be drawn to a box that is smelly or has some other problem, the same way you might go to a beach even if there's garbage on it and the water's too cold. Sometimes you just want to hang out at the beach, right? But proper litter box environment is multifaceted and ultracritical. Your home should have more than one clean, large, accessible, safe, well-lit, and well-situated litter box station. (The number of boxes depends on the number of cats; I'll get to how many stations in a moment.) A feline utopia in your litter box resources will prevent both unwanted urination and defecation outside of the box and other behavior issues caused by avoidable social tension between cats (see Chapter 7).

CAT'S-EYE VIEW

Signs that your cat is unhappy with her litter: She doesn't dig in the litter or sniff it, doesn't try to cover her elimination in the box, scratches outside her box after eliminating, stands on the edge, puts two paws in, or eliminates just outside of the box.

If your cat gets in the box only to struggle mightily, squatting for a very long time, she may have a urinary health or constipation issue. The same is true if she doesn't go at all, avoids the box, produces only a tiny amount of urine, or has pinkish or reddish urine. Vocalizations while eliminating can be a sign that your cat is in pain. If your cat is blocked, unable to produce urine, produces pinkish or reddish urine, or vocalizes while eliminating, take her to the vet *immediately*. These conditions can become quickly life-threatening.

Maintenance Litter Given a choice, cats instinctively prefer the sand used by their wildcat ancestors in the desert. But they'll happily use a manufactured litter that's close in texture. Unfortunately, litters are marketed toward *you*, as if you were going to use it, or your kitty shared your aesthetic preferences. But your cat is the ultimate buyer. I've found that for a maintenance litter (to use when your cat *hasn't* recently had elimination issues), most cats prefer an **unscented, medium-grain clump-**

ing litter, or a very fine-grain silica (or sandlike) litter. Both types of litter neutralize smell; the clumping litters do so even more effectively if they contain carbon. The silica sand litter looks and feels like white sand. It's very light, nontoxic, absorbs urine instead of clumping, and absorbs smell very well. It is the first choice of many veterinarians. There are some silica litters on the market that are full of chemicals and that are made up of large jagged pebbles that can hurt a cat's paws; you should avoid those. They can be a big deterrent for cats.

I do not recommend corn litters or wheat litters for adult cats. Many cats eat these litters, which can be unhealthy while also conflicting with the elimination drive, but cats instinctively do not like to urinate or defecate in a food source. As a result, I've seen hundreds of cats develop an aversion to food-based litters. These litters are also soft in a negative way: Cats' paws tend to sink in them, which they dislike. I can't tell you how often food-based litters have wrought havoc on good litter box behavior or made existing issues worse. I also recommend avoiding litters that smell of pine. Pine falls under the category of a (strongly) scented litter, which cats dislike and may avoid.

Kittens need litter that is expressly designed for them. Like human babies, kittens like to put things in their mouths, so I don't recommend using plastic pellets, clay, or clumping litters for kittens. See catwhispererproducts.com for current information on the best litter products.

It may be that not all of your cats like the same litter, so be sure to have a couple of different kinds of litter available. If you switch brands, do so by gradually mixing ever-increasing quantities of the new litter with the old litter, until the change is complete. That way your cat will get used to the new litter and you'll minimize the chances of any negative reaction.

Litter Box Cleanliness "The housekeepers clean the box twice a week," one of my clients proudly told me. Egad! If I could write and appear in a public service advertisement for feline health and happiness, I would put litter box cleanliness at the absolute top of my list of priorities. Your cat spends much of the day cleaning herself. You should not make her job any harder by failing to provide her with a sparkling-clean litter box.

- **Two scoops a day keeps the behaviorist away**. Ultimately, the frequency of your scooping will vary with your cats' need for clean boxes, how many they use, and how often certain boxes get used. As you begin the process of finding the right frequency, start with this rule of thumb: If your cats are eliminating properly, scooping once a day *may* be enough; but I recommend twice-a-day scoopings. If you go on vacation, make sure your sitter maintains the same cleaning schedule you do (or better). If that's not possible, then you may need to add extra litter boxes while you are out of town. I don't recommend covered boxes, but if you insist on using one, scoop two to three times daily.
- **Change the litter**. You can't keep a box clean forever just by scooping out soiled litter. The scents of feces and urine—so unattractive to kitty—adhere to the remaining litter even when the urine clump and stool is removed, so all of the litter will start stinking soon enough. A good rule of thumb is to completely change clumping litter every few weeks and non-clumping litter (pellets) every day to every week, depending on the cat, the litter, and the smell. To neutralize odors, you can also mist an odor-binding cleaner in your litter boxes. In one study, litter boxes sprayed with such a cleaner were used more than boxes without it, and cats showed greater satisfaction with their litter box.[3] See catwhispererproducts.com for recommendations.
- **Clean the boxes every few weeks** with a mild cleanser (not bleach), then scrub and rinse. If you wait until the box starts to smell, then you have waited too long to clean it—and you may have set your cat on the downward escalator to disliking his litter box situation. Boxes should be replaced every six months, unless they're made of a nonabsorbent plastic.

Enough Litter Boxes? Add More In a multicat household, it's important to avoid competition for litter box resources. Otherwise, dominant cats may try to deter other cats away from the box, and cats who want to avoid an altercation will avoid the litter box area—finding their own elimination resource elsewhere (in places you are almost certain not to be happy about!). Many cats also like to be able to choose a box that doesn't smell very strongly of another cat. One reason may be simple cleanliness, but they may also want to avoid what they perceive as other cats' territorial marking of the litter box with urine or feces. One sure way to reduce competition and social tension is to increase the number of boxes, locations, and options for the cats. Generally, you should have one box for each cat you own, plus at least one more, or at least one box per floor of a multilevel house, whichever is more. That means that if you have only one cat, but live in a three-story house, you'll need three boxes. If you have three cats in a single-level home, you'll need at least four boxes.

A Clean, Well-Lighted Place Litter box areas and the pathways to them must be well-lit twenty-four hours a day—at least with night lights. Good lighting will immediately make the litter area more visible and friendly at night. Cats can see very well in low light, as much as six times better than we can, but they see even more clearly with more light, and they feel better when they know they can see anything lurking nearby. Some would rather not walk into dark and shadowy areas even during the day.

Box Size and Type A litter box should be uncovered and should be one-and-a-half times the length of your cat. Given a choice, most adult cats (especially the obese) will opt for a jumbo-sized box. My cats revel in large, see-through, low-sided plastic storage containers. If you have soiling problems, and have the space, try them. These containers usually cost the same as or less than a litter box from the pet store, and because they're less absorbent, they last longer. I recommend boxes about six inches tall, sixteen inches wide, and twenty-one to twenty-three inches long.* The box's walls should be high enough to keep litter in, but low enough that your cat can step in easily. What if your cat likes to kick out his litter? Get a see-through storage container that's more than six inches high. Make your cat an entrance by cutting a U-shaped opening from the top to about six inches from the bottom. However,

---

* In centimeters, approximately 15 × 40 × 56. See catwhispererproducts.com for the most up-to-date recommendation.

if your cat is old, arthritic, or overweight, don't use a box any higher than six inches. And if you have a kitten that can't easily scale the side of a regular litter box, you can temporarily provide her with a low-sided litter box especially for kittens.

A note on automatic self-cleaning boxes: The quick answer? If you have or have had elimination issues, stick with your manual box. I've seen some cats who like self-cleaning litter boxes, but most would rather go scuba diving.* Many cats develop aversions to these boxes because their motors make noise during cleaning and the actual litter area is not big enough for most cats. However, most owners can't clean litter boxes immediately after every use, as the automatic boxes do, so the automatic box's greater cleanliness might appeal to certain felines. Still, the automatic boxes are by no means maintenance free. You must monitor the level of litter daily and make sure the cleaning rake or mechanism is not gummed up with litter, or worse. If you want to get a self-cleaning box, it should be *in addition* to an appropriate number of do-it-yourself boxes.

Litter Box Placement Naturally, people have their own vision of how many litter boxes they will have in their home and where they will be located. But our aesthetic sensibilities will never defeat a cat's instincts. At the end of the day, the *cat* decides! If you do add new boxes, do not move your cats' existing boxes unless the location is poor or they never use them. But in considering where to place the new boxes in order to create the feline utopia that will keep your cats happily eliminating where you want them to, use the following list of do's and don'ts as your guideline.

THE DO'S

Do make for easy access. Your cat should not have to run from the second floor down a flight of stairs to the first floor, hurdle a sleeping

---

* I had a pretty good idea of which automatic boxes available on the market actually worked before The Hammacher Schlemmer Institute recently asked me to do a more controlled study. After testing several models, The Littermaid litter box was my recommendation, just as the Littermaid was the box I'd seen work best in years of house calls for clients. See catwhispererproducts.com for the latest reviews.

dog, run a gauntlet of other cats, tumble downstairs to the basement, sprint through a maze of boxes, pole-vault over a baby gate, and crash through a cat door into a dark garage just to eliminate. Well, actually, he most likely won't do all those things. He'll go somewhere more attractive and convenient—to him, that is, not to you. Just as you always ask, in malls or airports, "Where's the closest restroom?" that's what he wants to know, too. As long as humans love to hide litter boxes away, cats will reciprocate that love by bringing their feces and urine out into the open.

Do spread them out. I've worked with many humans who had, say, six cats, and who had all seven litter boxes (a good start!) lined up . . . in the basement . . . accessible only by a single kitty door, on the other side of which was Buster the Bully Cat, looming. . . . *Oh! Terribly sorry for the interruption,* your timid cat says. *Don't mind me. I'll just go upstairs on the couch.* Aside from the competition and convenience problems, having just one location for boxes fails to respect

---

THE OVERCROWDING PROBLEM

Sometimes it's not just the litter boxes that are all located in one place but *everything* dear to a cat. Often set up in basements, these cat habitats are full of toys, litter boxes, food—and other cats. You may think this is like setting up a recreation room for your kids, but it's more like—to put it in child-speak—creating a situation where the peas touch the carrots and the ketchup *and* the soccer balls and Uncle Bob's sweaty gym shorts, too.

Whether you've just got a litter box line-up or a full-blown cat habitat, overcrowding of resources is guaranteed to make time-sharing more difficult and to increase the odds of tense meetings in a multicat household. If all the resources are in one place, that means there will be a limited number of pathways to that place, which makes your bully cat's job of intimidating and guarding that much easier.

the fact that some cats want to defecate in a place other than where they urinate. This is probably the biggest error I see clients make.

An example of good litter box placement is to put the boxes on opposite ends of the house in something like a north, east, south, west configuration. Think of your home as being made up of pathways that cats must take to get to important resources (food, water, resting/perching areas, litter boxes). Place litter boxes on different sides or ends of these pathways. If you increase locations, then, when Angel heads west down the hallway only to confront a waiting Buster, she can turn right around and light out for a box in the east, north, or south.

Do put them out in the open. Open placement of boxes increases your cat's sense of escape potential and her choice of ways to get into and out of the box. Cats have an innate survival instinct not to put themselves in a vulnerable situation. When she's in her litter box, your cat should have the best view of her territory in order to see who may be coming into it. When you're placing boxes, envision your cat in the box and see what she can see in the environment. Will she be able to see who is walking into the room? A common misconception is that cats want privacy, which humans conveniently interpret as a box wedged into a tight spot invisible to guests. For cats, a good vantage point and escape potential will usually outweigh any need for privacy.

Most people would rather not have a box right out in the open. But placement in closets and cabinets, or behind plants or furniture, should be the exceptions, not the rule. If you choose one of these hidden locations, make sure your cats have alternative locations that are more easily accessible and have better vantage points and escape potential. Do keep the litter box safe from dogs and short-legged humans by using a baby gate that your cat can easily jump over, or a pet gate that has a special small door for cats located at the bottom. This will keep Fido and Baby Fred out, but allow Fluffy to saunter in whenever she likes.

Whenever possible, *don't* wedge a box up against a wall. The box should have a foot or more of buffer on all sides so your cat can walk all the way around it, sniff, and decide which side to step into. Not only have you increased your cat's choice of entrances into the box, but the exits as well, which gives the cat her ever-so-important escape potential and, of course, choice.

THE PRIVACY MYTH

A cat's supposed need for litter box privacy is largely a myth sprung from anthropomorphism. I've seen cat owners re-model a part of their home just to seclude the litter box. Add a toilet roll holder and a few magazines, and some of the lit-ter box setups I've seen would look just like what a minia-ture human would want in a bathroom. Cats are not *embarrassed* to be going to the bathroom. What cats want is safety. When they're urinating or defecating, they need to feel safe from predators or competitors (real or imagined). That may mean they don't want to have to eliminate in front of the dog, but more often it means that while they're im-mobile and vulnerable, they instinctively want a location with good escape potential and vantage point.

Many of the don'ts are just the opposite of the do's, but there are a lot of other don'ts as well, summarized below.

THE DON'TS

Don't put the litter boxes in high-traffic areas like hallways. Cats' dislike of commotion is not arbitrary.

Don't deter your cat from the litter box with obstacles like piles of laundry.

Don't let him see an outside cat through a window in or on his way to the litter box (see deterrence in Chapter 8)

Don't put a litter box near anything that could startle a cat with a loud noise, such as a garage door, refrigerator, or washer or dryer.

But if you must, give your cats some quieter alternative locations, too.

Don't put litter boxes only in small, cramped places like the laundry room (which also has the disadvantage of reeking of strong smells such as those of bleach or detergents).

Don't put boxes in a location where anything bad—fights, hostility, or punishment—has occurred. Cats can have flashbacks. If your cat is near a box where he's had negative experiences, he may growl, hiss, and even piloerect. Or he may just not use the box.

Don't put boxes only in a bathroom. Some cats have no problem with their litter boxes in a bathroom, but to others a bathroom might as well be a major train station, given how much traffic in and out there is. They may also dislike the steam and humidity from the shower. If you do put a box in a bathroom that is in frequent use, place an additional box somewhere else so that if the bathroom is occupied and your cat would rather not share, she has a choice.

Don't put litter boxes next to "nest" items—food, water, and beds. Especially in a small room, nothing associated with a cat's nest area should be in the same room as the litter box. In the wild, stool or urine near the nest area attracts parasites, predators, and competitors. Keeping the nest area safe from threats is a hardwired survival instinct in a cat, which means that most cats will not eliminate near it. If you can't place litter boxes and food bowls in different rooms, place them diagonally across the room from one another or erect a visual barrier to create a sense of separation.

A COUPLE OF OTHER BIG DON'TS

Don't use covered boxes, especially in a multicat household. Covers are for humans, not for cats. There are no equivalents of covered litter boxes in nature; crawling into something like a hole reduces a cat's view of the terrain and of possible escape routes. Covers also trap smells and produce a Porta-Potty effect, keeping urine and stool moist and extra stinky. Your poor cat can't plug his acutely sensitive nose. My eyes burn just thinking about it, and I know your cats' eyes do, too.

If you're worried about your cat scattering litter, accidentally urinating over the edge of the box, or spraying against a wall while in the box, buy a high-sided storage container as recommended earlier and cut an opening in the side so your cat can easily walk into it.

I have seen many cases where a covered box was the one and only reason a cat stopped using the litter box. Obese, arthritic, and elderly cats often struggle to get into or maneuver about in covered boxes. These too-small boxes are almost always a bit too high-sided for cats with mobility problems. If you already have a covered box, I recommend that you either take the cover off or offer your cat at least two uncovered alternatives in different locations.

Don't use liners! The crinkly noise can be a deterrent to some cats, their claws get caught in the liner when they scratch to cover up, and if the liner doesn't exactly fit the box, urine may splatter up against them, which they definitely will not like.

If you've read this chapter carefully, you're well-armed to prevent a great deal of unhappiness in your cats, and the undesirable behaviors that often go hand-in-hand with unhappy cats (making for unhappy owners, too). After I briefly explain the relationship between medical problems and behavior in the next chapter, you'll be ready to apply the T of the C.A.T. Plan to all the behaviors that will be discussed.

SIX

Psychology and Physiology: Does Your Cat Also Have a Medical Issue?

*"Speak English! I don't know the meaning of half those long words,
and I don't believe you do either!"*
— The Eaglet, *Alice in Wonderland*

CATS' BEHAVIOR IS A PRODUCT OF THEIR GENES, THEIR ENVI-
ronment and social development, and their health. Many behavior
problems are medical in origin and should first be treated by a veterinarian. But even medically related behavior problems should be
referred not just to a veterinarian but also to a cat behaviorist (or this
book). In my experience with thousands of clients and their vets, vets
are great at dealing with medical problems, but they are rarely as successful at dealing with behavior problems, particularly those that have
become habitual. Let's look now at your cat's physical health and
behavior and the intersection between them.

Good Veterinary Hygiene

Did you know that cat owners take their cats to the vet less often than they take their dogs, not to mention less often than dog owners take their dogs? In fact, over the last two years, the disparity has gotten even worse. I recommend that you take your cat to a vet for medical checkups and teeth-cleanings as often as your vet recommends, but at least once a year, and certainly any time your cats begin to exhibit any unwanted or abnormal behaviors.

One possible reason that people don't take their cats to the vet as often as they probably should is that cats hide their illnesses more effectively than dogs. For example, it's been estimated that nearly a third of cats over the age of eight suffer from painful arthritis, but you'd never know it. Cats don't show it by limping, as dogs or horses do. Cats rarely even vocalize their pain; in fact, if they're not feeling well, they may even purr, because purring can be a form of self-soothing. Although a cat may also signal an illness by a sudden unwillingness or inability to jump or eat, or by sleeping more, and playing and hunting less, other signs that something is wrong—say, sudden aggression, spraying, or inappropriate elimination—may be misunderstood as signifying behavioral rather than medical problems. Hyperthyroidism, for example, is just one of many possible physiological causes of aggression. And I can't tell you how often an abscessed tooth has been to blame for all the cat fights within the home.

When was the last time *your* cat had a dental exam? The stress of a painful tooth or sore gums can transform the dynamics of the entire household—and not for the better! Poor oral health leads to pain or discomfort, which leads to stress, which leads to tension among cats.

Original Medical Causes Versus Habituated Behaviors

Because unwanted behaviors sometimes have a physiological basis, among the first actions you should take to cure behavioral problems is to make sure you've identified and dealt with any medical causes.

For most of the behavior issues in this book, I've included a sidebar called Medical Alert, which will give you an idea of possible medical causes you should consider consulting a vet about.

A visit to the vet will usually reveal any medical cause, and lead to effective medical treatment. However, as successful as that treatment is, it may not be able to change any behavioral habits that formed in response to the medical problem. The unwanted behavior now has another, separate cause: It's become habituated. For example, I often work with clients whose cats' urinary tract infections or crystals were cleared up prior to the owner consulting with me. But the cats are still urinating inappropriately because (1) they have associated the litter box (or substrate or location) with the past painful urination, and (2) they've developed a habit of urinating somewhere else, like on the sofa. Both association and habit can develop very quickly, resulting in a preference for a new location and a different material.

Our goal in this book will be to make sure you remedy both the original, medical cause of the behavior problem with your vet, and the habituated and environmental causes, all while we undo any negative associations and attract and retrain your cat to more desirable behaviors. Perhaps you can now see why one-note remedies, such as curing a urinary tract infection or adding more litter boxes to your home, are often insufficient.

CAT'S-EYE VIEW

Another possible catalyst for undesirable habits that aren't medical in nature is psychological trauma. If you yelled at or spanked your cat near her litter box, or forced her into it, she may associate the litter box with the painful or negative experience of your anger. Here, too, we must reverse an ingrained association.

Better Living Through Chemistry? Don't (Automatically) Drug That Cat!

Let me say, up front, that psychoactive drugs can save cats' lives and work where nothing else does. Sometimes it's the most responsible and even humane decision. However, I am concerned here with over-prescription of medication for normal and easily solved cat behavior issues. Just as pediatricians (sometimes with the complicity of parents) may overprescribe ADHD drugs for kids who are just, well, being kids, cats are often overmedicated for exhibiting natural and easily solved behaviors such as spraying or clawing.

To a person who loves cats, the results of unnecessary medication can be tragic. An unnecessarily medicated cat is a cat that may lose its catness. Go to your medical vet or a vet behaviorist, but go armed with empowering knowledge. While psychoactive drugs have a useful place in solving some behavior issues, there are a number of reasons to adopt a more skeptical stance toward medication than most cat owners do.

First, depending on their application, even the most effective med-ication for your cat's behavior issue may have a success rate of only 50 percent or so. The most effective medications for spraying, for example, have success rates of around 75 to 90 percent[1]—a lower rate than I achieve. (And that's assuming that the medication is actually the right one. It may take several trips back to the vet, either to mod-ify the dosage, or to find a different drug that works better than the first one that was prescribed.) My clients who have been medicating their spraying cats are usually able to use my methods to remove the un-derlying cause of the spraying and take their cats off the medications.

Second, even when drug therapy works, it usually works only as long as the animal is medicated. (One exception is when medication has been used to defuse cat-to-cat social conflict; the results may be lasting.) For example, cats who are put on and then taken off med-ication for spraying tend to resume spraying at rates of 75 to 95 per-cent.[2] Without a behavior plan, your cat may revert to her unwanted behavior once you stop the medication.

Third, medications may be prescribed in error. I've seen many cases in which a vet, sometimes pressured by the cat owner, prescribed an antianxiety medication (like most cat drugs, one first sold to humans) for a behavioral problem—while, ironically, overlooking the underlying medical issues for the problem, such as a bladder or kidney stone.

A VET'S VIEW: DRUG THERAPY FOR CATS

Dr. James Shultz, DVM

For about the first ten years of my career as a small-animal veterinarian I must have counseled thousands of pet owners on canine behavioral issues. For these clients the options were almost endless. Dog trainers, behaviorists, puppy whisperers, and animal psychics, all at their disposal and ready to help. Group training, individual training, in-home training, and doggy boot camps that would last three or more months and most certainly cost as much as a small SUV were the norm. Then there were the products: citronella collars, shock collars, spiked collars, pinch collars, tracking collars, muzzle leads—the list went on and on.

But what about cats? Cats were a whole other story. Clients would come in frustrated. Like most vets I know, I was not trained in cat behavior, but I did my best: We would rule out any purely physiological cause and then try a few things like changing the number and location of the litter boxes, changing the substrate in the box, and maybe we'd try enriching the cat's environment with a few toys. If none of this worked, the cat owner had but a few options: make the cat a "barn cat" or "outdoor cat" or try one or more medications. Since few if any behavioral medications are specifically designed for cats, it usually meant trying a human medication on the cat and then trying to find a dose that worked.

These medications worked about half the time, to some extent. In a few cases they made all the difference and the owner was elated, and so was I. Too often, though, there were problems, and lots of them. To start, how do you get cats to take the medication? We tried pills, tuna-flavored liquids, flavored treats containing the medication, and even transdermal gels. And not always successfully.

Then there was the cost. Nearly all of the cases treated, if successfully managed with medications, were only managed while the cat was medicated. In other words, there was no way to get the patient off of the drugs. On top of this, clients were reporting that not only were the medications lightening their wallets, but that there were other unwanted side effects as well. Even on some of the newer drugs, clients would note that the cat had lost his or her "personality" or seemed "out of it" most of the time — side effects not that different from those noted by humans taking these medications. (Note that with some medications it is common for cats to seem dazed for a couple of weeks, but once their bodies adjust to the medication, they often seem to normalize.) Since cats don't metabolize these drugs in the same way as humans (for whom the drugs were originally designed), it makes sense that undesirable side effects would be common.

Some variation on the above treatment plan was basically how we treated these cases until we met Mieshelle. What was so exciting about her methods is that she could consistently identify and correct the underlying *cause* of the unwanted behavior. This meant in most cases usually no medications were required at all, and when we did utilize them in conjunction with her methods it was only for a short period of time. By identifying the cause of the unwanted behavior (example: spraying), Mieshelle resolves the problem *for the life of the cat*, without the need for long-term medications, and without banishing your cat to the garden shed forever.

All that being said, there's no question that drugs are sometimes not only helpful but necessary, and even lifesaving. And sometimes drugs must be used when the problem has no medical basis but is as purely behavioral as it's possible for a problem to be. Imagine a cat that presents a danger to himself, another cat, or a person. Medicating a cat under those circumstances is certainly a better solution than abandoning or killing him.

But for problems that have no medical basis, I firmly believe that we should explore natural solutions before resorting to drugs. Based on my experience and a high success rate in solving unwanted behaviors through behavioral techniques and environmental modification alone, I believe most medication of cats with unwanted behaviors is unnecessary. It makes no sense to drug a cat against anxiety when the source of the anxiety can be easily spotted and removed from the environment. Medication is rarely enough by itself. There's a reason the behavior started to begin with, and it wasn't because the cat was missing Prozac in her diet. Just as a cat behaviorist should not hesitate to recommend the services of a veterinarian when a cat appears to have a medical problem, I consider it unethical to medicate a cat for a behavioral problem without first seeking behavioral expertise.

Now, are you ready for some fighting? We'll start with a common and challenging behavior of cats: aggression.

SEVEN

Feline Aggression: Accepting and Managing Your Cat's Inner Wildcat

[The Cheshire-Cat] looked good-natured, she thought:
still, it had very long claws and a great many teeth,
so she felt that it ought to be treated with respect.
—Alice in Wonderland

POUND FOR POUND, CATS ARE FORMIDABLE ADVERSARIES. They've been called the perfect carnivore. Dogs have one weapon— their teeth—but cats have many more. There's that wide-opening mouth with teeth sharp enough to neatly sever the spinal cords of animals of similar size or smaller. There are the four, almost prehensile, paws with claws as sharp as razors that cats can wield like swords. And cats have many other strategic advantages, too. They are quieter than a whisper but have explosive power and speed. They're harder to restrain than a Chinese contortionist channeling Houdini. Cats' backbones flex like noodles and they have no collarbones. Their shoulders can rotate in nearly any direction. Like the greatest human athletes, cats have an unerring sense of where they are in space. Everyone knows that a cat that falls upside down from high enough can usually air-right itself and land on its feet. (But *do not* drop a cat to test this claim, lest you cause your cat serious injury.) In her charming memoir-with-cat, *Homer's Odyssey*, Gwen Cooper relates how her blind cat Homer would stalk flies through the house until suddenly, springing five or more feet into the air, often complete with a back-flip, he would catch one in his mouth.

CAT BITES

Cat bites can contain particularly harmful bacteria and, about half the time, they cause infections in humans, adding an element of danger that most cat owners (it's fair to say) didn't consider when they picked little Hansele out as a kitten. Cat bites against both humans and cats (or other animals) can be very deep and should be treated immediately.

The cat's arsenal of weapons and defenses makes sense: Their African wildcat ancestors lived, stalked, hunted, captured, killed, guarded prey, and ate—all alone. They still do. They've never had a pack or group to rely on, as dogs and wolves do. And because cats have the status of being both predator and prey, they're all but unique in needing adaptations suitable for being the predators and *not* becoming the prey. Of course they're going to have serious skills, as teenagers say, both defensive and offensive.

So what are you going to do when a cat seems to be itching for a fight, *fight back*? Unfortunately, some people try.

What Not to Do: Punish, Reprimand, or Reach For

As I explained in Chapter 1, you should avoid giving punishments or even reprimands to your cat. Of course, if you're confronted with an angry or aggressive cat and are willing to risk scratched-up arms and (one can only hope) a good dose of guilt, you *can* overpower a cat, or even try to "punish" it (quotes here because that's the *owner's* notion of what they're doing). But *abuse* (my notion, and I suspect the cat's, too) will do nothing to help the problem. It has the potential to further anger the cat, or frighten him, or ruin your relationship with him, or both. So don't bother. Nor should you ever try to pick up or soothe an agitated cat. Cats, once aroused, don't usually calm quickly or benefit from human attempts at soothing. Some cats might even consider the attention a kind of reward for their behavior—another mistake. Better just to remove yourself from an upset cat's presence; otherwise the cat could injure you.

CONVENTIONAL ADVICE ALERT

Some people suggest that if you're dealing with a kitten who is biting or scratching, you should swat or growl to discourage the kitten's inappropriate play behavior, as the mother would.

I do not recommend this approach. Swatting violates our injunction against punishment, and because we aren't mother cats, we're not able to growl with the full range of vocalizations and body language that she employs.

Understanding Feline Aggression

Understanding aggression is the first piece of the puzzle. Then you must treat or manage aggression as quickly as possible, because aggression can be self-reinforcing. The longer you let it go on, the more entrenched it can become. It's precisely the cat owners who come to me after *years* of aggression who are my greatest challenge in cat behavior consulting.

Most domesticated animals—other than cats—are less territorial than their wild forebears were; they're more playful throughout their lives than their ancestors, they're less fearful and less suspicious of novelty, they exhibit less predatory behavior, and they're quite dependent on others for food and attention. But the cat? Its territorial and aggressive behaviors develop as it matures, so that by the time it's an adult, its behaviors are similar to those of its wildcat forebears—further proof of the cat's incomplete domestication.

KITTY JEKYLL OR MAD-CAT HYDE?

Cute and fluffy one minute, a fanged dervish the next. Seems incomprehensible that a cat could transform itself so fast and so completely, but aggression can be a normal response to situations that threaten him—or at least seem to him to do so. In fact, aggressive instincts are the main reason cats are such great survivors. A cat is and must be its own best protector.

A cat and his aggression are as natural as a kangaroo and his hopping. An aggressive cat is not a bad cat. The instincts we lump into aggression are those that helped cats survive: catching and killing prey, marking and defending territory, protecting themselves and their young. A cat's ability to protect himself at a moment's notice is a hard-wired instinct. It is simply a part of who he is and what makes him such a great survivor. Owners may have trouble seeing and understanding this wildcat survival mechanism, especially when it's buried beneath the cuteness and fluff. But every cat has the potential to be aggressive if the circumstances bring it out in him—and sometimes owners create those circumstances without being aware that that's what they are doing. I've never seen any of my six cats act aggressively, but I know the potential is always there.

The average cat owner has almost 2½ cats (this number being a statistical average, and not a literal description of, say, 3 or 4 Cheshires in various stages of disappearance), so aggression within the household is always a possibility. The more serious forms of aggression arrive, like marking, with the onset of social maturity, somewhere after about two years of age. While aggression can be common between intact toms in sexual competition, aggression between cats is less often related to sex than to social hierarchies, territory, and emotional responses. Most aggression between cats is covert, subtle, and passive, which can make it extremely hard to detect. Rarely will you see your cats facing off, snarling, over a food bowl. In fact, your cats could have a conflict right in front of you without your being any the wiser. One cat may subtly posture aggression, the other cat will subtly signal deference, and that will be that. Some conflicts are resolved just by staring—and just as with humans, the first to blink or walk away is the loser. More obvious signs of aggression in cats, whether they are being threatened or doing the threatening, often involve trying to look bigger than they really are—their way of bluffing and swaggering. They straighten their longer hind legs to raise their hindquarters, and the fur along the ridge of their spine and on their tail stands up (called *piloerection*). Some, though, will begin to look smaller, flattening their ears against their heads for protection, tightly curling their bodies, and leaning away from the source of their arousal. Or they may just decide to go passive-aggressive, getting their territorial point across with a little urine marking. But however bold or subtle the signs, when two cats don't get along, it can upset the entire household, cats and people alike.

What about aggression against humans? Aggression against humans is generally related to the human's behavior. One study found, for example, that nearly all cat bites fell into the provoked category, which didn't necessarily mean that the cat was being abused but that immediately before the bite, it was being petted in a way it didn't like or picked up at the wrong time or exposed to some other kind of treatment that caused it distress.[1] Since you may be completely unaware that you are doing anything to upset the cat, it will be useful to learn the types and signs of impending aggression in order to back off from it before it occurs.

MEDICAL ALERT

Aggression related to medical conditions could overlap with pain- or irritability-induced aggression. Be sure your vet can rule out medical conditions like localized pain or general discomfort, abnormalities in the central nervous system, Feline immunodeficiency virus (FIV), hyperthyroidism, partial seizures or epilepsy, infections, dietary deficiencies, toxoplasmosis, hepatic encephalopathy, feline ischemic encephalopathy, meningioma, toxicity, CNS pathology, dental issues, impacted anal glands, and even medications like corticoids and progestogens.[2]

PREVENTION

Before I explain the different types of aggression and provide C.A.T. Plans for treating them, let me review some general ideas about how to prevent aggression before it blooms.

Socialize and Properly Introduce

Aggression that results from a cat's lack of socialization to people as a kitten is probably the most difficult to treat. So before bringing a kitten or young cat into your household, see if you can find out about the kind of socialization it had, particularly during the important two-to-seven-week period. And if you yourself have kittens in the home, make sure to give them plenty of safe, supervised exposure not just to people but to any other cats or animals in the household, and also expose them to a variety of sounds, and to different locations and situations during that critical window between two and seven weeks of age. You should continue that exposure afterward, too, gently and carefully. Even one unpleasant experience can teach a kitten to fear, so do your best to make sure the kittens don't encounter a rambunctious dog, a territorial cat, or a tantrum-throwing toddler in the home—otherwise they might develop everlasting fears of dogs, cats, or children (just like some people you know).

Kittens who lack adequate socialization during their early days are more likely than their better-socialized peers to grow up to be both fearful and aggressive. People often tell me that on the basis of what they've seen of their cat's behavior, the cat must have been abused before they adopted it. In most cases, however, it was merely not adequately socialized. Socialization specific to humans can help prevent play aggression.

With adult cats, it's important to use the correct introduction process when you bring a new cat (or person, dog, or other pet) into the home. You'll be happy you did. Sometimes the only reason a cat has become fearful or territorial is that the owners introduced the new cat into the home too quickly, setting the stage for years of chaos. It's not enough to let them sniff each other under the door for a few days. (See Chapter 4 for the full description of the process for introducing cats to one another.)

No Body Parts

To reduce play aggression and unwanted predatory behavior, never use your (or anyone else's) body parts to play with your cat. I've seen people using their fingers, toes, and hair, or poking their faces into their cat's face, as part of their play. Not good. Instead, maneuver string and wand toys, throw simple toys, and let automated toys do their thing without any participation from you.

Spay and Neuter

Unneutered or unspayed cats are typically more territorial and aggressive (and more likely to spray). The urge to mate is one natural instinct of cats that can and should be eliminated. Cats are prodigious breeders. At least thirty thousand feral cats must die every day just to keep the population stable.[3] It should be clear that the enormous feral cat population, up to 70 million in the United States alone, constitutes a humane crisis. Cat owners' collective failure to spay or neuter leads to unhappy lives for millions of abandoned cats who become feral, and for their offspring, and leads to a host of other negative effects, such as:

> fouling of common areas, nocturnal fighting and caterwauling, leaving of corpses [of prey, not to mention the corpses of deceased feral cats], attacks on pets and people, entering homes uninvited, flea infestations within the neighborhood, health risks [to humans] from the cats in general (toxoplasmosis), killing of pet and ornamental birds and fish [and killing of wild birds], and digging of gardens.[4]

Millions more cats are cycled through animal shelters and euthanized every year, many of them due to behaviors that could be eliminated or reduced by neutering males. To reduce your male cat's instincts of sexual or territorial aggression, you should definitely neuter him at four to six months of age. About 90 percent of males neutered before the onset of puberty never engage in aggression with other cats. And it's never too late: If you neuter an adult male, there's still a 90 percent chance he'll stop fighting (50 percent stop immediately and 40 percent after a few months).[5] Early spaying of females may help not just to keep the cat population down but also to prevent mammary cancer.

Deter

Keep other animals out of your home and off your property. A very common cause of redirected, fear-based, and territorial aggression is your cat's sighting of a dog or cat outside, paw prints in soil, or feces on the ground, or your cat's smelling cats' urine spray on windows. If you know the owner of the outdoor animal, you can ask the owner to keep it away from your home and yard. (If you get no love from thy neighbor, see Chapter 9 to learn how to deter outdoor animals from your property.) If you feed feral cats, do not do so near your property.

TYPES OF FELINE AGGRESSION

We can describe the types of aggression in terms of their purpose or function. Aggression ignited by a particular purpose includes aggression induced by fear, petting, or pain (so-called "irritable aggression" could also fit in here); inter-cat aggression, which can be territorial, fear-induced, or sexual, or could also be maternal (if some other cat seems to threaten her kittens); aggression; and predatory behavior. Aggression can be further broken down into the fundamental emotional divide of offensive versus defensive. We won't deal here with fine parsings of aggression, such as irritable aggression, that fall into larger categories. We also won't deal with aggression related to medical conditions or with idiopathic aggression, which is Greek for "we really have no idea why your cat just did that," or, as Alice put it, "I think you might do something better with the time than wasting it in asking riddles that have no answers."

I'll start the in-depth discussion of the various kinds of aggression with unwanted play aggression and predatory agression, directed toward you or other people, as well as toward other cats, animals, or actual prey. First, I'll explain their different causes, then offer a C.A.T. Plan that will work for both kinds of aggression.

Play Aggression

Sooner or later, when you are petting or playing with your kitten, she may go too far and bite down on your fingers too hard, or unsheathe her claws on your ankles. Her bite pressure and scratching power seem uninhibited—Why, just look at the bloody scratches and puncture wounds she's left on your hands and ankles! She is doing what all kittens do to one degree or another, which is to sharpen their hunting skills— she just hasn't learned how to inhibit the actions that cause others harm. Such a kitten may be playful one minute and then, as if someone had flipped a switch, she'll flatten her ears, growl, and attack. A kitten or cat who is merely playing will usually be silent. If your cat growls or hisses, however, she may be in a fighting mood—either defensive or offensive.

Natural Play

Many humans (and not just first-time cat owners) have no idea that the hunting skills practiced by their kitten are normal, and that they didn't mistakenly purchase a tiny leopard. "Welcome to kittenhood," I tell them. Kittens begin to play by batting at moving objects at about two weeks of age. Social play behavior begins when a kitten is three to four weeks old—at around the same time it can actually move around well. The kitten paws and bites softly, assuming a series of postures designed to increase its eye-paw coordination and develop its hunting skills. Play has a diversity of purposes ranging from physical fitness and exploration of the environment to the coordination, timing, and maturation of the central nervous system.[6] The kitten repeats its hunting behaviors, or motor pattern sequences, over and over again, coupling instinct with (eventually) ability. Watch, and over time you will see your kitten display the following postures.

- belly-up
- stand-up
- side step with body arch
- pounce
- vertical stance
- chase
- horizontal leap
- the face-off

Kittens also practice catching different kinds of prey, from "mice" (pouncing on a small object and seizing it with the forepaws) to "birds" (intercepting flying objects and guiding them to the mouth) to "rabbits" (e.g., larger moving objects, such as my Teacup Chihuahua, who, when Josephine and Farsi were kittens, *lived* to be ambushed, brought to the ground, and, gently, neck-bit, in a replay of the ancient battles between saber-toothed cats and wolves). Like small children, kittens even have imaginary friends, and with great zest will engage in so-called hallucinatory play.

A kitten with healthy play socialization learns when she has gone too far: She gets a nip, a scratch, a low growl, or a swatting from her littermates or her mother. The mother or littermates will often leave or pull away from the overly exuberant player. The message: *Unnecessary roughness. Ease up or we won't play with you.* The kitten who is taught when enough is enough learns to calibrate her actions and reactions and the intensity of her bite or scratching.

Play That Has Gone Awry

Play aggression is most common in cats between the beginning of sexual puberty and the age of two, a period known as psychological adolescence. There are four common reasons for a cat playing too aggressively: It is feral, it was taken too early from its mother and littermates, its owner has socialized it to aggressiveness, or it suffered malnutrition. If a kitten was taken from her littermates and mother too soon (especially before the so-called sensitive period is over, at seven weeks, but even before twelve weeks), or her mother was absent or unavailable due to illness, a too-soon pregnancy, or death, look out: That kitten was deprived of valuable lessons. The same goes for feral kittens, who also didn't get the message about what is and is not acceptable about relating to people. The archetype of play aggression (or what some behaviorists call lack-of-socialization aggression) may come from the cat that was born feral and didn't interact with humans during the sensitive period. Imagine a child who was never told "No" during the Terrible Twos.

In addition, if the kitten suffered malnutrition for any reason, its coordination and responsiveness could suffer, and it might be overly reactive, fearful, or aggressive as a result. In other words, the best remedies—proper socialization and nutrition—for an adolescent or adult cat who exhibits play aggression are not available to you without a time-travel machine. But as you'll see later in this chapter, when prevention is not possible, treatment is. So don't despair.

Human-Caused Play Aggression

In too many cases, it is we humans who are, perhaps unwittingly, responsible for a great deal of play aggression. Sometimes kittens are adopted too early, often around six to eight weeks of age. It's detrimental to a kitten's continuing social development for her to leave her mother and littermates before she's twelve weeks old.

Another way we can help further the socialization that will guard against future behavior issues is by promoting the adoption of *two* kittens. By adopting two kittens, you will allow them the chance to continue to develop their social skills and decrease the likelihood of behavior issues developing later on. Your kitten also won't get so bored that she must direct all her playfulness onto you. I have always felt that taking a kitten away from all of her littermates was an unnecessary trauma. I strongly recommend a twofer adoption. The best course is to adopt two kittens from the same litter, but if that's not possible, pick up the one in the next cage at the shelter. Adopting two is even helpful for socialization when one or both kittens is already older than twelve weeks. Two kittens are just more fun, both for you and for the kittens, than one.

Owners who roughhouse with their cats too much during play, unable to resist the fun of wrestling with a tiny, toothy ball of fur, need to switch to more appropriate forms of play. I've heard more than a few owners admit that they hand-wrestled with their kittens, using their hands to roll the kittens around as the kittens (still gently) bit and clawed at them. When the cat is still a kitten, this can all be great fun. How cute! But be careful how you train that budding tiger. Even with dogs, many researchers and trainers strongly believe that supposedly violent breeds are not so much genetically violent as conditioned to violence by their owners.[7]

Owners who don't play with their kittens at all also need to change their behavior. The kitten instinctively has to practice hunting and looks for the best target. A moving target is the best, of course, and you can't just leave a catnip mouse toy on the floor and expect the cat to get what it needs. If you're not engaging your cat in interactive play with wand toys and other moving targets, then your moving feet and hands may become the targets of choice — by default.

Luckily the behavior issues related to inappropriate play aggression can easily be reversed or improved, and all without declawing your cats, as some ill-informed cat owners do. In fact, declawing can cause a cat to use its teeth more.

Predatory Aggression

Once, when I was eight, I was, as usual, outside inspecting the animal kingdom when I spotted a baby bird. He was fresh out of the nest, wobbling on a fence rail. I slowly made my way behind him, using my best approximation of the stealth strategy that I'd observed in cats, delighted that he was not taking flight. I had gotten myself right up to the fence and was just about to reach out to the bird when a flash of brown and black picked the bird off the fence and whisked it away. The flash was Spunky, one of the barn cats I'd worked so hard to socialize.

I had witnessed a prime example of feline predatory behavior. Spunky's emotional state was neither offensive nor defensive. It just was. Predatory cats are unemotional, all business. Predatory behavior, which starts at about five weeks of age with help from Mom, is a normal feline behavior when it's directed at cats' normal prey, like birdlings wobbling on fence rails. By just over a month of age, skills that will later be used for predatory behaviors have become part of healthy play. By five to seven weeks, kittens display some solitary hunting behaviors. Kittens mock-fight each other at seven to eight weeks and, as their neuromuscular control improves, become effective hunters at fourteen weeks. For a variety of reasons, kittens orphaned or hand reared may show more aggressive predatory behaviors as adults.

As with play aggression, owners often misinterpret predatory play behavior as malicious or spiteful. Thinking like that leads to abuse of cats. You may be sitting on the couch reading the paper and notice your cat peering at you around the corner of the sofa. The next thing you know he's crouched low, wiggling his rear, and then hurling himself toward your bare feet propped up on the ottoman, where he latches on to them only to quickly release them and run away. What you just witnessed was your cat's prey sequence.

Some experts think predatory behavior should not be called aggression at all, because it has no self-protective or social function and does not involve a shift in the emotional state, such as, *Now I'm really angry!* or *I'm terrified!* A cat in the throes of predation is emotionally neutral, just doing what is in his nature to do. Still, predatory behavior in the household, which is usually characterized by surprise attacks on the owner or other cats, is a behavior you will want to discourage.

INHIBITED PREDATORY AGGRESSION

If your cat is stuck inside, and the tasty fluttering bird is outside, he'll be inhibited from predatory behavior. You may see his tail switch back and forth, and you can see and even hear his jaws chattering slightly, like early Jim Carrey.

Play is a normal behavior in kittens still sharpening their hunting skills, and both play and predatory behavior are normal in adults. Play is not just normal, but also crucial to cats' mental, physical, and emotional health, as well as to preventing unwanted behaviors. That's why the treatment techniques in the C.A.T. Plan below are intended to allow the cat to continue to play or practice hunting, but without targeting you or another animal in the household with the unwanted behavior.

C.A.T. Plan for Play and Predatory Aggression

CEASE the Unwanted Behavior

It would be difficult and not very much fun to limit your cat's access to you, so the best solution is to be vigilant and anticipate the occasions when your cat likes to attack you, so that you can avoid them. You should be able to do this much more effectively than Inspector Clouseau, who is continually ambushed by his valet, Cato.

Avoid—No Hands, Ma

Avoid situations that cause your cat to want to prey on you in the first place. For example, any kind of movement can elicit his play/prey response, leading to biting or scratching, so be mindful of your activities. If you have been using your hands to play with your kitten, stop right away. It's tempting to entice a kitten into playing by wiggling your fingers above its head, but you are simply training him to go *after your hands*. No toe play, either! Try to make any body parts that he likes to attack unavailable to him. In order to avoid surprise attacks, put a belled collar on him so you'll always hear him approaching.

All of this may take some creativity on your part and even a bit of inconvenience. But the more your cat or kitten rehearses his play-and-prey instincts on you, the longer it can take and the more difficult it can become to end the biting and scratching.

Anticipate

Most important, learn to read your cat's body language so that you will know the signs of an impending bite or scratch.

The warning signs of play aggression are:

- hiding behind doors and other objects, waiting to spring on its victim
- lashing or twitching tail
- turning ears back or flattening
- unsheathing the claws
- stiffening the legs and shoulders
- engaging in the "butt-wiggle"
- lowering the head

Note, however, that some play and prey aggression postures may actually resemble those of fear aggression. These include:

- stalking—as when the cat flattens himself to the ground and moves forward very slowly
- growling

The warning signs of aggressive behavior that is predatory are:

- engaging in it regardless of whether or not he's hungry
- showing little or no mood change
- intense concentration
- silent, stealthy, deliberate stalking, rather than spontaneous actions
- after staring and stalking, performing the rest of the prey sequence (see Chapter 5), from the chase to the grab, or the pounce and bite, and the kill bite
- lying in wait, slinking, head lowering, butt wiggling, tail twitching (body postures of hunting)

Distract and Redirect

If your cat shows any of the signs of impending aggression, try to intervene before the actual aggression begins: Distract him by maneuvering a wand or string prey target away from you, or throwing a small toy away from you. Effective diversions allow him to exercise his perfectly normal prey urges and get him in the habit of attacking the right target; equally important, they keep him from rehearsing attacks on you that strengthen the habit you wish to discourage. His prey urge may include sinking his teeth into, say, a rabbit, so in case he wants to eat his prey, offer him food or treats. You'll further promote the idea that toys are appealing and rewarding prey targets. (See The Prey Sequence in Chapter 5.)

Place wand toys and other toys in strategic locations around the house, such as places where you spend a lot of time or where your cat often attacks you: near sofas, hallways, chairs, your bed, the kitchen. That way they will be handy to you if you see any signs of aggression. If your cat attacks only at certain times, such as when you come home from work, you can try confining him to a different room during the day in order to diminish his association with the triggering event of your arrival, or come in the door with a wand toy to divert his attention and redirect his play elsewhere. As a preventative measure, I recommend using toys with your cat even before you see any signs of imminent aggression, especially in contexts or locations where aggression often occurs.

Timing is very important. Do not wait until the cat is actually displaying aggression to distract him, or you will reinforce aggressive behavior. He'll think all he has to do is start attacking things in order to get you to play with him.

Ignore—The Snub of the Queen

You can learn a lot from mother cats. When one of her kittens engages in behavior that is too rough, such as biting hard rather than just nipping, the queen may simply disengage from that kitten by standing up and walking away. Withdrawal of attention can be very effective when done by a human, too. When your cat goes too far, immediately withdraw your attention. Leave the room for a few minutes. Cats learn quickly. It won't be long before he learns that biting or scratching too hard takes something away from him that is *very* important—*you!*

For Play Aggression Only:
Aversion Therapy and the Act of God

If your cat still relentlessly attacks you, it's time for an Act of God. Covertly use a water pistol or air in a can to deliver a very small squirt of air or water—just enough to achieve an interruption. You never want to traumatize or punish a cat with this technique, just mildly startle her. Do not squirt the cat in the face. Aim for the cat's side or rear end instead. Or just let the can hiss behind your back.

Finally, never run away from your cat when he's in predatory aggression mode. The sight of you running may excite his prey response even more.

For Natural Predatory Aggression Only:
Prevention and Management

Predatory behavior toward appropriate, or natural, targets is difficult to "cure" humanely. The best solution is to prevent your cat's access to targets like birds and other outdoor animals. Bell your cat so that his targets get forewarning and have a better chance of escaping. (Use a safety release cat collar that comes with a small bell attached.) Just don't consider it foolproof. Cats are like martial arts masters: I've seen cats intuit how to move in just such a way that the bell never rings. If cats could learn to handle a bow and arrow, they would be like the Zen masters described in *Zen in the Art of Archery* who hit their targets blindfolded, and then split the first arrow with the second. (That said, belling is still worth doing.)

If you see that the cat has started the countdown to his prey sequence by eyeing his target, use a distraction (Ping-Pong balls, etc.). If you miss interrupting the eye stare and your cat has moved on to the stalk or chase, he may be more difficult to distract.

ATTRACT the Cat to New, Acceptable Behaviors

Now we need to show your kitten or cat what *to do* in the environment. Cats need to play, bite, claw, and hunt. There is no way around this. It's what they are programmed to do at the kittenish stage in their lives. We just need to help them focus this behavior on to the appropriate targets.

Schedule a Regular Playtime

As with so many cat behavior issues, play and predatory aggression can also be diminished with routine and predictable play sequences—a homeopathic remedy, a little whisker of the cat that scratched you, so to speak. Play is also a good way for your cats to get exercise. Set up a daily schedule to maneuver inter-active toys for your cat. Predictable playtime schedules will also let a cat or kitten know when it's time to be active. For an adult cat, I recommend two playtimes daily, from ten to twenty min-utes each. For a kitten, I recommend as many as four playtimes per day, which mirrors kittens' natural preference. If your cat becomes bored easily, play for two minutes and then give her a five-minute break before resuming. (For a full description of the play/prey technique, see Chapter 5.)

You can supplement interactive playtimes with toys (such as battery-operated toys*) that you don't have to maneuver, so you can trigger his prey drive even when you're not around. If your cat likes to prey on you when you're sitting down after work or while you're in bed, think preventively and help him perform a prey sequence or other form of play *before* these times (i.e., thirty minutes before you go to bed) and have a battery-operated toy going while you're trying to work.

Reward Behavior You Want Repeated

It's easy to remember to correct (or worse, punish) a cat when it's doing something undesirable, but one of the most effective techniques is often forgotten. Reward your cat for play-attacking the appropriate target or for being calm or showing other desir-able behaviors. In addition to praising her with a soft voice, pet-ting her, and giving her treats or food, you can also use clicker training to promote and reward specific desirable behavior. (See Appendix A for more on the very effective, advanced solution of clicker training.)

TRANSFORM the Territory

The key words here are *environmental enrichment*. A bored cat is a cat who may want his fangs in your ankle. Give him ample

---

* See catwhispererproducts.com for the latest recommended toys.

opportunities to unleash his play aggression and predatory behavior on appropriate targets. Make your home a stimulating territory with lots of places to perch, hide, and play. (See Chapter 5 for full details, including the sections Toys and Scratching Posts and Other Stimulating Gear.)

For Play Aggression Only: What? Another Kitten?

If you have only one kitten and he remains relentless in his attacks, consider adding another kitten of about the same age and size into the household. A second kitten is sometimes the best way to give your kitten another outlet for play. When I mention this idea to most owners, still nursing puncture wounds, they're not usually in the frame of mind to have yet another kitten in the household. But when they do add another kitten, the attacks they have to endure usually either disappear or are cut by at least half. If adding another kitten is not in the cards, then you will need to concentrate on expanding the number of play outlets and interactive toys for your cat.

Be patient. Habits take time to break as well as to form, and your cat is doing what comes naturally to him. In most cases, when kittens get older, the play aggression goes away.

Next up is redirected aggression—aggression redirected from a desired but unavailable target to someone or something nearby. Redirected aggression usually starts with a fear response, and sometimes it can lead to a vicious cycle of aggression *between* cats.

REDIRECTED AGGRESSION

The literature on cats reports a case in which the sounds made by a talking doll so startled the family's cat that the terrified animal flew at the little girl holding the doll and bit her in the face. Although this is an extreme version of the phenomenon, redirected aggression—against a nearby person or animal—is a typical response when something provokes a cat's feelings of fear, but he's unable to get at the trigger itself. Redirected aggression is the most baffling kind, because often we can't see the cause and have no idea what triggered the sudden attack. About half of all feline aggression toward people is actually redirected aggression, which is commonly misdiagnosed as unprovoked aggression. But the cat is *not* malicious; he's just in such a highly reactive state that he is compelled to act upon his primal urges.

Here's a common scenario of redirected aggression: Your cat Moe is sitting on the couch, looking out the window. He sees a neighbor cat walking through his territory, safely on the other side of the window. Hissing and screaming, Moe suddenly turns and attacks the Great Dane sleeping next to him. Moe saw something outside that triggered his fighting response, probably by first making him fearful. Fit to burst with aggressive energy surging through his system, he chose fight over flight, yet was unable to express his aggression onto its natural target. Therefore he redirected it onto something nearby—the dog. But windows, furniture, and largely innocent lampshades have all been known to take a good beating under such circumstances. It could also be you, sipping a cup of coffee nearby; another cat in the household minding his own business; or your spouse fast asleep on the couch. Anything or anyone in the path of an upset cat can be a target. And because cats can remain aroused for a while after the triggering event, you may never know why your cat just took a swipe at something.

I recently had a client who had purchased a large cat tree. She placed the tree by a window so her cat could enjoy basking in the sunlight, but after a few days she noticed her cat becoming agitated and sometimes aggressive. She reported to me that sometimes when she walked by the cat's tree, her cat would lash out and attack her with unsheathed claws. After a little investigating we discovered that the placement of the new cat tree had permitted her cat to see the neighborhood cats traversing the yard. Redirected aggression strikes again! Needless to say, we moved the cat tree. Case solved.

NYUK, NYUK: REDIRECTED AGGRESSION ON THE SILVER SCREEN

If you're old enough to have seen *The Three Stooges*, or you watch a lot of YouTube, you've seen redirected aggression in action. Moe pokes Larry between the eyes. Larry kicks Curly in the behind. Larry has just redirected his aggressive feelings toward Moe onto Curly. (Moe is usually redirecting his own aggression. He usually starts off the slapping because he's upset at something in his environment.)

As the Three Stooges teach us, humans actually relate to the impulse of redirected aggression better than they do to most aspects of cat psychology. I once explained the concept of redirected aggression to a cat owner whose cats were exhibiting redirected aggression. "Wow," he said. "I think my *wife* has that."

> *But ask the animals, and they will teach you.*
> — The Book of Job

I have always felt that we humans are more animal-like than we think. We can learn a lot about ourselves and our motivations by studying our companion animals. Reverse anthropomorphizing?

Redirected aggression can come suddenly and seemingly out of nowhere, and it can be quite upsetting to the innocent victim. Redirected aggression can be so profoundly terrifying to other household cats, and so effective at rewiring both aggressor and victim, that it can up-end the entire social hierarchy. It takes only one instance of a cat redirecting his aggression against a fellow cat to start a vicious cycle of (barring professional intervention) sometimes-permanent instability between cats. It can traumatize one or both. Imagine two cats just resting peacefully. There is a loud noise. Both cats startle and puff up and assume a defensive posture. Each then sees the other in that defensive posture and says to himself, *Unbelievable. It looks like that cat is actually about to attack me.* Each one *then* reacts even more defensively, or perhaps one becomes the aggressor. Maybe there's a fight, and after that they're aggressive whenever they see each other. Each cat may act as if the other started the fight. A cat who sees himself in a mirror may do the same thing, becoming more agitated as he sees his counterpart puffing up more and more. And for better or worse, when it comes to built-up associations, cats have *very* long memories.

"The victim's fear becomes a sort of conditioned paranoia," writes veterinary behaviorist Stefanie Schwartz, "transmitted in defensive body language that triggers renewed attacks by the 'bully' long after the initial context is forgotten."[8] To add more twists, a victimized cat may even become the aggressor at a later time. This may be the most likely outcome if the cat who initially redirected his aggression was actually inferior in status to his target. Oops. On *The Three Stooges*, there's a reason you don't see Curly slapping Moe. You don't bully a superior cat! The superior cat will reassert his status and the poor cat who first launched an attack may find himself incessantly victimized.

If *you* were the original victim, your cat may now be conditioned to see you as a stimulus for attack.

Luckily, there are solutions.

MANAGEMENT OF REDIRECTED AGGRESSION

You don't fix or cure an incident of redirected aggression. First you manage the immediate consequences—the fighting, the agitation—and then, to prevent it from happening again, you try to remove the fear triggers.

Break Up Any Fights and Separate Because they don't have clear dominance-based hierarchies, cats can't work things out as dogs do.

Instead, generally, the more they fight, the worse their problem becomes. So if your cat redirects aggression onto another cat in the household and a fight breaks out, you will want to safely separate the cats right away. Do not get between the cats. Break up the fight by wedging a pillow or large piece of cardboard between the cats, or throw a thick towel over one of the cats. Do not use aversive interruptions like an Act of God! Adding a negative to a negative situation only makes the situation worse. If you can lure the aggressor into a separate room without picking him up, do so. A quiet, darkened room is best. If he stays where the triggering event occurred, he may feel the same tension. He might even generalize the trigger to *anything* in that location. If he continues to be exposed to the trigger, consciously or unconsciously, his panic response will be reinforced and a cure can be difficult.

If you can't lure him out, leave him alone so he can calm down. Make sure he has food, water, litter, and, ideally, calming pheromones. Whatever you do, do not touch or pick up any agitated cat or dog that was in the room during the aggression. You *may* get bitten or scratched. Nothing personal, of course. It could take hours or even days for all the cats to calm down. The stronger the initial stimulus, the longer the recovery period. Just gently herd any other animals or people out of the room with you. Then look for any fear triggers to eliminate.

Later, you'll use play therapy and food in the area to build positive associations. It's possible to change your cat's emotional state from fear to a calmer state by getting him to either actively watch a toy or engage in play (see Chapter 5).

Remove Fear Triggers I explain how to keep foreign cats off your property in Chapter 9. If deterring outside animals from your cat's perception is not possible, Chapter 9 also explains how to block the windows your cat can see out of. You don't need to block the entire window, just the portion through which he can see out.

Even if the fear triggers are gone for good, your cats' relationship may be damaged. If so, you'll want to follow the C.A.T. Plan for Territorial, Fear, and Cat-to-Cat Aggression coming up next. Pay special attention to how to bring the cats together through controlled exposure. If things are really extreme, however, you may need to perform a full reintroduction (Chapter 4).

If an incident of redirected aggression is part of an already ingrained pattern of behavior, or becomes one, you will then need to proceed to the C.A.T. Plan for Territorial, Fear, and Cat-to-Cat Aggression.

I'll now address these three types of aggression, and give you a C.A.T. Plan that will work for all of them, and can be effective for redirected aggression, too.

TERRITORIAL AGGRESSION

Territorial instincts often lead to the aggression displayed by the solitary hunter whose instincts say, *I must keep the competition away from my important resources.* Territorial behavior is normal in cats after they reach social maturity, often being set in motion between ages two and four, when their biological clocks tell them it's time to establish social rank and territorial rights. Status and territory are intimately intertwined: To get more territory or even be entitled to time-share it, your cat may try to establish equal or higher ranking; to establish higher rank, your cat must acquire more territory. Territoriality typically begins gradually, so much so that it can be invisible to the owner, which is why it may seem to have erupted out of nowhere when you do finally notice it. Often what happens is that you have two cats who are best of friends . . . until suddenly they're not. Instead of curling up together to sleep, grooming each other and playing happily, they're growling and hissing at the sight of each other.

Although cats may be more tolerant of neighbor cats they've seen before than of total strangers, even your gentlest cat can run another cat right off your property (and his). You may have seen him laying the groundwork for his territorial challenge: patrolling his territory and chin-rubbing and scent-marking things inside or out with his urine and scent glands. Indeed, urine marking (see Chapter 9) should be considered an alert to the underlying tension that can lead to overt aggression.

Territorial aggression toward a feline intruder is surprisingly effective: The intruder is at a psychological disadvantage and usually withdraws at signs of aggression from the resident cat. Actual fights are rare; given cats' arsenal of weapons, the risk of serious injury is too great. Instead of outright violence, both offensive and defensive territorial aggression tend to feature highly ritualized posturing, some of it very subtle—but effective. However, if the cats do fight and the resident cat loses, he may not only be injured but lose any primary breeding status in the colony and even be psychologically castrated.

One of the most common causes of territorial aggression is the introduction of a newcomer to the household—whether it be a new cat, a new member of the family, or a guest. (See Chapter 4 on making proper introductions.) Typically, it's the resident cat who will display territorial behavior toward a new cat, but sometimes it's the upstart newcomer. The victim cat may begin to hide to avoid his enemy, and may even stop coming to the litter box. (See Chapter 8 for solutions to the resulting inappropriate elimination.)

Foreign smells can also make a cat aggressive, even when the cat who carries that smell is a cat he knows very well. Let's say one of your cats, Curly, has been to the vet. He returns home. Moe begins to slap him silly.

MOE: Uggh! What's that awful smell on you?
CURLY: It's vetsmell and it's not my fault, leave me alone!
MOE: What I'm gonna do is smack you again.

This returning-home-from-the-vet crisis is very common. Moe may be feeling territorial, he may be redirecting his fear as aggression, or he may be suffering from what some behaviorists call nonrecognition aggression.

When you bring your cat home from the vet (or any other outside location such as a boarding facility), he may have a foreign smell. Resident cats may have negative reactions not just to the "vetsmell" but to the appearance and behavior of the returning cat. Perhaps still not feeling well, coming down from anesthesia, or merely stressed from the car ride, the returning cat may act strangely. Faced with this goofy-acting, scent-unknown intruder (remember, cats rely on scent to distinguish friend from foe), and perhaps sensing distress in your own emotional reaction, the resident cat may cycle through fear and redirected aggression and straight into territorial aggression.

A SENSIBLE SCENTS STRATEGY

You can minimize the potential for scent-related aggression by a form of allogrooming. Before you bring the returning cat into the home, rub the resident cat with a dry towel and then use the same towel to rub down the returning cat. The home cat then smells on the returning cat . . . himself! What could be less threatening? Do *not* do this the other way around, wiping foreign scents all over the householders! Doing so could trigger fear and territorial behaviors in the cats who stayed home.

I've heard of or dealt with many cases of territorial aggression (possibly mixed with status-based aggression) against not only other cats but people: a cat who wouldn't let a hospice nurse get close to his dying owner; cats who guard their food bowl even against their owners; cats who won't let other cats near their litter box or sleeping area. I knew one cat who sat atop a video game console and took a swing at anyone who tried to touch the controls. Some cats will try to attack any visitor. (This can tend, over time, to diminish the number of guests who come to your home.)

PREPARING FOR GUESTS

If you're having guests over and you think your cat is likely to be fearful or aggressive, put the cat in a separate room while the guests are present. The "Cat's Diary" quoted in Chapter 1 put

it this way: "There was some sort of assembly of [the humans']
accomplices tonight. I was placed in solitary confinement for
the duration of the event." Give her plenty of food and water, litter, toys, and even a treat, and leave a TV or radio on to create a
noise buffer. Be sure to play with her before you close the door.
For those occasions when you can't guarantee keeping her away
from a surprise—or surprised—visitor:

- Trim the cat's nails to prevent serious scratches.
- Warn guests against approaching the cat, making eye con-
  tact with her, or causing big sounds or movements.
- Keep on hand an interactive toy or a few toys you can toss.
  These are not only a distraction, but can help change a cat's
  mood and emotional state for the better.

FEAR-INDUCED AGGRESSION

A certain amount of fear is a useful, adaptive response. Fear is what
keeps all living creatures from doing unwise things that would prevent
the perpetuation of their gene pool—in other words, things that could
lead to injury or death. In animals, fear evokes one of four responses:
fight, flight, paralysis, or submission. Sometimes a cat will freeze and
urinate in fear, but cats rarely traffic in such paralysis. And the weight
of authority says cats are never submissive. Instead, your cat will usually choose fight or flight. Which one he chooses will depend on a
split-second decision about what he senses will best ensure his survival, but I have found that when a cat is able to flee the scene easily,
he usually will. It's when a cat is feeling cornered, unable to locate his
options for escape, that his level of arousal redlines and he chooses to
fight. This fighting response has undoubtedly made cats the great survivors that they are, but it can pose serious consequences for owners,
vets, children, other household animals, and even the cat itself.

Anything can cause a cat's fight-or-flight response to veer into fearful aggression. Learned reactions to a particular pain (e.g., pain experienced at the vet's office) may quickly lead to fear-induced aggression, which you see in a cat fighting not to be removed from its carrier when you take it to the vet. Other things that may cause fear— followed by aggression—include: having a pill pushed down his throat, seeing a dog or a toddler running in his direction; hearing a sudden loud noise, such as a dish or piece of silverware being dropped on the floor nearby; and even (this is unusual but it does happen) seeing a wand toy in motion in his vicinity! Fear aggression is the most common type of aggression between cats who suddenly find themselves living in the same home without having been properly introduced to one another. Every cat has a fear-sensitivity threshold, but for some cats, this threshold is low.

BODY LANGUAGE ALERT

A fearful cat may roll over on its back, turning its head to face the aggressor with all four paws ready for protection. This might appear to some observers as a submissive posture, like that of a dog, whose belly-up posture is intended to discourage an attack by signaling *Okay, okay: I'm lower ranking.* But cats do not have specific dominance or subordinance displays. They convey their relative social status by a combination of offensive and defensive aggressive behaviors, avoidance, immobility, and deference. A cat on her back is a formidable opponent. Her seemingly submissive postures—*This is not to say, by the way, that I bow to your authority*—are simply attempts to inhibit an attack. She has at her disposal a mouth ringed with knife-tips and all four sets of claws. With her forelegs, she can grab a four-legged aggressor near his mouth while her hind legs rip away at his belly, as cats also do with prey. You have seen cats play with prey toys this way, rolling on their backs and then kicking ferociously at the toy.[9]

If the fear-induced aggression is directed at you, it may be that your cat had too little human interaction during the sensitive period of two to seven weeks. If the deficiency of interaction was pronounced enough, your cat's neural wiring may be so fixed that it's virtually impossible to retrain him to be less aggressive toward you or your visitors. (Some behaviorists call this nonsocialization aggression, the classic example of which is kittens born and raised feral, like my very first cats. A great deal of time and love will help all of them to become at least a little more sociable, but there are limits—variable as they may be. Depending on two feral cats' genetic inheritance, one may become quite friendly, while the other will never be comfortable with human touch.)

CAT-TO-CAT AGGRESSION

Cat-to-Cat aggression can have many causes. Cats may fight due to redirected, status-related, fear-induced, or territorial aggression gone amok. Or they may fight for reasons known only to themselves. But whenever it happens, and for whatever reason, it's a bad moon rising.

ARE YOUR CATS PLAYING OR FIGHTING?

Chances are they are playing if:

- The cats are familiar with each other, without a bad history.
- They don't scream, hiss often, spit, growl, or swat with claws out.
- They take turns being the pretend aggressor.
- If, after wrestling, one cat does not chase the other cat away and neither cat seems afraid.
- There are no signs of blood or flying fur.
- Ears are not rotated and flattened.

If your cats are playing, let them be. Play—even when it looks like fighting to you—allows kittens and cats to show off their assertiveness and strength. It helps establish social ranking within the home and so smoothes out territorial and social issues. As long as the cats aren't really attacking each other in a hurtful way, and their bout doesn't appear too lopsided, let them finish so they can find the social equilibrium they need. Otherwise, their conflicts may only intensify and become more frequent. Fortunately, if the play-fighting does start to go nuclear, many cats will end it on their own.

However, if you see two cats wrestling and they don't typically get along or play together, it's probably aggression. And if, after wrestling, one cat chases the other cat away or they avoid one another, it's even more likely they were being aggressive, not playful.

C.A.T. Plan for Territorial, Fear, and Cat-to-Cat Aggression

If your cats are already locked into a physically hostile, even violent, relationship—in other words, if they are actively fighting—you will need to implement the C.A.T. Plan below, *and* also reintroduce your cats as if they've just met (see the reintroduction process in Chapter 4).

But for cats who are *not yet fighting*, or are able to coexist with infrequent or low-level spats, here are some tips on relieving the tension before it gets worse.

CEASE the Imminent Aggression

Anticipate

Watch for the following.

Signs of Imminent Territorial Aggression*
- staring
- lifting the hind quarters
- hissing (when defensive)

* Be aware that predatory behavior may look similar.

- swatting
- lying in wait (on the way to the litter box is a popular strategy)
- ambushing*
- spraying
- vocalization
- one cat's relentless pursuit of another animal, such as another cat

Signs of Brewing Cat-to-Cat Tension

Before the arrival of outright aggression, the alert owner will spot the signs of brewing tension.

- staring
- tail flicking, lashing, puffed up like a bottle brush (piloerection)
- piloerection of fur along the spine (your cat suddenly looks fluffier than usual)
- ears flattening or rotated outward
- body stiffening
- walking with a slow, tense gait, tail held low
- dilated pupils
- head hunched
- lip licking
- vocalizing—hissing, growling, or yowlings

Signs of Imminent Fear-based Aggression

- crouching, especially backed up against a wall
- ears back, paws tucked under body, body hunched so as to appear smaller, or a combination of attack and defensive posturing (ears flattened, back arched, drawing in the neck)

---

* A territorially motivated cat will not do the butt-wiggle (a playful or predatory behavior) but will ambush. The aggressor will lie in wait for his unknowing victim to mosey by, minding his own business, oblivious to the rodeo about to start.

- back paws aimed somewhere other than straight ahead, anticipating escape
- dilated pupils (the classic panic response) and narrowed eyes
- whiskers flattened against cheeks
- ears flattened and out to the side (like airplane wings) or rotated back
- hissing and growling
- piloerection of fur on back and tail
- avoidance of eye contact
- salivation (tongue will lick quickly)
- sometimes sudden defecation, urination

Distract

It's really important not to let aggressive posturing or staring continue, because either one can easily lead to fighting, and you do not ever want to let your cats fight it out. Interrupting staring is particularly important, and effective. Once your cats get to the stage of spitting, hissing, relentless chasing, and fighting, it can be very difficult or impossible to interrupt. And once cats have fought, they establish negative associations to each other that usually lead to more fighting. So if you happen to notice one of your cats displaying any of the signs described above, even if it's just staring at another cat in a very intense way, create a gentle, covert interruption. (Although staring is a way that cats can safely work out territorial rights, it can also be a six-lane highway to stalking, chasing, and thence fighting, especially if Mr. Eyeballed Cat ignores the warning.) Try tossing a Ping-Pong ball, toy, wadded-up piece of paper, small throw pillow, or other small or lightweight item on the floor nearby.

If you choose to go one step further and perform an Act of God, make it a really nice Act of God. Don't opt for an unpleasant, annoying, negative stimulus, like shooting a squirt gun, yelling, or clapping your hands. When cats are highly aroused, you don't want to do anything to rile them up even more, or to create any kind of negative association with each other. We want each cat to walk away from their mutual encounter without memories of even more bad things happening when they are in the other's presence.

Redirect to Prey Target

This is a good technique to use immediately after you have interrupted your cats' staring or posturing. It can also be a kind of distraction in and of itself. Say you walk into a room and you immediately sense it may be heading toward a bad scene. You can feel the tension yourself. If the cats are not already fighting, pick up an interactive string or wand toy to distract an aggressor cat and redirect his energy. Timing is of the essence. You must distract and redirect him with a toy *before* he launches an attack. If you play with him after he has attacked, you will reinforce the undesirable behavior with the reward of play.

If you have two wand toys and are coordinated enough to maneuver them separately (one in each hand, far apart), that's a great way to work play with two cats in the same room. Stop maneuvering the toy if one or both of the would-be combatants have gotten too close. The last thing you want is for the cats to duel over the scarce resources of one prey toy and your attention. If there's only one toy or the cats seem to be too tense to play in each other's presence (or have a history of disliking it), place them in separate rooms and play with them sequentially to change their moods.

For cats who have gone past the imminent aggression stage and actually started to fight, different strategies are required.

HE STARTED IT!

Cat owners usually think the aggressor is the one who started the fight, but sometimes the attacked cat is the one who tried to intimidate the attacker by staring at her.

Break It Up!

The very first priority is to stop the fighting and remove them from each other's presence in order to give them both some breathing room. See Break Up Any Fights and Separate in the Redirected Aggression section earlier in this chapter.

Separate Them

The length of the separation depends on the cats. It could be a few minutes to several hours or even days. When both cats have begun to act like themselves—not as stressed and reactive, eating again, wanting to play—it's time to put them in the same room again.

Control the Exposure: The Importance of Happy Endings

If you have noticed that your cats can usually be in the same room with one another for, say, twenty minutes before the hissing, chasing, or fighting starts, then try to time their exposure to each other so that you separate them before they get upset. If you wait to separate the cats until someone becomes upset, each cat will simply file the event in her memory bank under, *Bad Mojo Happens When I'm Around This Other Cat.* That makes for even worse mojo.

Keep the cats far apart in the beginning, ideally in opposite cat trees or at opposite ends of the room. As long as they're not showing fear, decrease the distance and increase the time they're in the same room, very gradually over the course of days. For example: Leave them in the same room for fifteen minutes for several days in a row, then twenty minutes for a few days, and so on, over a period of thirty days, or longer if necessary. Try to end sessions on a positive or at least a neutral note. If they've been calm, give them treats. Over time, you can increase both the cats' tolerance for one another and the amount of time they can be around one another. You want to carve memories in their cat brains along the lines of, *Heeeey. Wait a minute. Every time I'm around that other cat*, nothing bad happens. Or even better, *Last time I spent time with him I got a treat!*

These periods of the cats' exposure to each other should be under your supervision, so that you will know if the tension starts to build or hostilities break out. If you see any of the signs of impending aggression—especially staring, ears flattening, tails lashing—separate the cats immediately. If you see signs of backsliding, reduce the time they spend together over the next few days.

Trading Places Therapy

If there is a clear bully and a clear victim, their status may have become too lopsided. You can help to right the balance by placing the bully cat in a room that is less-favored territory—not a favored room like the master bedroom or the living room, or a room with his favorite things in it. If he's a *real* bully, keep him in a space where he will be near to the ground—with no cat tree to climb on or shelves to jump on. Meanwhile, put the victim cat in another and more favored part of the territory, making sure she has access to high-status locations, such as a room with a cat tree, or a window she likes to look out of—or, best of all, on your lap. Then play with the victim several times a day to build her confidence, and, separately, with the bully to help him release his aggression and any pent-up energy. Establishing these two territories will help the victim become more confident and take the aggressor down a peg or two. Pheromone plug-ins can help both cats. Cats, like people, tend to take on the status they feel themselves living out. The aggressor may start to believe the victim can't be so easily bullied, and so may the victim. Her body postures will even change to reflect her new belief.

If there's not a clear bully, try to keep the cats' territories about equal in size and desirability, and switch them back and forth at least every other day. Play with them both every day, albeit separately.

For Fear of Other Cats Only

Reintroduce

If your cat has a serious fear of another cat in your household, then you must use the reintroduction techniques in Chapter 4.

Drug Therapy

Another thing you can try, with your vet's counsel, is psychoactive drug therapy. If it's clear that one cat is the aggressor, and the other the victim, there are medications for victim cats that a vet can temporarily prescribe. It can lower anxiety and give the victim increased confidence. The victim cat will likely stop hiding and begin standing her ground. She may even chase the aggressor! All of this can correct a severely lopsided social dynamic beyond the end of the prescription. But medication should be part of a behavior plan, and not used on its own.

For Fear-Induced Aggression Only

Identify and Eliminate the Triggers

The best way to stop aggression caused by fear is to eliminate or avoid the stimuli that caused the fear, if that's possible. For example, if the cat is afraid of dogs, don't expose him to dogs. If there's a dog in the home, either resident or guest, keep the dog and the cat in separate places until you're ready to enlist a behaviorist to help you reintroduce them. Removing triggers like outside cats is discussed in the Redirected Agression and Territorial Aggression sections earlier in this chapter. Still, it could be a lot of work, removing fear triggers all the time. That's why helping cats form positive associations *may* be a better long-term strategy.

Desensitize, and Create Positive Associations

For example, if your cat objects to visitors, have one or more of your cat-loving friends come over on a regular basis. Ask your guest to move slowly and quietly, in stockinged feet, as he enters the house, making as little noise and commotion as possible, and avoiding any eye contact with the cat, whom you have placed in the room where you and your guest are going to be. Then have your friend *sit* down, preferably on the floor, or, if that's not possible, on a couch or chair (the lower the better). Keep your guest as far away as necessary to keep your cat calm. Your cat can move closer on her own as she relaxes. If your cat looks at or approaches the guest, speak gently to her and give her treats. Next, have the guest dispense the treats—and lots of them, more than the cat is accustomed to getting from you. If the cat won't come close, the guest can slowly toss a treat, and also maneuver a wanded cat toy to improve your cat's mood and emotional state.

Another thing you can do, over the course of several repeat visits from the guest, is to feed your cat while the guest sits quietly in the same room. If the cat eats without arousal, the guest can move closer the next time—or the cat herself will move closer. When your cat gets close enough to play with a string toy, the guest can play with her.

Watch for the signs of aggression and try to end all sessions while they are going well. Of course, this all takes time and patience. But your cat is smart. She will make the positive association you are trying to instill: *These guest-types sort of rock. I think I will not bite them.*

RADICAL DESENSITIZATION

Flooding is a technique in which you expose an animal to the source of its fear in overwhelming doses.

Flooding is risky in any animal, and I *never* recommend trying it on cats.

Make It Easy and Safe to Flee

Cats can get relief from fleeing as well as from fighting, so to make your cat more likely to choose fleeing, give him cat trees and access to other elevated locations that will get him out of reach of whatever is triggering his fear. Also give him tunnels, empty boxes and pieces of furniture to hide in or under. If he has safe places to retreat to, his general level of fear may go down, making him more relaxed.

Picture this: A toddler walks in to the room waving a yellow plastic shovel. Your cat, seeing his five-foot cat tree nearby, dashes to the top of it, where he now sits calmly, confident that he is safe. If he were instead on the floor, backed into a corner by the child, with no escape route or safe hiding place he could easily sprint or jump to, he might react more fearfully—which is to say aggressively. Empty boxes on the floor can serve as buffers that allow cats to navigate around one another, too.

ATTRACT the Cats to a New Behavior

Play with Them

Playing with your cats helps change their mood and emotional state for the better. If they've been tense or actually fighting with each other, play with them immediately—before you bring them together again, while they are together, and after you've separated them, so that they have lots of happy associations with their reunions. End the sessions on a positive note.

Bring on the Happy Scent Brush

Use the group-scent technique from Chapter 4. Helping cats to maintain a group scent can reduce or eliminate hostility between cats and promote affiliative behaviors.

Reward Them When They're Calm

Praise your cats and give them food or treats when they are calm and relaxed. See Appendix A to use clicker training to promote positive or neutral behaviors, such as when they're calm, not fighting, sleeping near one another, etc.

TRANSFORM the Territory

Your cat's wildcat predecessors did not have to share food, elimination areas, or perching or resting areas with other wildcats. They wouldn't have liked it one bit. Your cats' swatting, hissing, and fighting is a genetic remnant from their ancestors, one only amplified by the way you may be crowding them and their resources under one roof. As I mentioned earlier, feral cats, outdoors, are known to fight much less than our indoor cats. The more cats under one roof, the more chances for friction.

In remedying territorial aggression, transforming the territory is *critical*. Your cats' competition for important resources could be the *only* reason for territorial aggression in your home. And again, that competition may be so subtle as to fly beneath your radar.

Implement the advice from Purrtopia: Transforming Your Cats' Territory, Chapter 5, in its entirety. Be sure to create lots of vertical space and disperse and add around the home more scratching areas, food, water, and litter stations, environmental enrichment activities, food puzzles, and more. Also be sure to add plug-in pheromones, and maintain the cats' group scent with the group-scent technique (see Chapter 4).

For Territorial and Cat-to-Cat Aggression Only

CREATE BUFFER ZONES

You may notice that certain areas of your home, such as hallways, stairways, and doorways—places that put the cats in close proximity if they happen to encounter each other there—are common arenas for fighting and intimidation. If a cat is fearful because he feels cornered, without an adequate escape route, his body language may send a message of uncertainty that the other cat may seize upon to intimidate him. Or maybe there's tension when both cats are trying to hang out at the windowsill to gaze at birds in the backyard, or when they're both running to the kitchen after hearing the sounds of their cans being opened or their food rattling around in the bag. Fostering a buffer zone between them at such times and places can help keep the peace.

Place buffers in the center of hallways for cats to maneuver themselves around. The cats can steer clear of one another and avoid altercations. Buffer items include cat tunnels, empty boxes, even cat toys. I once had a client who decided on his own to put a strip of blue painter's tape down the center of his entire hallway. Amazingly, he reported that when his cats walked through the hallway at the same time, they stayed on opposite sides of the tape. As with all effective buffers, fights and tension were greatly reduced.

If All Else Fails . . .

If this C.A.T. Plan doesn't solve the cat-to-cat aggression problem, and you have truly been very patient, then you will need to do any or all of the following: Reintroduce your cats (see Chapter 4), see a vet about behavior medication, and consult a cat behaviorist.

PETTING-INDUCED AGGRESSION

This is a very common form of aggression. You're sitting on the couch. Your cat comes to you asking to be petted.

Meow. Meow.

Oh, how sweet. Let me pet you.

Purrrrrr.

You like that, kitty? Is that good? Yes, you like that, don't you?

Purrrr.

You really love it, I can tell!

Silence.

Ow!

Now your hand has reddish pinholes in it, and your feelings are smarting too. What just happened? There are a few possible reasons for this kind of bait and switch.

- **Overstimulation** Cats are wired to be extremely sensitive to stroking and you may have overstimulated him by petting. Cats' touch receptors can get their signals crossed in the brain so that the feeling of pleasure turns into pain.
- **Undesirable Style of Petting** Many cats do not like being petted or stroked on their sides, below mid-back, or near their tail, and may tolerate it only for a short time. If you think about it, body petting is not a natural activity for cats, whose grooming of one another is focused mostly on the head and neck.
- **Improper Socialization** If your cat was not petted often as a young kitten or had a negative experience with a human hand, such as a punishing whack, your own hand may not be welcome, or may be welcome only briefly.
- **Feeling Confined or Confused** A cat puts itself in a very vulnerable position when it sits on your lap and allows itself to be stroked. While you're petting your cat, he may become very relaxed, drifting in and out of awareness of his surroundings, but if the world suddenly comes back into focus for him, he may feel overwhelmed or confined, at which point his fight-or-flight response may kick in and he may bite. And not in a spirit of play!

In some cats, petting-induced aggression may overlap with pain- and so-called irritation-induced aggression, or even status-related aggression.

STATUS-RELATED AGGRESSION

Cats have control issues. It's just part of their charm.
— Internet wisdom

Leave me alone! or I'll *decide when you handle me and when you stop!* Like petting-induced aggression, what behaviorists term status-related aggression is directed at humans—usually a particular human whom a cat has somehow designated as someone to control. This cat may stalk the human, stare assertively at him, block his path, even hiss or growl, or bite when the person tries to pet him or pick him up—all in the name of control. This kind of aggression may appear unprovoked, or it may appear when your cat is being petted or feeling territorial. (It's also called, variously, control, competition, or assertion aggression.)

C.A.T. Plan for Petting-Induced and Status-Related Aggression

CEASE the Unwanted Behavior

Avoid

If your cat is aggressive during petting, try petting him only around the head and see if the behavior improves. If your cat is facing you, make sure you don't make continual eye contact with him.

"Don't you eyeball me, boy."
—Sgt. Foley (Louis Gossett Jr.) to Zack Mayo
(Richard Gere) in *An Officer and a Gentleman*

Like Sgt. Foley, cats often see eye contact as threatening.

Anticipate

Watch for the body signals listed below and end petting immediately if you see any of them. If you wait until he tries to bite you and then you pull your hand away, you can actually reinforce the biting behavior by teaching him that biting pays. It gets you to do what he wants you to do (such as move). Try not to react strongly. Of course, your *not* pulling your hand away can get you bit, so set yourself up for success and stop any petting as soon as you see the early warning signals. Watch for the signals if your cat has been showing status-related aggression against you, too.

- tail twitching or thumping
- skin rippling
- body suddenly looks or feels tense or still, head may be hunched
- shifting body position
- purring stops
- low growl
- ears go back
- pupils dilated
- whiskers rotate forward and fan out
- a light grab of the petting hand (or foot)
- direct stare (status related)
- mouthing your arm or leg (status related)

For Status-Related Aggression Only

Put a belled collar on the aggressor to alert the human victim of the cat's whereabouts. Use a distraction or Act of God technique to interrupt the cat's unwanted behaviors. If you use an Act of God like a water gun or compressed air, you must use it at the exact time your cat is engaging in the unwanted behavior or it won't work. Remember to be covert or your cat will view your actions as a challenge, and this will make the situation worse.

If your cat is showing signs of status-related aggression (growling, direct stares, mouthing), don't pet him or pick him up for a while. If he's on your lap when he shows these signs, stand up and let him gently drop to the floor. Do not use your hands to set him down or you might get bit. These cats will also try to control you by blocking your path, so be sure to have the squirt gun ready if he tries to bite or scratch you as you pass. Do not simply avoid him in the hallway, giving in to his controlling behavior, or you will have reinforced the behavior and taught him that you can be easily controlled. To further establish your control, don't free-feed him. Feed him yourself, so he knows where his food comes from, and put the food down only when he is not demanding that you do so.

ATTRACT the Cat to a New Behavior

Besides avoiding and anticipating petting-induced aggression, you can also increase your cat's petting threshold. Over time, if you are careful to end petting *before* your cat displays agitated body signals, he'll learn to trust that you know his limits and he'll become more and more comfortable with being petted by you. So if you know that you can usually pet your cat for thirty seconds before he bites or puts his ears back, end the next few petting sessions at twenty seconds—and give him a treat if he has remained calm. This will further help him associate petting with something positive. Over time, you can increase the amount of time you pet your cat and your cat will start to enjoy the petting sessions—and the treats—instead of feeling anxious that you might go too far. Again, remember to pet him only where he likes to be petted.

For Status-Related Aggression Only

The person who is the target of the cat's aggression could use clicker training (see Appendix A) to train the cat to do tricks for rewards and to promote behaviors you want to see repeated—

such as when he allows the victim to walk by him or pet him without the usual outright aggression—and to acknowledge who is in control. The target can also dish out the cat's food so that the cat forms a positive association with him—and remembers where his food is coming from. I also recommend that the target conduct frequent play sessions with the cat, followed by a feeding. The target, in other words, should be the source of food and entertainment.

TRANSFORM the Environment

Utilize pheromones in your home to help soothe your cat. Holistic remedies are also calming (see Chapter 5 and catwhispererproducts.com). The status-seeking cat should also have plenty of toys and other diversions with which to exhaust himself.

Be patient and continually adjust your expectations. Your cat can sense any frustration, and that can dampen his mood and further delay progress. This can be a very long process, and some cats may never learn to enjoy being petted or sitting in a lap—at all, or for an extended period of time.

In a multicat household, aggression between cats, whether latent or in the form of outright fighting, is a frequent cause of misplaced urination and defecation and, of course, urine marking. Now that you understand tension and aggression between cats, we'll discuss an occasional symptom of feline intimidation and aggression—outside-the-box elimination.

EIGHT

You've Got to Elim-i-nate the Negative: Thinking Outside Your Box to Get Cats into Theirs

We're all mad here.
—Alice in Wonderland

THINKING OUTSIDE THE BOX IS AN ADMIRED TRAIT, OR AT LEAST so people claim. But the last thing we want to see is our cats getting creative with what Parisians, faced with very public human unzipping, call *urine sauvage*, or wild urine. (Lovers of the city of light will be happy to know that Paris now boasts, in response, a crack 88-member Brigade des Incivilités, or Bad Behavior Brigade.) I knew of a Siamese who urinated in anything with an opening: an empty laundry hamper, the kitchen sink, the recessed area of a stove top, the basket with the dog toys, the woodbox next to the fireplace—and finally, the owner's purse. I've heard of cat owners finding unwelcome gifts from their cats inside shoes and coffee mugs. I once solved the curious case of a smelly toaster.

The feline instinct to dig into a substrate (which we humans hope will be the substrate in the litter box) and eliminate is so strong that kittens do it instinctively, without training. It's been suggested the instinct comes from our cats' wildcat ancestors, *Felis silvestris*, who have lived in the semideserts of North Africa for thousands of years. The sand-rich soil conditions there made it easy to bury feces and urine. Okay, you say, but why did they bother to do *that*? They probably did so both for reasons of hygiene and because reducing their scent around their resting and sleeping places made them less conspicuous to predators. Contrary to popular belief, though, cats do not always cover their feces; they rarely bother at all when their territory is large enough—witness feral cats—that their scats lay far from their sleeping and resting areas.

Some domestic cats should open housekeeping businesses: They will cover not only their own feces but any other feces they find in the box. It makes sense that this is a behavior that we would see in domestic cats, since cats that through the ages covered up were probably the ones more likely to be taken in by humans, who would have preferred having the more hygienic cats around and in their homes.

AN UNNECESSARY TRAGEDY

Unwanted elimination is a serious but preventable problem. Experts estimate that between 40 and 75 percent of all cats with behavioral problems have an elimination problem. It is the *number one* complaint of cat owners and the number one reason *millions* of cats are surrendered to shelters each year, and even killed. It's crucial that owners get help for this unwanted behavior, because it is—believe it or not—not just one of the most distressing but one of the most easily solved.

Most of the circumstances that contribute to this problem are obvious enough that, with the advice in this chapter, you should be able to make the necessary changes to fix it yourself. I have helped thousands of cats over the years with their out-of-the-box issues. In the early days of my work as a behaviorist, I felt that in order to offer help I had to see the cat, the owner, where the litter boxes were kept, and the locations of the inappropriate urination or defecation. But over time I fine-tuned the forensic questions I asked my clients and perfected my behavior modification techniques to the point that I could almost always get cats using the box again without an on-site visit. Now I've refined my approach even further, so that in most cases you will need neither a house call nor a personal consultation with a behavioral expert. In this chapter, I will retrain *you* to make the changes needed for your cat's happiness. Then we can just sit back and let the cats do what cats do.

OUT-OF-THE-BOX DEFECATION

CASE #1: And the Owner Called her Yum Yum

Let's look at an example of a cat who, in the days of old, without the benefit of a particularly adoring owner, wouldn't have had much of a chance of getting to stay in the hut.

The Problem: Defecation Outside the Litter Box for Four Years and Counting

Owner Stefan's description of the problem (excerpted from a lengthy questionnaire):

I adopted Yum Yum as a kitten in 2004. In 2005 she started defecating outside the box, and then later on the living room carpet. Sometime after that, she developed an ongoing habit of running throughout the house dropping a bit of poop or two as she went. She also defecates on the fluffy bathroom rug, after which she turns the rug over. Oddly, she still urinates in the box just fine. The vet says there's no medical reason for it.

I've tried spraying pheromones around the house in case the problem was stress related, but that didn't help. I scoop her litter box at least three times a week.

The Consultation

When I met Yum Yum and Stefan at their Seattle apartment, I could see immediately that Stefan loved his cat and was doing his best to create an environment where she could thrive. A five-year-old gray-and-white Persian, she had every cat toy known to man and cat, numerous cat trees of every size situated all around the home, and cat perches in the window to maximize her bird-viewing pleasure. On Stefan's big screen TV he'd even thoughtfully arranged for a viewing of a bird video made especially for cats. Stefan himself was very into shoes. His apartment floor looked like that of a shoe store during a big sale. Shoe boxes lined every wall of his apartment and stood, at odd angles, Stonehenge-like, in other seemingly random places throughout the home. As I later learned, he had placed them as barriers to the locations of Yum Yum's fecal offerings because he thought they made it less likely she would return to do it again in the same spot—as cats are wont to do.

Yum Yum was extremely friendly. As soon as I stepped into Stefan's foyer, she rubbed up against me, purring. She then ran straight over to one of her cat trees and batted at the pom-pom dangling down, glancing coyly back at me, or so I liked to imagine, as if she assumed I was there as a playdate the ever-attentive Stefan had arranged.

"I give Yum Yum everything a cat could want," he began. "I don't have any kids, so she's it. This is a lifetime commitment, you know, so I could live with her pooping around the home for another fourteen-plus years." He paused. "Of course, I'd rather not."

Stefan added, "And what if I want to get married some day? Who's going to live with me and my pooping cat?"

"You have a point," I said. "Clients whose spouses dislike their pooping cats give me a chance to save more marriages than most marriage counselors.

"Okay. Let me ask you some questions," I continued. "I always like to rule out any possible medical causes first. Have you ever taken Yum Yum to the vet to see if there is a physical explanation for her behavior?"

"Yes, before she was a year old, she sometimes had very dry, hard stools and wouldn't go for days at a time. But the vet recommended I feed her wet food in addition to the dry food, so the stools are now normal-looking and happening every other day. He also prescribed a stool softener just in case."

"Did he make any other kind of recommendations to resolve the problem?"

"When the change in diet and the stool softener didn't help, he decided her defecation issue was behavioral. For a while he put her on an antidepressant, but it didn't work and I don't really like her to be on meds if it's not necessary."

I turned to the cat. "What do you think, Yum Yum?"

She shrugged. *Well, I was in the box a long time ago once and I did the thing and I was like, ow, that really hurt, and I didn't want to go there anymore, the hurting place, and then, like, I used the carpet over there, and that hurt, too, just like when I used the box, so I kept running around to different places, and finally it did stop hurting and so I just kept going outside the hurting-box, but I kept peeing in the box because that never hurt, you know, and—*

"I think I understand at least a big part of the problem," I told Stefan. "Yum Yum's behavior," I said, "had one sure cause and maybe a combination of two or three. So one other thing I need to know is, does she ever defecate right next to the box?"

He thought for a moment, picturing in his mind, I imagined, every location of his cat's stool.

"She used to do that a lot, and I guess she still does a few times a week."

"Okay, that might mean that the litter box has been too dirty. You've mentioned that you clean the litter box three times a week, but that's just not often enough. And you should have at least two litter boxes. As for the other causes, let me explain. . . ."

The Diagnosis: Pain While Defecating and Habituation, and More

"First of all, it was premature to conclude that there wasn't any medical reason for Yum Yum's problems. The dry stool made defecating in the box uncomfortable and possibly even painful, and if you weren't seeing any stool for several days at a time, that's probably because she was constipated. Constipation is a normal consequence of having hard stools; the stools are so painful to expel that cats hold on to them. Even worse, the longer the cats hold the stool, the harder they can get! And constipation can cause elimination problems."

Stefan looked a bit doubtful. "Even if she is no longer constipated?"

"Yes, because the pain she felt when she defecated in the box could have conditioned her to associate the box with that pain, which then caused her to develop a habit of defecating outside the box. Your description of her running around the house dropping feces sounds to me like a cat who was running away from pain—or from the box, because she thought the box itself was causing the pain she felt when she tried to defecate in it."

So Yum Yum once had a health issue, the original cause, and that had probably turned into a behavioral habit. One not helped by the single, dirty litter box. Even if the health issue was now resolved, a habit, once established, often continues, despite the fact that the reason it developed in the first place no longer exists. However, given that Yum Yum was now having bowel movements only every other day, it sounded to me as though she might *still* be constipated or having problems with hard or dry stool. Generally, animals have at least one bowel movement a day. Outdoor cats may have as many as five, with an average of about three, though a diet of the newer, concentrated foods *might* reduce the number to less than one per day.[1] I suggested that Stefan make another visit to the vet, who later confirmed my hunch and gave Stefan additional dietary advice, including how to increase the moisture content of Yum Yum's stool, which helped to relieve her constipation.

After looking over the detailed questionnaire that Stefan had filled out, and talking to him for about an hour, I had everything I needed to know in order to prescribe the C.A.T. Plan for behavioral change that you'll read about later in this chapter. I'll spare you most of the other questions I asked Stefan in order to narrow down possible causes for the problem, but I address one of those questions in the next section.

MEDICAL ALERT

Any stool that is not normal consistency, whether it's hard stool, soft stool, or diarrhea, can be the original cause for defecation outside of the box. A cat with diarrhea may not even be able to make it to the litter box in time. Using the carpet instead, she discovers that it seems just fine, and—*voilà!*—a new habit or preference for the location and substrate is formed.

The pain of defecating through impacted or very full anal glands can cause cats to hold onto their stool longer. I've seen cats become terrified when it's time to defecate. Their eyes dilate as part of a fear response, and their tails may lash with agitation. Some cats will even growl at their litter box. Cats also hold stool when tension between them expresses itself in territoriality over the litter boxes: A lower-ranking cat may stay away from the boxes and hold his stool. Holding stool can be both the result and cause of constipation and dry stools, and dry stools are of course also painful to eliminate.

If the anal glands are full or impacted, you will need to have a vet express them. In my experience, about 70 percent of all unwanted defecation is initially caused by cats having hard or dry stool, diarrhea, constipation, or anal gland issues. But even when the medical or other issues have been resolved, you may very well *still* have a cat with an habituated behavior—defecating in another place—and a negative association with defecating in the litter box, so you will need behavioral cures.

HAVE YOU EVER BEEN INVITED TO A FECAL BALL?

The physical causes of misguided stooling are not limited to medical issues. A common problem with medium-to-long-haired cats like

Yum Yum is that stool can get stuck on the long, soft hair on the backs of their legs, and under and around the tail. When such cats go too long between groomings or don't manage to get in the right position during elimination, the fecal ball can get stuck and you may be witness to a furious feline flamenco, as the cat dashes helter-skelter, trying to get rid of its unwanted dance partner. Though this had not happened to Yum Yum, it's not uncommon among long-haired cats like Persians and various domestic longhairs. I remember one client telling me about her orange-and-white tabby Persian tearing through the house like an orange creamsicle with a gargoyle latched onto it. Her husband had a different term for the mess he cleaned off the little guy as he squirmed in the sink. This "fecal ball" can be a horrific event for our fastidious feline friends (and their owners), and the afflicted cats may blame it all on the litter box where, so far as they can tell, the trouble began. Sometimes the bad association with the box will get a cat urinating around the home, too.

I recommend keeping the hair around the cat's behind and back legs clipped short enough to prevent the problem. I also recommend having a professional groomer, your vet, or a veterinary technician do the job. Do not try grooming on your own without first being shown the correct way, or you risk cutting your cat's skin, after which she may never allow you to clip or shave her again.

MADDENING MIDDENING, OR JUST A STOOL AWAY FROM HOME?

Sometimes a stool is not just a stool. Stools left around the walkways of the home or on a favored sofa or other elevated areas might be a form of marking done by your cat to delineate territory. This "middening," which usually begins only when the cat enters into social maturity, is to simple defecation as spraying is to mere urination. *Middening* comes from a little-known English word that derives from the Old Norse term for a dunghill or manure pile.

If you type *middening* into a search engine, it will, maddeningly, try to correct your spelling. "Was it maddening you were looking for?" Just say no. The fact that the search engine thinks you can't spell, and won't give you much information on middening in any event, is an indication of how rare middening is, at least indoors (free-ranging outdoor cats midden as much as half the time, but in housecats it's much rarer). But when it does happen, middening *can* be synonymous with maddening!

More dominant or confident cats may midden to send territorial messages. Middening is not only a strong visual signal, visible from a distance, but, because the anal sac secretions that lubricate feces are so foul smelling, it's a very strong olfactory signal as well. Because cats who are middening are trying to send a message, they usually deposit their midden in very prominent locations so it's not easily missed by other cats (aka the competition): in hallways or the frequently walked paths of household cats, near doorways leading outside or to favored rooms in the house, on elevated locations, and near other important pieces of real estate about which a cat may feel competitive. Cats may defecate (rather than mark) in these prominent listed locations as well, but it's more common for them to defecate in *less* prominent locations like the corner of a dining room. Typically middening is done away from the core territory of the nesting area's food and cat beds. However, a dominant cat who wants to deter other cats may even midden territorially in front of litter boxes or food bowls.

You'll know your cat has tried to cover the stool if you find it buried in clothing or bed linens left on the floor, or if you see claw marks on the carpet near where he left the feces. Cats will not cover a stool if they're leaving it for marking purposes. They want it to be seen! That said, there are some cats that don't try to cover their defecation even when they are *not* intending it as a message. So when you find an uncovered stool by the front door, it can be difficult to know for sure what your cat's intent was.

As far as Yum Yum was concerned, I had ruled out middening, in spite of the public displays she'd left around, because she was the only cat in the household and saw no other cat competition from her fourth-floor apartment, and she'd started defecating. Just outside of the box, and at one year of age, *before* she entered social maturity at around the age of two. In addition, her hard stool pointed to the likelihood of painful defecation. All of these factors made it very unlikely that her behavior was a form of territorial marking— as did the fact that she had tried to cover her stool with the bathroom rug.

Ultimately, it may be difficult to know for sure if your cat is middening or just defecating. Follow the C.A.T. Plan for Inappropriate Elimination, and if it doesn't work, your cat could be middening. In that case, you'll want to check the next chapter for additional techniques to address possible stressors in your cat's life, including competition with other cats for important resources.

Now let's look at a common scenario in the annals of unwanted urination, and then I'll present the C.A.T. Plan for both defecation and urination issues.

OUT-OF-THE-BOX URINATION

CASE #2: The Basement Cat Habitat, and Other Human Mistakes

The Problem: Urinating in Multiple Areas Around the Home in a Multicat Household

Owner Franziska's description of the problem (excerpted from a lengthy questionnaire):

Jelly Bean, Pasha, Nutella, and Helmut (all between two and three years old) get along perfectly about 95 percent of the time. They've been thoroughly checked out by the vet and have no medical issues.

Jelly Bean and Pasha started urinating outside the litter box when they were about two years old. At the advice of my vet, I have tried adding litter boxes and using different litters, but nothing has solved the problem. Please help! We are getting very close to leaving Jelly Bean and Pasha at a no-kill center. But this would be emotionally devastating!

The Consultation

I met Franziska at her home. "Oh, hi," she said to me, "come on in—" and to one of the cats, "you get back in here!" Franziska herself was giving off serious stress pheromones—I could sense that immediately. One of the cats greeted me at the door and was all meows, flashing her sparkling green eyes at me.

"This is Jelly Bean," Franziska said with a big sigh, "one of the urinators."

"Since you have four cats, how do you know who the urinators are?" I asked, wanting to be sure that she had the right culprits.

"I isolated different cats to my master bedroom. Over time, it was easy to find out who the offenders were. I have also caught Pasha and Jelly Bean in the act many times."

She went on. "Jelly Bean is the friendliest and sweetest cat otherwise, but she knows when she is being bad. If I walk into the room and she's just urinated, she will slink off with a guilty look on her face."

Cats don't by nature think urination itself is a bad thing, but if you yell at them while they are doing it, they *can* learn that urinating *around you* is not a good idea. Cats lack the cognitive equipment for a true sense of shame, and you can't feel guilty without a sense of shame. (I learned this not through my cat studies but by observation of an ex-husband.)

I asked to see where the cats had been eliminating, and, still agitated, Franziska began to walk me through the first level of her two-story home. There was not one cat toy, food bowl, or cat bed anywhere. The only sign that she owned cats was sleek, black Jelly Bean herself, weaving in and out of my legs as I walked.

"Wow," said Franziska, watching her. "It's been a long time since she did that trick. She used to do that every time I came home from work. Can I ever get her to like me again? I miss—" She let out a gasp and pointed to the couch.

"*See!?*" Jelly Bean and I both froze in our spots, our eyes wide. "A *new urine* spot on the *couch!*" At the sound of Franziska's outraged yelp, Jelly Bean tore off and up the stairs. I could feel the empathetic urge to tear out with her.

CAT-PARENTING FAUX PAW: REPRIMANDING

People often admit to me that they've rubbed their cats' noses in urine or smacked their cats. In so doing they've created in their cats a negative association with themselves, and possibly with the location of the punishment. What they haven't done is stop the problem. A cat that avoids the owner when it's time to eliminate may eliminate in hidden locations—which will eventually be discovered—or hold her urine, fearful of setting off more yelling or hitting. Holding urine is unhealthy for the urinary system and, ironically, can contribute to medical issues that cause unwanted urination.

"I'm sure you can get Jelly Bean to like you again," I said. "Cats can be very forgiving, if you want to pretend they have the human idea of forgiveness. But you need to stop all that shouting immediately. Your reaction really scared Jelly Bean. As you've seen, it doesn't work. But it does cause her to associate you with feelings of negativity and fear, which can damage the cat-human bond."

Franziska assumed an authentically guilty look, but she recovered well enough. "I just cleaned this area yesterday and someone urinated here again," she said. "I want to get a new couch but I'm afraid it will get ruined, too."

"We should get the behavior under control before bringing in a new couch," I agreed.

She pointed to the table in the breakfast nook, where she had displayed her English teacup collection on saucers neatly arranged around the table. "One day I invited my mother-in-law over to tea. We both went into the breakfast nook to sit down and I saw urine in her teacup! And Jelly Bean had tried to cover it up with a lace doily!"

I had to laugh. Franziska started laughing, too.

"What did you do?" I said.

"Why, I snatched it right out from under her nose! Said I'd seen a fly on it."

Franziska then took me on a sort of Magical Mystery Tour to show me all the other places Jelly Bean and Pasha had been urinating. There were many places, but the cats seemed to concentrate on the carpet in the corners of the bedrooms. Less frequently strafed were the bed and things left on the floor, like magazines, plastic bags, and paper. "The items are always tousled and scratched on, right down to claw marks in the carpet next to the urine." She'd now mentioned for the second time the cover-up attempts, which, along with the locations and impersonal nature of the targets, were good clues that the cats were not *marking* with their urine but *eliminating*.

Next I asked Franziska where the litter boxes were.

"Right this way!" she said. "I gave the cats their *own* finished basement for their main habitat. All their litter boxes, toys, food, and water are down there," she said with pride.

Here was another clue. I walked down the stairs to see it for myself. The light coming through the basement windows was dim. She had to turn on a light so we could see the five litter boxes lined up on one wall. A few feet away were the food and water bowls. Dispersed throughout the rest of the basement were cat trees and cat beds, toys, play mats, and even tunnels.

The other three cats were there, too: Nutella, Pasha, and Helmut. Helmut was perched on a cat tree, looming over the litter boxes. Nutella lounged on an ottoman located directly on the path from the basement door to the litter boxes.

"You wrote that you thought your cats got along about ninety-five percent of the time," I said. "What about the rest of the time?"

"Someone will hiss or growl at someone else, or someone will go a little too far when chasing somebody, until somebody becomes upset. It happens quite a bit on the stairs into the basement, but they were fine up until six months ago."

After some more questioning, I'd heard enough. If you've read Chapter 3, on cats' territoriality, and Chapter 5, on creating a proper feline environment, you will have already spotted many of the issues.

THE DIAGNOSIS: COMPETITION FOR
RESOURCES, TERRITORIAL CONFLICT,
UNATTRACTIVE ELIMINATION AREAS, AND MORE

Franziska's cats were most likely suffering from any or all of the following problems, any one of which could have caused the inappropriate elimination *all by itself.*

- a cat habitat consisting of all the key resources—litter boxes, food, prey targets, and other toys—crowded into one room, which created competition among the cats
- the cats' recent social maturity—they were all between two and three years old when I met them—and the resulting territorial behaviors
- too few pathways leading to key resources—only one set of stairs to the basement, and only a couple possible routes within the room, which were closely guarded by Nutella and Helmut, who were clearly deterring Jelly Bean and Pasha from using the basement litter boxes
- boxes too close to allow the cats to separate two drives— urination and defecation—that many cats instinctively want to keep separate
- boxes too close to the eating area, which cats like to keep separate from their elimination area
- inadequate lighting in the litter box area
- dirty litter boxes, since they were cleaned only once a day, in spite of the fact that the cats probably used some boxes more than others

Let's look at a few of the main potential causes.

Only One Location? But I Want to Pee *Here*, I Want to Do the Other Thing *There*

If litter boxes are all lined up next to each other in *one* location, they appear to the cats as *one* box. Each cat then perceives the resources as being limited, and will feel more territorial. Yowl! The seemingly unitary grouping of boxes may also conflict with the feline instinct to separate urination and defecation behaviors.

Sure, one box is okay for number two, but where am I going to go for number one? Hey, this Tibetan rug works like a charm!

Increased Aggression: Another Result of Excessive Competition for Resources and Difficulty Time-sharing

I knew the other cats weren't happy with the overcrowded cat habitat. Dominant cats like Helmut and Nutella may deter cats like Pasha and Jelly Bean from resources in cat habitats because they do not enjoy sharing limited resources. A cat habitat can actually increase territorial behavior. Forcing the cats to share resources all in one location may have also caused the swatting and hissing that Franziska didn't seem to think was a problem. If she was seeing tension 5 percent of the time, you can be sure there was social tension at other times that was just too subtle for the average cat owner to see. There's often more to a sitting cat than meets the eye. Pasha and Jelly Bean may have tried to remedy the situation on their own by increasing their territorial resources, that is, by making themselves a litter box of their own upstairs, wherever it seemed safe and attractive at the moment (like that couch Franziska was so upset about).

Intimidation

A cat like Helmut may lie in wait for other cats and just stare to intimidate them away from an important resource. In Franziska's household, there was only one entrance and exit to all the cats' critical resources, and that was the stairway to the basement. And once downstairs, there were very few pathways to the litter boxes themselves— so few that they could effectively be guarded by Helmut and Nutella. Big mistake. Hallways, stairs, and narrow passageways are prime vantage points from which dominant cats can guard resources and bully other cats. Such problems are particularly likely to begin when cats enter social maturity, for this is the time when they start to look at their environment through a territory scope.

AFTER YOU

When cats *are* getting along, access to pathways may be on a first-come, first-served basis, having nothing to do with dominance! In fact, cats have been known to sit for a very long time, each waiting for the other to go first.

> **Cat 1:** No, you.
> **Cat 2:** No, I insist, you go first.
> **Cat 1:** Only after you.

Toe Amputation—a Common Cause of Litterbox Aversion

Happily, Yum Yum and Franziska's cats had all of their toes. But after a "declawing," or amputation of the toes, cats suffer from ultra-sensitive paws—some for the rest of their lives. It should come as no surprise that the pain they experience may cause them to be turned off by many litter substrates and to begin searching the home for softer, smoother surfaces on which to eliminate—a practice that can then become habituated. The cat's paws can be so sensitive that *any* type of litter substrate causes pain, so that the cat develops a negative association with the box itself, even after the pain subsides or disappears. Another problem is that in the immediate aftermath of a toe amputation procedure, people are typically instructed to provide paper pellet litter or shredded newspaper instead of sand litters so that the sand granules don't get inside the cat's toe incision (which can further traumatize or infect the paws). You might think this would prevent the pain problem described above. But paper-based litter gets soggy quickly, which cats do not like. So this, too, can become a possible cause of litter box aversion, and another reason that the cat may develop a habit of soiling in new locations and substrates around the home. I'll talk more in Chapter 11 about the problem of amputation in cats.

MEDICAL ALERT: URINATION
AND DEFECATION

Fifty-five percent of cats that urinate outside the litter box have medical problems.[2] These problems must be addressed before or during the steps you take to solve the resulting behavioral problems. Not all medical causes can be found through a basic screening. Your vet may advise more than one urinalysis, a urine culture, or other diagnostic tests to reveal complex medical causes, which may include:

Too-Frequent Urination[3]
* urinary calculi
* interstitial cystitis
* urinary tract infection
* renal problems

Urination or Defecation Outside the Box
* Feline Lower Urinary Tract Disease (FLUTD)
* Feline immunodeficiency virus (FIV)
* Feline Urological Symptoms (FUS)
* urinary calculi
* viral infections of the urinary tract
* funguria, or fungi in the urine
* idiopathic/interstitial cystitis
* urethral plugs, stones, or strictures
* inherited/congenital disorders of the lower urinary tract
* neoplasia (cancerlike growths)
* Inflammatory Bowel Disease (IBD)
* colitis
* giardia or other intestinal parasites
* bacteruria
* loose or unusually smelly stool (conditions that may be caused by giardia, IBD, and numerous other medical conditions)

- polyps or other colon issues
- arthritis and joint problems
- occult abdominal pain, rectal pain, other pain associated with defecation
- polyuria (e.g., renal disease, diabetes)
- hyperthyroidism (a tumor of the thyroid that causes excess production of thyroid hormone)
- kidney or bladder stones or abnormally sized kidneys

The most common medical issues that result in urination issues are urine crystals and occult bacterial pain and interstitial cystitis. I see many cats with crystals in their urine. Because crystals wax and wane (often with stress) and don't always show up in any one urine test, I recommend that, to rule out crystals, you take your cat to a vet more than once to have the urine checked. I can't tell you how many times a cat's second urinalysis was found to be packed with crystals, where just a week before, a test was completely clear of them.

C.A.T. Plan for
Inappropriate Elimination

This C.A.T. Plan can be applied to problems with either defecation or urination—or both. I'll explain it using the examples of Stefan and his cat Yum Yum, the defecator, and Franziska and her group of urinators and squabblers. In this plan, you must put in place the Cease, Attract, and Transform techniques simultaneously, so read the whole plan before beginning.

CEASE the Unwanted Cat Behavior

Since constipation and hard stools are often a cause of elimination problems, examine the cat's stool. If you pick up a fresh stool with a tissue and the tissue doesn't cling to the stool, that's an indication that the stool may be too hard. The same is true of stool that emerges in balls or short segments rather than longer pieces. If you want to try to improve the stool consistency, increase the moisture in your cat's diet by adding some water to the canned food you already feed your cat, making it a soupy mixture.

Change the Cat's Diet

If you currently feed your cat only dry food, consider adding wet food to her diet. But you should consult with your vet before making any diet changes. Vets can recommend other ways to soften stools or help cats become more regular.

Add Water

You can entice a cat to drink more water by providing filtered water fountains made especially for cats. Placing water resources in an area separate from your cat's food can also make water more appealing. Instinctively, cats like to drink fresh water that isn't contaminated with bacteria from "dead prey." Your cat's store-bought food is its dead prey; his survival instinct is one of the reasons he may enjoy drinking from your water glass or the sink more than from a water bowl next to his food bowl.

Treat, Blockade, and Reassociate the Soiled Areas

To stop your cat from eliminating where it has been, we need to make the soiled areas *unattractive* for soiling. This involves a multistep simultaneous process for transforming those sites.

STEP 1: CLEAN THE SCENE.

Nothing will undermine my C.A.T. Plan for unwanted elimination faster than residual urine or stool odor. Why? When cats smell urine or feces, it's a message to them: *This* is a place to eliminate. The more often they eliminate in the same place, the more

ingrained the habit becomes and the more likely that they'll even
develop a preference for the new substrate and location.

It doesn't matter if *you* can't smell anything. Cats can smell
things our human noses can't; less sensitive than dogs' noses,
cats' noses are still at least one hundred times more sensitive
than ours.[4] So any place where a cat has eliminated in the past,
regardless of whether you smell anything there, should be
cleaned with a good cleaner. The more quickly you clean up
the mess, the better the chance that your cat will not associate
the area with urination or defecation. Also, the better the
chance that a *different* cat will not find the soiled spot and decide to start eliminating there, too.

To remove all urine or stool odors, I recommend that you
clean the soiled areas with an enzyme-based cleaner or an odor-
bonding neutralizer. As of this writing there are a few that I particularly recommend for cleaning residual urine or stool odors.*
For best results, don't waste your time on just any pet store
cleaner, nor on a homemade mixture. I have found time and
time again that total removal of odor is a matter for serious
chemistry. And definitely don't use strong-smelling cleaners,
such as bleach or ammonia, either. They could present a challenging new scent (not to mention that ammonia is a con-
stituent of urine) and may compel your cat to return to urinate.

If there's a chance that your cat is not simply urinating but
urine marking, refer to Chapter 9 for additional instructions—
and for additional insurance that you're addressing the right
problem.

URINATING VERSUS MARKING

The Great Cover-Up

The cover-up is a good way to identify mere urination. If
you happen to see your cat pawing the urine site before or

* See catwhispererproducts.com for the latest products and recommendations.

after, or you find a piece of laundry or paper pulled over the site, or you see rake marks in the carpet, he's almost certainly just urinating outside of his box.

However, if your cat does *not* cover up, but leaves his urine for all to see, he could still be one of the cats who just don't cover up their urine—and not a urine marker. Some cats simply do not have good covering habits, even in their litter box. But even a cat with good covering habits might feel that there was no good substrate to cover with, and therefore he won't even try. Another possibility is that he might have gotten frightened by something and run off before he had a chance to finish covering. Such exceptions notwithstanding, in general, covering up versus not covering up can help you distinguish between marking and nonmarking behaviors.

When a place has been soiled with urine over and over again, you may wish to try an effective carpet-infuser system to clean underneath the carpet. (Such systems use needle-like implements to inject enzyme cleaner deep into a carpet. See catwhispererproducts.com for more details.) In extreme cases, you may need to replace the soiled carpets or rugs and either replace or treat and seal the subflooring.

STEP 2: IF THERE ARE MANY SOILED AREAS, YOU MAY WISH TO TEMPORARILY BLOCK YOUR CAT'S ACCESS TO SOME OF THEM UNTIL YOU HAVE A CHANCE TO CLEAN THEM.

The million-dollar technique is to reassociate *all* of the soiled areas with feline drives that conflict with soiling (as explained in Step 3). However, reassociation takes time—from applying the cleaning solution and waiting for it to dry to going through the reassociation steps. If there are a lot of soiled areas, you won't be able to go through the reassociation process on all of the areas at the same time. Until you can get to them, you may want to temporarily make some of the soiled areas inaccessible or un-attractive by means of various barriers. Few clients like barriers, but they are only temporary, and they will protect the area from the cat until reassociation can be done. Barriers and other minor deterrents for the cat include:

- a plastic tarp over the area
- upside-down plastic carpet runners with the pointy, uncomfortable side of the nubs facing up
- aluminum foil
- furniture or other large items
- scratching posts or pads (larger ones help block areas)

For barriers to protect furniture, consider:
- a large plastic drop cloth (from a paint supply store)—make sure it's thick enough that a cat cannot easily chew on it
- a fitted waterproof mattress cover for the bed, and a plastic shower curtain liner on top of the sheets, blankets, pillows, and other bed coverings
- a sheet of heavy vinyl (from fabric stores)

TIP: STOPPING ELIMINATION IN THE BATHTUB OR SINK

For thirty days, fill the sink or tub with a couple of inches of water. For shower stalls, place at the base of the stall a cooking tray or plastic storable container with a water-soaked towel or an inch or two of water. (Obviously, if you have small children do not use this technique.) If there is a place nearby, or on the way to the sink or tub, where you won't mind a litter box for the longer term, use it now to give your cat an alternative. You should also place a retraining litter (see catwhispererproducts.com) in the boxes for at least thirty days.

Keep in mind that by themselves, barriers will probably not stop unwanted elimination. Cats often just find somewhere else to go, especially if the litter box situation hasn't been made attractive. In fact, if you simply left the barriers in place and didn't follow through with the reassociation process, you would actually *prevent* that place from being reassociated with activities other than urination or defecation. Putting up *temporary* barriers is a useful way only to buy some time until you can reassociate an area with activities that conflict with the unwanted behaviors.

CONVENTIONAL ADVICE ALERT

I do not recommend trying to deter cats from an area by using mint, which can make cats sick, or deodorant-scented soap, which can be toxic, even deadly. I also don't recommend Scat-Mats or cacti (yes, I still see this recommended), both of which I consider to be inhumane.

STEP 3: REASSOCIATE THE SOILED AREA: STAGE A HUNT.

How often do you sleep in the kitchen? Or eat in the bathroom? Unless you're an especially interesting person, I'm going to guess your answer is "never" or "very rarely." Doing either one would just feel kind of weird, right? So you should understand the concept of *drive separation*, and the idea that cats form associations between places and the activities that are supposed to occur in those places.

Cats tend not to eliminate in the same areas where they carry out competing instinctual drives such as catching prey and eating. Not only is it unsanitary, but the strong smells of urine and stool could alert predators or competitors to their presence. Even a cat that lives alone in a Manhattan high-rise will typically, and instinctually, cover her stool and urine. If you help the cat to form competing associations in a location where it has formerly soiled, the habitual urge to eliminate will lose out to the other instinctual drives, and the place will no longer be attractive for elimination.

Reassociating soiled areas with competing drives is probably one of the least-known but most successful of the techniques I recommend. Because cats build associations (and very quickly!) and will remember what an area was used for, *reassociation works best and delivers lasting results*. If you do not reassociate the problem locations, however, they may very well remain a problem.

CONVENTIONAL ADVICE ALERT

You may hear advice to place new litter boxes at the location of the former soiling. I do not recommend this unless you don't mind having a box in that location forever. Remember, we are trying to *reassociate* the soiled area with *different, competing drives*. If you put a litter box in the formerly soiled place, you are reinforcing your cat's association: *This place? Pee!*

The single best way to activate the reassociation is to stage a hunt, complete with prey and even feasting, twice daily in the areas that were soiled. This puts your cat's hardwired survival instincts at the service of your goal—stopping all elimination in those areas. The sooner you can start this after the soiling, the better—twenty-four to forty-eight hours being ideal (but never start it before you have done a complete cleaning of the area and allowed it to dry).

Complete instructions for performing a prey sequence with your cat can be found in Chapter 5. I'll briefly summarize those instructions here, while focusing on a few new instructions that are specific to litter box issues.

Since you can play with and give treats to a cat only so many times in one day, and if there are simply too many soiled areas to try to reassociate at once, you should focus first on the most heavily targeted areas. Use temporary barriers to block off the other soiled areas (see Step 2) or shut the doors to the rooms where they are located, and then start the reassociation process with the blocked-off areas as soon as you can.

And now for the hunt: First, collect a wanded cat toy and some cat treats or food that you know your cat is likely to eat right away. With your cat, go to a recently soiled area (now cleaned). Then go through the complete prey sequence, including the offer of food at the end. It's critical that you offer food in the same area where the soiling occurred. Doing so will help your cat reassociate the area where she eliminated with a different, conflicting behavior—hunting and eating. If your cat seems nervous about playing or eating in areas she's soiled, that just goes to show you how strongly these behaviors can compete. (Or her fearfulness may be in response to having been punished in the soiled area, in which case the playtime will also be critical in rebuilding her confidence.) So in order to get her to play or eat in the soiled area, you may need to start the prey sequence in the general vicinity of the previously soiled area and gradually move her, and the food you leave, closer to the soiled area.

It doesn't matter if your cat is not hungry before the hunt, or doesn't eat the treats you offer afterward. If she doesn't eat, leave the food in the soiled spot and she may come back to it later. If she doesn't come back to it, move it a foot or so away from the soiled spot. Spend five to ten minutes or so doing the reassociation process at each soiled area, twice a day. While reducing the time you spend at each area is not the best course, a shorter time is better than nothing, and the food you leave in the soiled area will also help to form the desired association.

To get a headstart on reassociating the soiled areas that you're not able to get to right away, you can try the following very simple technique: Leave several pieces of kibble on paper plates and distribute the plates in or near the soiled areas. Even without your performing a prey sequence, the food in those locations—or a memory of food—will compete with the elimination drive and make it less likely that the cat will eliminate there.

It can take a few weeks before you notice improvement, so be patient. If you have more than one soiler, play with only one soiler at a time so as not to create competition among your cats for the prey target. Many cats don't like another cat to be nearby while they play.

By now you will have made huge strides in stopping the unwanted behavior. Meanwhile, by following the suggestions in the Attract section, you'll be making the litter box a happy alternative for your cat. Remember, all parts of the plan— repelling the cat *from* the soiled areas as well as attracting the cat *to* the litter box—must happen simultaneously. Do not try to rely solely on transforming the litter box environment. Probably the biggest error I see in owners' independent efforts to cure elimination issues is that of only adding litter boxes or trying different litters. You could deploy a dozen or more litter boxes all over the house and the cat might still perform the habituated behavior on the dining room carpet. The reason? If he has not formed any conflicting associations with the area, habit or preference may continue to make the carpet seem like a great place to eliminate.

ATTRACT and Retrain Your Cat Back to the Desired Alternative: Litter Boxes!

During the retraining process, you should make your cat's litter box as attractive as possible. As Don Vito Corleone's cat in *The Godfather* might put it, *Make your cat an offer he can't refuse.* Here is a summary of adequate litter box resources, as well as actions specific to unwanted elimination. (For full information, see Chapter 5.)

EEEW!

You can tell that your cat doesn't like the litter, or find it clean enough, if she perches on the edge of the box to do her business, scratches outside of it before or after, won't put her paws in, does very little digging or covering, shakes her paws, tries to urinate or defecate just outside of or a few feet away from the box, or runs out quickly. A cat might also want to get in and out of the box fast, without doing any digging or covering, if she feels intimidated by another cat nearby, or has been pounced on while in or near the box.

Provide Enough Boxes

During retraining, you need to set out at least one more litter box than the number of cats you have, but sometimes I have my clients temporarily double that number so their cats simply can't miss a box. No, that was not an extended typo. I said *double*. This is what Franziska did. It can be a big help.

Put the Boxes in Suitable Locations

In the beginning of a behavior plan to cure elimination issues, I like to have the boxes located in places that the cat can't miss: not in high-traffic areas, but not in the far-off corners of your home either. Boxes should be placed in such a way that when the cat walks into a room, there is no doubt that he will immediately notice the box. If you say to yourself *I can't put a box here*, then, for the absolute best and fastest results, that is probably where you should put one of the boxes, at least at the start of retraining. Clients email me every day to tell me that the more-exposed litter box has become the preferred box. Remember, cats prefer to have a good vantage point while they're in a litter box, and they don't like to go into areas where they might feel cornered.

After your cat has stopped eliminating out of the box for at least a week or two, continue using the appropriate number of boxes (equal to the number of cats or floors plus one) throughout your home. If you have put the boxes in a place where you really don't want them to remain on a permanent basis, you can experiment with gradually moving them to new locations that you *and* your cat agree on. This is a process of trial and error, and you should move the box only an inch or so a day, so that the cat doesn't catch on to the fact that you are making sudden changes. Cats don't like sudden change.

If your cat begins to eliminate outside the box again, he is disagreeing with your interior decorating, so nudge the boxes back to his preferred locations. Too much movement may also signal to your cat that *any* location is fine. It's a negotiation, a dance, a *paws de deux*, if you will. But in the end, your cat will get to decide the best place for the litter box.

By increasing the number of litter box locations, you increase not only the number and availability of such resources, but the number of pathways to them, so that not all of them can be presided over by a bullying, staring cat like Helmut. If a timid cat is running toward the litter box with his legs practically crossed with urgency and a cat, dog, or child is blocking the way, he should know that he's got other boxes available to him, and other routes to those boxes. Giving the timid cat more boxes to choose from will increase his options—and with them your chances of having him eliminate where you want him to go. (See Chapter 5 for more information on setting up the ideal cat territory.)

Clean—Two Scoops a Day Keeps the Behaviorist Away

Insufficient cleanliness is one of the top reasons cats develop an aversion to the litter box and a habit for eliminating somewhere else. Cats are revolted by dirty, smelly litter. They don't like to have their paws touch soiled litter, even if it's their own, but especially not another cat's. They don't like to walk to a box and think, *This one smells too much like what'shername.* Would *you* like to eliminate in a filthy toilet?

During retraining, scoop at least twice a day to keep the box very clean (remember, an offer they can't refuse). Once you've scooped the boxes twice daily for two weeks, you can, if you must, experiment with once-a-day scooping. But if you notice that some boxes get used more often than others, make a point of cleaning the former more than once a day. Keep in mind that in a multicat household, you're also dealing with litter box competition. Cats rely strongly on their sense of smell. If a lower-ranking cat finds a high-ranking cat's urine or feces in the box, the low-ranking cat may shrug, turn around, and go somewhere else.

I have six cats and five aren't too picky, but unless I scoop twice daily, one of them will go outside the box. She really insists on a clean box!

If you are using covered boxes, uncover them.

WHEN THE OWNER'S AWAY . . .

Many cat owners forget that when they go away on a trip, they need to make sure that whoever watches their cats in their absence is told to clean the boxes as regularly as the owners do.

For a Fast Track to Success, Use Retraining Litter

Your cat may have been avoiding the box in part because she disliked her litter. But even if you have no reason to believe your cat disliked the litter, if you want the highest assurance of speedy success during retraining, I strongly recommend that as part of your C.A.T. Plan you use a special *retraining litter* or a litter attractant that can be sprinkled on regular litter. I see some on the market that work and some that don't, so visit catwhispererproducts.com for my recommendations.

The retraining litter I like best, which is a staple in almost all of my litter box consultations, is a medium grain, unscented litter that has an organic attractant mixed in with the litter itself. The litter grain is large enough that it doesn't easily stick to the paws, but small enough that it doesn't cause discomfort. I've found this to be highly attractive to most cats. They will literally visit the box several times a day, which is very important for retraining and instilling new habits. If your local stores don't carry any of the retraining litters that I recommend, try sprinkling a separately sold organic litter attractant into any unscented, medium-grain litter.

Spread the retraining litter two to three inches deep in all your cat's new litter boxes and at least one of the old ones. You may soon notice your cat visiting the boxes more often and scratching around more, before or after elimination. If your cat scratches at the litter for more than four seconds, it's safe to say he likes the litter. Many cats love retraining litter so much that they will sit in the box for half an hour. Use the retraining litter for at least thirty days. If your cat likes the new litter, be sure to add it to your cat's *old* boxes, too.

Is your cat still not attracted to the new boxes after several days? First, honestly assess whether the box locations are optimal from the cat's point of view rather than yours or your spouse's. If not, here are some things to try. First, try moving some of the boxes. Second, use an empty litter box. Cats who like urinating on tile or other smooth surfaces may actually prefer the smoothness of an empty box. Third, you can place a substrate that you know your cat likes—such as a puppy training pad (whose soft absorbent texture mimics the softness of the bathroom rugs your cat may currently enjoy). Once your cat begins frequenting these boxes, you can begin gradually adding a little litter to the boxes each day.

Litter Substitution Once the unwanted elimination is solved, you may decide not to switch from the more expensive retraining litter to a maintenance litter. If you do switch, do so gradually, one box at a time, mixing increasing amounts of maintenance litter into the retraining litter, until, box by box, each one contains only the maintenance litter. I also recommend having more than one kind of litter available if you have a multicat household. Chances are, some of your cats might like one litter over another.

During retraining, praise and even reward your cat for using the litter box. But you know your cat better than anyone: If he would rather be left alone than receive any attention while in the box, then leave him be.

TRANSFORM the Territory

Cat owners often set up their cat's environment to please themselves, or, with better intentions but not necessarily better results, in a way they mistakenly believe will please their cats. (See Franziska and the cat habitat she created for her cats.) In most cases, the litter boxes and other parts of the environment are set up in such a way as to *cause* unwanted elimination. Interestingly, we can help decrease tension over the litter boxes by decreasing tension over *unrelated resources within the same environment*. That means providing plenty of toys, perching places, boxes, tunnels, diversions of all kinds, and spreading them out instead of concentrating them in one place.

Some of the methods of transforming your cat's territory may have already been implemented in the Cease and Attract sections, depending on what the territory was like at the time of the problem. Transforming the territory is one part remedial and three parts preventative. It is very important. My goal is not just to fix immediate behavior issues and prevent new ones, but to make your cat's life better. Refer to Chapter 5 for all the important details, and see the handy checklist in Appendix B.

In the next chapter, I'll discuss urine marking, a slightly more challenging behavior that's often confused with mere urination but has entirely different causes.

NINE

"X" Marks the Spot (or Spots)!: Urine Marking

"It must be a very pretty dance," said Alice timidly.
—Alice in Wonderland

ON YOUR WAY OUT THE DOOR IN THE MORNING, YOU TAKE ONE last look at those beautiful red and gold drapes. They're a month old now, and were so very, very costly, but worth every penny because they bring the whole room alive, especially when the wind catches them, as it does now, and sets them in motion. As you turn to walk away, you catch a movement just below your field of vision. Your gaze focuses and drops like a vaulter's pole.

Ah, love! You sigh. It's kitty.

The Aslan-like all-white Maine coon with gooseberry eyes, that extra beat in your heart, has come with his leonine grace into the room. You love to watch him walk. Tail straight up in the air at the moment, like a king holding up the banners of his own royal procession. Is there anything so regal as a cat? His nose comes to a point like one of the Great Pyramids; the tips of his ears could puncture a Doberman. Magnificent.

Moved, you decide to call out to him, to say good-bye one more time before you leave. Before you can do so, you see him stop near the drapes. His tail, you now notice, is shivering, quivering—*vibrating*. *How fascinating*, you think, like a proud mother. These cats and their idiosyncrasies. Now he's picking up his rear paws and setting them down, up and down, like a little person marching in place. Such curious quirks in him today! Maybe it's a good-bye dance. Poor little guy, he's obviously missing you already. Pawing in place, his tail vibrating, he makes your heart just about want to burst, and you are again about to call out to him when something catches your eye, something that makes you realize that what is emerging from Sasha is not an emanation of reciprocated love but a mist of urine, parallel to the floor and surely destroying its target, your gorgeous eight-hundred-dollar drapes. The wind that had toyed with them a minute ago now carries to your nose one of the most foully pungent of animal odors.

QUIZ

Your beloved cat has just:

    a. forgotten where the litter box is
    b. lost his mind
    c. engaged in a catlike expression of excitement that you need to learn to accept, because it's utterly incurable
    d. spray marked
    e. urinated to show you that he resents you for something you did or didn't do

(Hint: The answer is *definitely* not c or e, two common fallacies.)

Sometimes when I speak to a cat owner for the first time, he will start our conversation about his cats with a big sigh, and I, without having heard anything at all about the cats' behavioral issues, will interject and say, "You must have a spraying issue." I then have to talk him out of the notion that I'm a cat psychic. I'm no psychic, but the sense of frustration and hopelessness that I hear in that sigh tells me everything I need to know.

Spraying is a major reason that cats get sent to shelters, or put out on the street. My job is to end the spraying and change the storyline. Like the director of a movie, I insist on my own ending, the happily-ever-after ending with the cat and the owner staying together. And I always get my ending, because spraying is surprisingly easy to remedy. Let's start by understanding feline marking behavior, of which urine marking is only the most upsetting variety.

MARKING FOR COMMUNICATION

Feline marking is inspired by complex emotional and territorial motivations. A territorial animal, the cat has quite sensibly evolved many ways of advertising what it considers to be the boundaries of its territory, and conveying information about itself. An animal that hunts

FACIAL MARKING AND BODY MARKING

When a cat rubs its face or parts of its body on vertical surfaces like chairs and chair legs, posts, and trees, it is depositing secretions from various facial and bodily glands in order to add its scent and pheromones to these objects, making the environment more familiar and comfortable for himself. Facial marking and body marking are harmless, but they're important to the cat, so they should not be discouraged.

Friendly cats may exchange face- and body-gland secretions with each other to aid in developing a group scent and a feeling of identification with the household group. This habit further debunks the myth that cats are solitary. Cats have rich and elaborate means to communicate with one another and even to form close and lasting bonds.

alone cannot afford to be out of commission due to avoidable fights among its own kind. So, to avoid fights, the cat has evolved an elaborate communications system, which involves various kinds of marking. Most of the time, cats use one of the several forms of marking that are no problem to their owners.

Friendly Marking, or the Cute Stuff

All marking by cats leaves scent, and some marking is easy to observe, once you know what to look for. But if you don't, you may not even recognize some forms of marking *as* marking: facial marking, which includes chinning, bunting, cheek marking, and lip marking; and other forms of rubbing with various body parts. These are just plain cute to watch. In fact, many times when you see your cat doing something adorable, she is either scent marking or issuing an invitation to decrease the distance between the two of you. When she rubs against your legs with her face or flanks, do you think she's stroking you with affection? As a Hemingway character once said, wouldn't it be pretty to think so. What she is most likely doing is leaving her scent and friendly pheromones and mixing your scents together. These important ingredients all help to form a social glue.

However, I believe that a cat may sometimes rub your leg as a sort of proxy for your head, which she can't reach—and then she may be trying to express something closer to affection.

When a cat head-bunts your head or face it's more about bonding and closeness—reminiscent of kittenhood with Mom—and, I think, closer to a true sign of affection. My Jasper Moo Foo is a master bunter. He lowers his forehead and pushes it insistently into mine, over and over, followed by nuzzling into my neck, chin, or cheek like there's no tomorrow. Considering that his "arms" are already around my neck, it's utterly heartwarming. Recent studies have shown that cat pheromones and human pheromones are similar in make-up. This may be one reason cats and humans can become so attached to one another.

What about that business of rolling around on the carpet? Also cute, but it's often a way of scent marking. Rubbing her chin on something like she's scratching it? You guessed it. Cats will also rub against one another as a greeting, to create a group scent that reinforces their place in the group, or to carry with them a sort of olfactory seal of approval from a recently rubbed superior. A group scent helps cats to feel affiliated with other cats in the group, which makes them feel more secure, and better able to get along with each other, thus less in need of urine marking.

FRIENDLY VERSUS ANXIOUS OR AGGRESSIVE MARKING

When a cat rubs his face on objects, he's releasing and depositing pheromones that are friendly and help him feel confident that he's in familiar surroundings. Other forms of marking, however, may signal less-positive feelings. Spraying and middening are emotionally intense behaviors, driven by either aggression or anxiety (or both). They're very different from the calm, affiliative forms of facial marking. Claw marking, except when done for exercise or to remove old claw sheaths, is a form of territorial marking that helps cats feel more confident. Cats may also claw to release pent-up emotions or tension.

Urine and the Not-so-Friendly Forms of Marking

Compared to fighting, urine spraying conserves energy, which is vital to every animal's survival. If a cat regularly puts out more energy than it takes in, it cannot survive. Most sterilized cats find that marking their territory by claw marking (see Chapter 11) gives them enough confidence that they don't need to resort to marking by spraying—which can be destructive, foul-smelling, or both—or by middening (see Chapter 8), which are more emphatic forms of marking. Excessive urine or claw marking may be the only sign you'll get that your cat is trying to make himself feel better in his environment.

Because urine marking is not only a way that cats mark territory, but a way to communicate and gather information, it's not uncommon to have more than one sprayer in a multicat household, though some spray may be overt and some covert. Confident or high-ranking cats may spray while another cat is watching, either to bolster their already high self-confidence, or to send a clear territorial message, or both. How convenient that nature endowed spraying with such theatrics! Less-confident cats may spray in secret while no other cat is watching, perhaps as an outlet after a recent distressing encounter with an aggressor, once the two have separated. Because other cats can perceive spraying as a sign of aggression, doing it in secret, while no other cat is present, is a must for the less-confident or lower-ranking cat, or he could invite attack.

There are several ways in which cats deposit urine.

- Elimination urination (see Chapter 8), which is not a form of marking
- Spray marking, which you saw in Sasha the Maine coon, usually done on a vertical surface, though some cats switch it up a bit and spray, from a standing position, on a horizontal surface
- Non-spray urine marking (from a squatting position). This may be done on horizontal surfaces (like the carpet) if the cat is not confident enough to spray urine vertically. If done on an owner's items, this could be considered associative urine marking (see the Associative Marking section).

Your goal, of course, is to restrict your own cats to elimination urination, and specifically elimination urination that occurs in the litter box. But before I turn to how you can assure that your cats only urinate, and only in the box, let's look at the other kinds of urine deposits—spray and non-spray urine marking—to get a better understanding of why your cats might be moved to resort to them.

VERTICAL VERSUS HORIZONTAL SPRAYING

The higher on a wall or vertical surface that a cat sprays, the higher the threat or challenge he's intending to convey. Urine marking on the horizontal may be done for territorial purposes or emotional release, as with vertical marking, but it's generally done more by a lower-ranking or less-confident cat.

Spray Marking—Not-So-Good Vibrations

What you witnessed in Sasha at the start of this chapter was the most common kind of spraying, in which a cat sprays on a vertical surface, standing up, tail raised in the air (the curious vibrating tail), paws treading the ground in a sort of march or kneading (perhaps to mark with paw scent), an intense or euphoric look on the cat's face, and then of course the urine, forcefully shooting straight out onto a vertical surface: walls, windows, curtains, doors, sofas, cabinets, stereo speakers, television or laptop screens, your leg, a pile of laundry, the outside of the litter box or the wall behind it, and fences and bushes outside—you name it! And it can be a little bit of urine or a lot.

So what's with the good vibrations? Think of the vibrating tail as a sort of lightning rod. Indoors, you'll most often see cats' tails vibrate whenever they are overly excited, agitated, unsure, and just need to relieve the tension. I see it most often when a cat has decided, for whatever reason, that he needs to hold still in a certain spot. My cat Jasper likes to jump up on his cat tree or other elevated surface where he eagerly waits for me to pet him. He is overcome with excitement, yet he knows it's in his best interest to wait and stand still in the spot where I usually pet him. During the agonizing wait, his upright tail vibrates like the leaves of an Aspen tree. A cat's quivering tail seems to release energy. A dog's wagging tail or fit-to-burst wiggling of his whole body might be in the same category. The pent-up, intense, emotional energy needs to flow out *somewhere* while the cat is holding still. So a vibrating tail by itself is not a bad thing. It's all about releasing an intense excitability that could be caused by something either positive *or* negative. It's only when the vibrating tail is a prelude to spray marking that the vibrations cease to be good (as far as you're concerned, anyway).

Spray marking is particularly unnerving to cat owners because of the damage it can do to expensive objects like couches, television or laptop screens, and silk curtains, of course! One cat was reported to have started a fire by spraying an electrical outlet.

This may seem surprising to you, but some cats tend to spray near their core territory, which is where their food, sleeping, or resting resources are located. Others spray more on the perimeter or home range: on walls, doors, and windows. Generally, if your cat is spraying near his core territory, or along internal pathways and borders like hallways or entrances into the place where you feed your cats, it's because he's in conflict with other cats within the house (or perhaps even a dog or child) who use the same areas. If your cat sprays around the inside perimeter of the house (on or under windows, on furniture near windows, or on walls and doors that lead outside), he's spraying the boundary line of his home range as a message to outside cats and even as a preemptive strategy in case an intruder makes its way in. (He's also making himself feel a lot better. Spraying decreases any feelings of stress or worry.) Some cats may be in conflict with both indoor *and* outdoor cats.

WHAT IS THAT LOOK ON HIS FACE?

Do you want to know where cats are urine marking in your home? Then watch to see where any of them open their mouths a bit, or gape, and sometimes grimace. That's a sign that they are taking in not only the scent that's been laid down, but the taste as well. For cocktail party chatter, you will want to know this is a *Flehmen response* and that it involves something called the *vomeronasal* or *Jacobson's organ*. A cat can take in the taste and scent of something simultaneously with this organ, which is just behind the incisors in the roof of the mouth. (Horses, cattle, and sheep also have a Flehmen response.)

Horizontal Urine Spraying Versus Horizontal Non-Spray Urine Marking

You might conclude that if you find urine on a horizontal surface, like a floor or bed, your cat is just urinating outside of the box, not marking. Not so fast. First of all, if you see a puddle on the floor, the urine might actually have been sprayed onto a wall before it ran down the wall onto the surface beneath. Or your cat could have been doing a form of spray marking called horizontal urine spraying—perhaps standing on a bed or on a table and then urine spraying the surface behind him. It has the same motivations, and is done with some of the same postures and theatrics, as the more usual kind of spraying, just with a horizontal target. You can identify horizontal urine spraying by the long thin stream of urine left behind, instead of the roundish puddle that signifies other motivations. Your cat can also squat on the floor and place urine as if he's urinating in the litter box, but his motive is to mark. This is called horizontal non-spray urine marking and it can be done on any flat surface like a table, carpet, counter, or bed.

Horizontal non-spray urine marking can be particularly difficult to distinguish from regular inappropriate urination, but if (as explained in Chapter 8) you actually got the chance to witness the act and saw the cat smell the location beforehand, and *not* sniff at his urine afterward, there's a chance he was marking. A merely urinating cat will often do the opposite: He's indifferent to smelling the location ahead of time, but he may inspect his work afterward in order to decide whether he has covered up sufficiently. Of course, many cats who have been caught in the act and reprimanded have learned to run off immediately, which can make it difficult for you to discern whether the cat is horizontal non-spray urine marking or just urinating. When in doubt, make sure your cat's litter box situation follows the guidelines in chapters 5 and 8 and that he has been thoroughly checked out by your vet for medical issues. If all is well in terms of the cat's health, then there's a chance that he is horizontal non-spray urine marking. Because flat-surface marking is less of a threat or challenge to other cats than full-on vertical spraying, less confident cats may perform this behavior to claim certain locations, but confident cats can as well. If your cats are doing this kind of marking, you will need to address how they are getting along (see Chapter 7).

SERIAL SPRAYERS AND GRAFFITI ARTISTS

Cats may have their own individual signatures when they spray. One cat I knew, Atticus, sprayed his signature like an urban graffiti artist, or tagger: His squiggle marks always formed a perfect upside-down triangle on his chosen canvas, the owner's velvet-tufted couch. There should be studies on this, or at least a gallery opening.

Atticus's owner told me, "He is quite proud of his work. When it starts to fade, he will even touch it up." It's true: If the scent of their spray is fading, that can trigger cats to re-mark a sprayed area to make sure there is no misunderstanding about whose area is whose—and when they last patrolled it. Cats can also spray out of habit long after the original trigger for the spraying is no longer present.

Associative Marking

Your cat may squat and deposit urine on items belonging to you. It can make a cat feel very confident to mix its scent with that of the owner. This is called *associative urine marking*. Your cat will single out your bed or other items that smell like or signify you. He may even do it in front of you. This is not contempt for you, or dislike of you. It could be that your cat feels his relationship with you is not optimal. The most common cause of associative marking? Your being away for an unusual period of time. The location of the marking? Your bed: It smells like you, and it is a symbol of you and of safety. Schedule changes are another common cause. A somewhat less-common cause is that of an owner punishing or reprimanding a cat, so that the cat associatively urine marks on the owner's bed and clothing. He does this to restore his self-confidence and lower his anxiety—but not out of spite. Associative urine marking, in short, is most likely an indication that your cat is having anxiety about something in the environment (which could include you) or is under stress because of a health issue. I view associative marking as even more emotional in its causes than other forms of marking.

WHAT CATS COMMUNICATE WHEN THEY SPRAY: TERRITORY MARKING, INFORMATION GATHERING, RELATIONAL PMAIL, SEXUAL ADVERTISING, PICK-ME-UPS

Once you have determined that your cat is spraying, you can best figure out how to stop the behavior by understanding why he's doing it. Spraying is animated by motivations very different from mere urination. Sprayers may be marking territory, gathering information from other cats in their territory, advertising their sexual availability, building confidence, or releasing emotions. Among house cats, spraying breaks down as follows: They have had conflict-ridden encounters with outdoor cats (49 percent) or aggressive interactions with indoor cats (28 percent); they've been restricted from going outdoors without having been given compensatory outlets for their energies, emotions, and needs (26 percent); they've been moved into a new home (9 percent); they have found new, perhaps alarming, objects in the home (6 percent); or they've had poor interactions with their owners (6 percent).[1] We have email; cats have pmail.

What are these messages that are delivered by such oddly behaving little postmen? What are they trying to say? When a cat marks with urine, think of him as leaving a personal business card with his pertinent information (age, sex, health), including even *when* he was last at that location and his level of assertiveness. Outdoors or in a multicat household, the network of messages among many different cats can start to resemble less a pmail than a chat room or social media like, say, MySprays or Spraysbook.

Marking Territory, Avoiding Conflict in Shared Territory

Spraying is one of the most visible consequences of the increased territoriality that cats experience when they reach social maturity. Spraying among wildcats or feral cats is quite normal—about as natural as breathing. Outdoors, tomcats during breeding season have been observed to spray twenty-two times per hour in one study, and over sixty times in another. Nonbreeding males spray about thirteen times per hour, and females four to six times.[2] Not unlike a rancher digging post holes for a fence, toms may spray every fifteen feet or so along their paths. Because other cats will spend more time investigating the urine if it is recent, sprayers put a premium on that zesty freshness.

Some people think that sprayers want to expel other cats from their territory, but although spraying does give a clear message to other cats that they're in someone else's territory, spray marks have rarely been observed to act as a deterrent.[3] The sprayer leaves a message about when he was last there so that other cats can consult their calendars and rearrange their schedules accordingly. Spraying may help cats to share a hunting range or overlapping territories without coming into contact and risking altercations. Such time-sharing is like a détente in a Cold War: The cats are trying to avoid all-out nuclear war. A cat may time-share until he finds that he has the confidence to take over the territory altogether.

(Sniff here)
Mr. Happy Paws

I was here: After sundown
Reason: To spray mark 5 locations in my home range
Assertiveness: Strong
Health: Excellent (just need a teeth cleaning)
Message: Try not to come around after sundown

Sample Calling Card

Information Gathering

Cats will also spray to *gather* information about other cats in the area. This is pmail in the truest sense: They actually want to see if other cats will write back, so to speak. A response would tell the sprayer whether another cat is in the area or even sharing his hunting territory. Why does he care? So he can protect himself, either by marking again, ceding territory, or avoiding the other cat. Much of urine marking of any kind is about territory. Marking helps cats figure out how to time-share their overlapping territories without having to risk fighting.

I come here on Tuesdays — What about you?

The Sexual Politics of Spraying: Intact Toms and Estral Queens

Only in unsterilized cats is sexual advertising a common motivation for spraying. Spraying to convey reproductive information is most common in intact toms and estral queens, where it is uniquely accompanied by a bansheelike yowling absent in neutered and spayed cats. Intact males spray more frequently around estral females, and the girls spray more often around the intact boys. The spray clearly gives off information about reproductive status, because males will spend more time investigating the spray marks of estral females than of those not in heat. For the majority of cat owners who have not spayed or neutered their cats, I recommend doing so. Among other benefits, most or all spraying goes away; sterilization decreases marking behavior about 90 percent of the time.[4]

That doesn't mean that a spayed or neutered cat will stop spraying completely. Far from it. Although altering a cat does eliminate most spraying—and all sexually motivated forms of spraying—the fact is that most of the thousands of spraying cats I've worked with had been spayed or neutered long before they began to spray. The sexual motivation to spray may be nonexistent, but the territorial drive to secure resources and to feel safer and less anxious may still cause your cat to spray. Both males and females, altered or not, may spray. Yet the assumption that only males spray is so strong that many a cat owner in, say, a household with one male and one female cat, has taken her *male* cat to a shelter—only to discover that the culprit is still with her. While it's true that males are more likely to spray than females, you shouldn't take *anyone* to a shelter. I can help you end the spraying, and quite easily, in most cases!

Spraying and Conflict

Sometimes spraying can follow the stress of fighting. Conversely, spraying may cause tension between cats that then leads to fighting. (For information on cat-to-cat aggression, see Chapter 7.)

I'm Feeling Worried

Cats may spray when frustrated, upset, or subject to competition or challenge. A spraying cat may even have separation anxiety. A cat sprays to increase his sense of security by surrounding himself with, well, himself. The more anxious your cat is, the more he'll need familiar odors such as his own in his surroundings.

I'm feeling threatened. I don't feel good about what just happened. This will make me feel better. Ahhhh.

Why *does* your cat spray? It's not always easy to say. A cat's stress thresholds are set both both by genetics and by developmental, social, and environmental factors. Nature: If the cat's parents were nervous rather than confident (the father's heritable temperament is especially important), the cat is more likely to react badly to stress. Nurture: If the cat had too little exposure to a variety of stimuli during the sensitive period of two to seven weeks of age, it may be nervous and anxious when exposed to anything at all out of the ordinary. And, of course, your home environment is also a factor: who else is in the household (both people and animals), what resources are available to the cat, the degree of competition for those resources, etc.

We usually represent a source of contentment and safety to our cats—just as they can signify contentment and peacefulness to us. We feed them and give them the attention they need, helping them feel like life is good and their survival secure. But for cats who are particularly anxious, we can find it challenging to anticipate their every need. Picture one of those particularly anxious cats meowing adamantly, demanding to be petted. What if the owner's hands are full or he's busy doing something else and doesn't want to be distracted? Stand back! The cat may be so in need of lowering her anxiety that she backs right up to a wall to spray. The resulting feelings of contentment can last for days, which is why you may be baffled to see spray marks appear only every three or so days. Clients often tell me their sprayer is the "sweetest" cat of the bunch (quotation marks alert you to the anthropomorphic trap). But sweet may actually translate as needy, anxious, fearful, as in the cat who seems to have a constant need for attention and follows you from room to room. It makes sense that the neediest or most worried cats are the ones who are most driven by the urge toward confidence building and release that comes with spraying.

"My cat is spraying to get back at me or out of spite." People often give this reason for their cat's spraying, but cats never spray because they're trying to get back at you. They simply can't think that way. Don't assume they're being insubordinate or disrespectful. It might lead you to yell at them, swat them, or rub their nose in the urine. This kind of behavior from you will not change your cat's, but it will make your cat afraid, and you far less popular. One more thing: Upsetting your cat will sometimes make him spray *even more*.

CASE STUDY OF BABYTAT: THE CAT WHO WANTED TO COME HOME

Babytat, a four-year-old orange male tabby, was spraying all over a beautiful home. He'd gotten a full checkup, urinalysis, blood work, and X-rays, prior to our consultation. Susan and Jeff, his owners, had first introduced him to me by email, then fleshed out their description of his problems in the questionnaire I'd sent them to fill out.

The Problem: Spraying All Over the House

Excerpted from the owner's description:

We have had Babytat since he was twelve weeks old. He has been the best cat ever until he turned about two years old and he started spraying everywhere inside our home.

One of the items sprayed was my husband Jeff's solid mahogany antique apothecary chest. The brass knobs now sport an oxidized patina.

He has sprayed the back of the couch near the living room window every other day for the last year, every custom drape in the house, the front door, the wall next to the sliding glass door, and Jeff's leather office chair in the den. The last straw was when he sprayed inside the grand piano that my husband bought for me for our anniversary!

The kids and I love Babytat and we do not want to give him up to a shelter (who would want a cat that sprays?). As a compromise we have decided to put Babytat outside. It kills us to see him scratching at the door to be let in while we're all inside enjoying ourselves, but he will spray as soon as he comes in the house. Our Babytat wants to come home (and I really don't want to get rid of my husband!). We are at an impasse. Please help!!

The Consultation

As I drove up to Susan and Jeff's house for an on-site visit, I saw an orange tabby sitting like a statue at the bottom of their long, winding gravel driveway. Glancing in my rearview mirror, I could see him gamely trotting behind the car, striped tail held high, as if he had shepherded many a visitor to his front door.

Even before I opened the car door to step out, I could already hear his loud cries. "Meooww, meoow, *meoooow!*" These were the kind of drawn-out meows that signified he was really anxious or in great anticipation of something. Once out of the car, I knelt down to say hello for a few moments and scratched him under the chin. As I headed for the front door he was already several steps ahead of me, meowing and looking back every few steps to make sure I was following him. He was probably smart enough to know I was currently his best chance to get inside the front door.

This must *be Babytat*, I thought, who, as Susan had put it, was "the cat who wanted to come home."

From the sounds inside, both Babytat and I could both sense the exact moment the door was to be opened. He was like a sprinter in the blocks.

"Hi, I'm Susan," said the woman who opened the door a small crack. She expertly stuck her leg in the opening to foil Babytat's dash inside. "We're so glad you're here! I can see you've already met Babytat."

Once I was inside, Jeff stepped forward and shook my hand vigorously. "It was either me or the cat," he said.

Suddenly the voice of what was most likely a teenage girl rang out from upstairs. "*You*, Dad! *You* need to be the one to go!"

They all laughed a bit but then caught themselves. Outside, Babycat was frantically pawing at the window.

I remembered from Susan's email that a number of the places he sprayed were near windows and doors.

"Do you ever see him run from window to window?" I asked.

"Yes!" said Jeff.

"Sometimes hissing all the way," said Susan. "Strays run around here sometimes."

I asked Susan to show me the other places she'd mentioned his marking, including Jeff's office chair and the grand piano. They, too, were near windows. After reviewing the questionnaire and talking to Jeff and Susan at some length, I deduced that the most likely reason for Babytat's marking was also the most common one.

The Diagnosis: Territory Marking

Babytat was clearly worried about the perimeter of his home range being breached. Anxious about outside cats, he was marking the perimeter of his territory.

In a nutshell, Babytat had been spraying inside the home for at least one reason — as a territorial or emotional response to seeing outside cats — and maybe other reasons as well. According to Susan's email, the spraying had begun when he entered social maturity, at around the age of two. Keep in mind that the outside cats had probably always been out there, but Babytat just wouldn't have cared when he was younger.

C.A.T. Plan for Spraying, Other Forms of Urine Marking, and Middening

There are veterinarians, certified animal behaviorists, and even "certified behaviorists" who will hold up their end of a discussion about cat spraying only to conclude, "Regardless, the key to treating spraying is pharmacological." This is where I part ways with many of the experts.

As long as we can identify and remove the reason your cat is spraying, my C.A.T. Plan works to eliminate marking without your having to drug your cat, and it will fit any cat, including yours. Before embarking on the Plan, identify the sprayer. And keep in mind that in a multicat household, the odds that you have more than one sprayer (even if you've caught only one) go up with the number of cats you own.

CEASE the Unwanted Behavior

Step 1: Clean the Scene

Clean the soiled areas with the special enzyme cleaner and methods discussed in Chapter 8. It's crucial to remove the urine smell as soon as possible to prevent a sprayer like Babytat from forming an association between the soiled area and his spraying instinct. If you find new spray at any time, be sure to clean it immediately.

Step 2: Remove the Triggers

Removing the stress triggers that affect a cat's mood and emotional state and cause him to mark is the single most important
part of the spraying C.A.T. Plan. We could work on all the rest
of the C.A.T. Plan, but if you don't remove or address the trigger for spraying, the cat will continue to mark. Here are some
of the most common triggers, from most common to least.

- The number one reason cats spray inside the home is that
  they see, hear, or smell another cat outside and feel threatened about safety or territory. Your cat may have perceived
  an outside cat from within the house, or on an outdoor
  excursion, or—much worse—might even have encoun-
  tered the strange cat inside the house if you brought it in or
  it entered through a cat door. *There were barbarians at the
  gate! And she let one in!* However, even a cat you've
  adopted and brought home can be less threatening to your
  cat than one whose progress he's been monitoring outside.

  Cat owners have said to me, "But I don't ever see any cats
  in the yard or in the area." Aside from the fact that humans
  just aren't looking (and listening) as hard as cats, outdoor
  cats tend to come out to hunt between three and five in the
  morning, when all the rodents are out and the people are
  not and there's usually just enough light for easy hunting. If
  your cat is awake, prowling his territory, he will notice them.

- Conflict.
  - The sprayer is not getting along with a cat inside the
    home, he's feeling territorial about important resources
    in the home, he is getting bullied by another cat, or
    he's anxious about changes occurring in the hierarchy
    of your multicat household social system. It's also fairly
    common for the sprayer to be reacting to having been
    victimized by *another* indoor cat who saw a cat outside
    and redirected his aggression onto the sprayer-to-be.

- The cats have to share food and water resources that are all located in the same place.
- You installed a cat door so your cat can go outside — but he feels more unsafe because his territory is now more easily breached.
- You have been punishing or reprimanding your cat — or even another animal in the house.
- Your schedule has changed (you're home for shorter, longer, or different periods of the day than before).
- You feed your cat on a schedule in which food is not sufficiently available, or you have simply changed his feeding schedule.
- You have stopped allowing your cat to sleep with you.
- Your cat is not getting as much attention as usual.
- You changed cat food brands or flavors, or switched to another kind of cat litter.
- You or someone else brought an unfamiliar item or scent into the environment. It could be anything — a new couch, a visitor whose clothes smell of cat or dog, a shopping cart whose wheels have picked up some worrisome outside smells on the way home, or even the soles of your shoes, which have brought in the smell of outdoor cats crossing your property (in which case you might want to remove your shoes as a precaution before coming indoors).
- You're having work done on your home. Remodeling brings in strangers and noise and dust and literally upends a cat's world. Remodeling is a huge stress trigger, especially if done in poor taste.
- You moved to a new home.
- A new person or animal was added to the household (baby, spouse, dog, cat) or there's tension with someone or some animal in the household.
- Medical issues are causing your cat to feel physical stress, which usually causes emotional stress, which can in turn also negatively affect how your cats get

along, which can in turn—are you ready?—lead to
marking.

After reading this merely partial list you'll probably ask yourself, When *doesn't* a cat spray?! You might even be grateful that,
given the many possible reasons to spray, you have cats who
aren't spraying. But for cats who are spraying, there are many
things you can do to put an end to it. Let's start with the number one reason for spraying—outside cats—and how you can
remove that particular trigger.

The problem of outside cats is greatly underappreciated; outside cats can have an enormous impact on the lives of your cats.
For best results, I strongly recommend that you act as if there are
outdoor cats even if you haven't seen any, and carry out the following techniques accordingly.

BLOCK THE WINDOWS

For the next thirty days, you are going to have to block any windows that permit a view of areas where there are outdoor cats so
that your cat can no longer see them.

I can hear you setting this book down. "Did she just say to
'block' the *windows*?" you ask your housemate.

"Surely not, dear," your housemate says. "I'm sure she must
have said to *knock* on the windows."

Nope. I repeat: Block them.

And while you're blocking your windows, you'll also work on
deterring outside cats from your yard, which I discuss below.
After you have successfully deterred the outside cats, but rarely
before thirty days have passed, you can uncover your windows.

Blocking does not mean covering the entire window, just
those parts of the window through which the cat can see intruders. How much has to be covered depends on what kind of
vantage point your cat has. You should prevent the cat from having access to the windowsills if possible—perhaps by putting
plants on them (assuming the cat doesn't like to eat plants, and

making sure that the plants are not poisonous, just in case). If there are chairs or other perching places near the windows and you can move them away, do so. There are different ways to go about blocking windows. The easiest and least expensive is to use wax paper and painter's tape. Put the material high enough that your cat can't see outside cats by climbing on top of something, or by standing on his hind legs atop the windowsill. In a more decorative vein, you can apply a roll of decorative window film—removable, opaque—from a home-improvement store. Merely closing the drapes is *not* likely to be effective. Cats can easily figure out how to get behind them for a catbird seat on the world outside.

KEEP OUTSIDE CATS AWAY

To keep cats off your property, I recommend remote deterrents. The type to use in smaller confined areas, or to guard a sliding glass door or window, is motion triggered and expels air from a can day and night. Another deterrent comes in the form of a motion-sensing water sprinkler; one manufacturer claims it will spritz invaders throughout an area up to 1,200 square feet. Finally, there is a deterrent with a motion-activated ultrasonic sound that the manufacturer says monitors up to 220 square feet. It emits bursts of ultrasonic sound that, like most rat sounds, cats can hear but you can't. The sound startles cats and teaches them to stay away. Turn off these deterrents when your own cat goes outside, so that he doesn't trigger the motion-sensor himself. Do they work? Actually, yes, as unlikely as that may sound. Cats are looking for a low-maintenance yard to prowl in; they have a lot of choices. A hint of unpleasantness in your yard, and they're off to visit the Joneses. Just follow the manufacturer's directions for your particular property layout. As always, see catwhispererproducts.com or the most up-to-date recommendations.

If outdoor cats are an issue, it's also a good idea to remove outdoor bird feeders and any food left outside, so as not to attract the cats. You can still feed the birds and even the cats if you want to, but in a location where your cat will not be able to see the outdoor cats.

Deterring outside cats can have a ripple effect of curing other behavior problems within your multicat home, such as reducing redirected aggression, which can in turn reduce spraying or unwanted elimination.

REINTRODUCE INDOOR CATS

If the stressor causing your cat to spray is not outside cats but conflict with a fellow cat in the household, then, in addition to adding more resource locations (per the Transform the Territory section later in this chapter), review the suggestions for dealing with cat-to-cat aggression in chapters 3 and 7. If none of these interventions help, you may need to reintroduce your cats as friends. (See Chapter 4 for the reintroduction process.)

If the problem is not outside cats or conflict with a cat inside the house, it's easy to see how to deal with a lot of the other triggers on the list. You could give the cat more attention if she needs it, stop yelling at or trying to punish her, be consistent in the food or litter you are using or make changes to them very gradually, feed more often, or in places where the cat won't feel encroached upon by other cats or animals.

If your cat seems to be marking in response to someone new in your home, have that person make friends with your cat by feeding, grooming, and playing with her. (See Desensitize, and Create Positive Associations in Chapter 7.) If the new person is a new baby who can't do any of these things, much less duck a stream of spray, then just make sure to pair the presence of the baby with good things for your cat, like extra treats, play time, and affection.

If your cat marks on new items brought into the home, such as furniture or rugs, drape a sheet or towel with your scent over the items for several days. You can also add pheromones to the sheet or towel, whether synthetic or harvested from your cat (see Chapter 4). And while you are implementing the C.A.T. Plan for spraying, keep foreign-smelling items that might get marked (including things that your guests bring into the house) out of your cat's reach. Items such as new purchases of yours, or things belonging to your new spouse, should be put inside a closet or cabinet or behind closed doors. Another option would be to mix these items in with familiar items belonging to you, whose scent the cat is accustomed to. You can also try misting synthetic pheromones on the items one to two times a week.

When you move into a new home, put your cat in a fully equipped safe room (see Chapter 4) and introduce him slowly to the rest of the house, playing with him and giving him treats as he explores.

Step 3: Gradual Reacclimation

If you have left your cat outside because of the spraying, as Babytat's owners did, let him back in. I advised Susan and Jeff to start the process gradually, allowing Babytat into only one room at first, and then letting him out into more and more of the house each day, making sure to reduce his anxiety and build his self-confidence by playing with him before, during, and after his entrance into each of the rooms.

Step 4: Interrupt the Pending Behavior

CONVENTIONAL ADVICE ALERT

The traditional advice for dealing with spraying in progress is to stop it with a negative outcome such as yelling, clapping your hands, or stomping your feet. These may be effective at the time, but they may also *elevate* the cat's background level of anxiety and increase his spraying *elsewhere*. It's also possible with some cats that they may perceive the attention as a reward—or just learn to spray when you're not around.

If you see your cat in a location where he typically sprays, especially if he's intently sniffing the area, or performing any part of the dance that signals a spraying is about to begin, the best advice is to calmly deter or distract him before he's actually started to spray. If at all possible, you want to act *before* the spraying begins. Bring out a toy; if it's an interactive toy, lure him away from the area, and then give him a little playtime. If you have only a noninteractive toy on hand, toss it near him without hitting him. In addition to interrupting the pending behavior with a toy, you will change his mood and emotional state for the better.

If your cat ends up spraying anyway, calmly remove him from the scene and clean up the mess. Do not try to distract or interrupt, and do not yell or punish.

Step 5: Prevent Re-marking

Make the marked areas inaccessible or otherwise not attractive. You can use any of the barriers mentioned in the last chapter, or you can place over the soiled areas a product called Catpaper, a sort of diaper for your floor or wall that consists of an absorbent pad with a polyethylene backing. You can also try hanging strips of aluminum foil on sprayed objects. Your cat may be deterred by the noise and splash of spraying on the foil, a concept that has even been put into practice by Parisian architects who've designed jagged "anti-pipi" walls to splash urine back onto intrepid human urinators.

ATTRACT Your Cat to New Behaviors to Replace the Marking Behavior

While you're carrying out the Cease (and Transform) steps, you are also going to help your cat build up new, positive associations in the locations where he once felt stress or worry. You will also be helping him decrease his anxiety by getting him to perform other acceptable forms of marking in place of urine marking.

Encourage Facial Marking

After you've cleaned up the urine with the appropriate cleaner, it's time to help your cat reassociate the marked areas as a place for facial marking as opposed to the conflicting drive of urine marking. You can do this in one or both of two ways. The first is to spray feline pheromone (see Chapter 4) two to three times a day in the urine-marked locations for at least thirty days, and then once a day for an additional thirty days. In one study of a feline pheromone sprayed onto marked areas, the pheromone reduced urine marking in 74 to 91 percent of households, and middening in 33 to 52 percent of households.[5]

The second thing you can do is to gently pet your cat's face with a sock (see Chapter 4 for full details) in order to gather the cat's own pheromones onto the sock, and then rub the sock on the sprayed area (after it's been cleaned, of course). Do this one to two times a day for at least thirty days. It can take two weeks before you notice any effects from your use of pheromones, so don't stop too soon.

But the success of both of these actions is higher when combined with the rest of my C.A.T. Plan. And remember, if you don't remove the stress trigger that's causing the spraying, and you don't use a cleaner that removes the urine smell completely, you probably won't have much luck with the pheromone products.

Facilitate Claw Marking

Claw marking—in which your cat scratches on cat scratchers, not on furniture!—is another form of territorial marking and a way that your cat can release pent-up stress. Particularly if anxiety is a major cause of your cat's urine marking (and even if you're not sure), I highly recommend facilitating his claw marking on scratchers as a substitute outlet for his urge to urine mark. If he has already *claw* marked his territory, why would he need to mark again, with urine? Not only is the scratch a visual mark, but the glands in your cat's paws also leave a scent mark. Even if your cat is declawed, you can promote paw marking. Here's how.

Place cat scratchers in the marked areas. They should be several feet away from pheromone spray or plug-ins. You can start with inexpensive corrugated cardboard scratchers, but you may need to experiment with what your cat prefers. (See Chapter 11 for promoting claw marking where you want it.)

Encourage Body Marking: Rub and Roll

Body marking is another way cats scent mark their territory. To encourage it as a substitute for urine marking, loosely sprinkle dried catnip or catnip spray in the now-clean marked location in an area about two to three times the size of your cat. Every time your cat rolls around in the catnip, his mood and emotional state will improve! Do this no more than two to three times a week so as not to diminish the effectiveness of the catnip on your cat. You can also install kitty combs on the protruding corners of walls to promote body rubbing, and even facial marking.

Do a Prey Sequence

Getting your cat to play and complete a prey sequence in a previously marked area for approximately thirty days can do two things. First, it helps him build confidence in an area where he previously experienced stress. A cat that has successfully acted like a cat—stalking, chasing, killing, eating prey, venting excess energy—is a more-confident, less-tense cat. Second, it helps him associate the area with the hunting and eating behavior instead of the urine marking behavior. These behaviors conflict with one another. Review the instructions for a complete prey sequence in Chapter 5.

Place Food Strategically

Placing food on or near soiled areas is an old-school technique that can work, as long as it's used for approximately thirty days *and* you've also eliminated any anxiety-inducing triggers. If you haven't addressed the anxiety-inducing triggers, your cat will still mark with urine, just in different areas.

Why does it work? For reasons of hygiene and so as not to attract predators or competitors to important resources such as food, cats will usually not urine mark in areas where they eat. Because the drives compete so strongly, in the beginning you may need to experiment with placing the food in the *vicinity* of the spraying—to ensure that your cat continues to eat rather than avoiding the area he associates with spray. Then you can move the food toward the exact location over a period of several days. In the beginning, your cat may still spray in a location where you've recently placed food. Be patient. Replacing an old behavior with a new one is a process and can take time.

TRANSFORM the Territory

At the same time that we Cease and Attract, we need to Transform the cat's environment by de-stressing it.

Create Calm in the Environment

To increase your cat's confidence and calmness, add pheromone plug-ins throughout the home, and apply the pheromone spray in urine-targeted areas, as well as applying it once a day, at about eight inches from the floor (cat-nose height), in additional locations throughout the home that are frequented by your cat (see diagram below for suggestions). Such locations might include the corners where walls meet, the frame of a doorway, the edges of furniture and the legs of a chair. (See Figure 2.) Cats will facial mark in such locations in order to lower their anxiety and increase their confidence. You should also rub your cat's cheeks and head daily. This kind of rubbing can have a real calming effect, which can reduce urine marking.

In the Transform part of the C.A.T. Plan, you will also use the prey sequence and other forms of play to help him express a

normal repertoire of hunting and prey behaviors and thereby improve his mood. Think of how exercise improves your own mood and makes you that much less likely to snap at someone.

You should also increase your cat's resources and their locations. If important resources are in abundance, your cat will not have so much to worry about. In many multicat households, competition for territorial resources is the first cause for relationships that go downhill and lead to marking. See Chapter 5 for more detailed information on territorial transformation, including the full details of litter box maintenance and how to decrease competition for this important resource. In a multicat household, having all your litter boxes in one location could be the only reason your cats are spraying!

Follow-up with Babytat

Within two weeks, Babytat had stopped all spraying and, now that he was back indoors, was a much happier cat. Susan told me that he was also a much more playful and cuddly cat, rubbing up against Jeff and even bunting Jeff on the forehead — the ultimate form of affection from a cat. Susan said the look on Jeff's face was priceless. Babytat also loved to run over to his cat scratchers and scratch, and then to zoom up his new cat tree. Susan saw how much pent-up energy he had to exert and how much more he seemed like, well, a cat. He curled up and slept on the sofa more, too; he had never done that before because he was busy worriedly sniffing around the house, as if his only job was to patrol and secure territory. If he did ever happen to look out the window and see a cat again, he now had a new way of reducing anxiety, and that was by claw marking on the cat tree and scratchers that were now located in the previously urine-marked areas. Most important, Babytat was able to come in from outside and be a part of the family again.

TEN

Yowl! — Excessive Meowing

"Do they never go to sleep?"
—*Mowgli,* The Jungle Book

I'VE HAD MANY CLIENTS WHO CAME TO ME SAYING THEY HAD NOT had a good night's sleep in years because of middle-of-the-night meowing. Others were about to be evicted because of their cats' non-stop or early morning meowing. Some are simply dumbfounded that their cat can consistently beat a 6:30 A.M. alarm clock by meowing at 6:28 A.M. The excessive-meowing consult has become my favorite over the years because I can so profoundly change the lives of the cat owner and the cat. Finally able to get some rest, they say I've added ten years to their lives, helped them keep their apartments (and their jobs, now that they're no longer so sleep deprived that they can't function), and even saved their marriages.

The most common meowing complaint I hear has to do with the early morning wake-up call, the most popular time being in the most wee of hours of three to five A.M. Even with your head buried under a pillow, that meow can sound like an airplane during takeoff. The cat will relentlessly try to pass himself off as a rooster until you show signs of waking up to give him attention or feed him. Why? Maybe his hunting clock has been set to go off around dawn. (But it can be reset to evening, as I will explain.) Or maybe he was aroused by some commotion nearby. Cats have excellent hearing and can hear rats' high-pitched calls and even (according to one recent study of tickled rats) rats' giggling, not to mention outside cats in the midst of territorial fisticuffs, and mice or squirrels in your attic or behind your walls. These are among the many possible reasons your cat could be meowing (or yowling—making an even louder and more insistent sound) excessively or at inappropriate times.

The original cause might also be a medical issue. I've seen quite a few diabetic cats who ate continually yet were still unsatisfied and feeling hungry: *I'm eating and it's not working!* If your cat is geriatric and has both increased her meowing and reversed her day and night behaviors, she may have feline cognitive dysfunction (a fancy way of saying she may be senile). Given how many medical problems can contribute to excessive meowing, it's very important to have your cat fully checked out—with blood work, urinalysis, and any other diagnostic testing your vet might recommend.

MEDICAL ALERT

Health issues that could cause a cat to meow excessively include diabetes, thyroid issues, arthritis, an impacted or full anal gland, tooth pain, or any other kind of pain.

Besides health issues, the situations leading to excessive vocalization, in approximately descending order of likelihood, are:

- a hunting clock that is set for morning instead of evening
- separation anxiety
- cat trained by you to meow to get what he wants (a problem that can be involved in many of the other issues in this list)

- pent-up energy or emotion needing to be released (boring or stressful environment)
- change in environment (e.g., after a move)
- change in schedule (yours or his)
- loss of family member
- hunger
- meowing has become a self-rewarding habit and just feels good!
- a cat that is just naturally more vocal than others
- a talkative owner may have a more talkative cat
- the cat had been living outdoors and has been brought to live in the house
- the cat is in heat—in which case the yowling will be temporary but will recur periodically for as long as she remains unspayed

Interestingly enough, meowing is a form of communication that is mainly directed at us. Adult cats rarely choose vocalization to communicate with other cats, and when they do it's usually to communicate fear or aggressive intent. Cats communicate with one another primarily by way of scent marking and body language. But being the most vocal of all species, we humans respond most readily to vocalization, so cats who live with people have learned that meowing is the best way to communicate with us and get us to pay attention to their wants and needs. In fact, a recent study demonstrated that many domestic cats have evolved a sort of purring (or gurgling) meow that seems specifically targeted at humans, who apparently find it hard to resist. When in Alexandria, do as the Egyptians do. Not only do cats speak to us, but they listen, too. Cats can learn the meanings of certain words, especially if the words are associated with things they like, such as food, treats, or various activities they enjoy. Of course our tone can be just as important as our words in communicating our meaning.

If at all possible, you should try to find out why your cat is meowing, so that if there is any environmental stressor involved, or medical issues, you will be able to address it. However, even if you're not sure

why your cat is meowing, the techniques in the C.A.T. plan will eliminate or dramatically decrease excessive vocalizations. The sooner
you start on these techniques, the better, because you want to prevent him from rehearsing the meowing behavior over an extended
period of time, creating a habit that will be harder to eliminate.

C.A.T. Plan for Excessive Meowing

CEASE the Unwanted Behavior

Drug therapy is usually not necessary. Consider medication only
if you've followed all of the instructions below and the meowing
or yowling continues. Please visit catwhispererproducts.com for
holistic remedies that address excessive vocalization.

Daytime or Nighttime Vocalization — No Reaction

Most cat owners unwittingly cause or exacerbate their cats' excessive vocalization by reacting to it, usually with some form of
attention. No matter what, do not give your cat any response
when he meows. Do not tell him "No!" If it's nighttime, do not
even roll over in bed. *Nothing.* Do not even dream about him.
Never, never pick him up, not even to put him in another
room — the pick-up is a reward, never mind the subsequent ban-
ishment. If your cat meows at five in the morning and you get
up, you have just trained your cat to meow at five in the morning. The same is true if he meows and you feed him. The *worst*
thing you could do would be to let your cat meow for thirty minutes and *then* react. If you give in after a half an hour, you have
successfully taught your cat to meow for up to half an hour.
See? Cats *are* trainable.

They can even train you!

Daytime Vocalization—The Snub of the Queen

If your cat meows when you're in the same room, leave. His mother did the same when he did something undesirable, and he still remembers it. (If he follows you, go to another room and shut the door behind you.) Return only after he has ceased his meowing for a full three seconds. Over time, your cat will get the idea that meowing leads to the immediate withdrawal of your presence and the end of any chance of receiving attention from you—and that when he is quiet he can enjoy your presence again.

I must warn you that when you withdraw your attention, your cat's meowing may increase temporarily. If this happens, you will know that you were definitely reinforcing the meowing. Now he's acting as if you've lost that lovin' feelin' and he's trying his hardest to get the old familiar response out of you. He may even hit upon ingenious solutions like knocking over the bedside lamp or dragging books from their shelves. But stick to my plan. He'll stop.

Distraction

If your cat typically meows at particular times or in particular places that you have learned to identify, you can anticipate the meowing and distract him with a toy or other activity *before* he starts it. Use the toy or activity to lure him away from the area where he usually meows. But be sure not to bring the toy *after* he begins, because then it becomes a reward for meowing. Battery-operated or hand-maneuvered toys can provide him with a release for the pent-up tension or emotion that can lead to excessive vocalization. You can also offer your cat a box filled with toys and catnip, or food puzzles to engage his mind.

Strategic Feeding

If you're able, free-feed your cat to reduce any meowing for food. If you feed your cat on a schedule:

- then, for daytime vocalization, put the food down *before* he starts meowing. Do not wait until he begins asking (and asking) for food or he'll draw the clever causal connection that you are manipulable by meowing. If it's feasible, you might consider having your cat rely on a timed feeder instead of you. Timed feeders have been a boon for many of my clients whose cats once crowed like roosters.
- and he meows in the middle of the night or early in the morning, make sure he has a chance to eat something before he goes to bed, preferably right after playtime.

Take a good look at your cat's feeding schedule. Is he getting fed enough food, often enough, throughout the day? Meowing can be a normal response to hunger. If you are not free-feeding, or making food available at all times (see Chapter 5), you should feed your cat several times a day. Use a timed feeder to dispense the food.

A Nice Place to Sleep

Make sure you have addressed the problem of outside cats or rodents. Deterrents (see Chapter 9) are the best way to discourage outside cats from coming around.

NIGHTTIME VOCALIZATION—CONFINEMENT?

Should you confine your cat for nighttime or predawn vocalization? In short—no! Many people try to resolve the problem by confining the cat in a room of the house (or, to avoid possible destruction, a kitty playpen or crate) where they can't hear him. If they can't get the cat far enough away, they play music or white noise to cover the most insistent meowing. These attempted solutions will only keep you from *hearing* your cat's meow. Except under circumstances too rare to be worth mentioning, they won't stop the meowing, or eliminate the source of any distress your cat is feeling.

If you turn down the heat at night, make sure you provide your cat with a warm place to sleep, or a heated cat bed. This can be critical for older cats.

ATTRACT the Cat to a New Behavior

Accentuate the Positive

If your cat likes to be brushed, talked to, or played with, or to receive treats, give him what he likes, but only when he *isn't* meowing. Cats learn by experience and they will repeat behaviors that give positive outcomes. For added insurance, try clicker training to reward positive behavior, as described in Appendix A.

Reset the Time Clock

If your cat is vocalizing only at night or in the early morning, then, in addition to all of the above, you *may* need to reset his internal clock for evening instead of morning. To do a reset, complete a ten- to thirty-minute prey sequence every night about a half hour before you go to bed, for two to four weeks. After the playtime, feed your cat something. It can be a few treats or his regular food. If one of his feedings is normally in the afternoon or early evening, save a portion of that food for play-time right before bed. (See Chapter 5 for more on how to complete a prey sequence.) You'll usually see consistent results with this technique after about two weeks. I've had clients report results in just a few days. With some cats, you may need to continue the prey sequences every so often to continue the good behavior.

TRANSFORM the Territory

Most cats sleep a good chunk of the day, but if you have a job that keeps you out of the house most of the day, you have no idea how much your cat is sleeping. Your cat may be meowing only or largely because he's bored out of his wits. He meows to release pent-up *catness*. The solution is to provide him with stimulating daytime activities to keep him up during the day and give him dark rings around his eyes by nightfall. I recommend more play of any kind. Throw balls for your cat, wake him up during the day, or even get another cat to keep him on his toes. Clients tell me that after putting in place daily workouts for their cats, their roles became reversed, and it was the clients who, in the mornings, woke up the cats, who were as dead to the world as teenagers. (See Chapter 5 for a full explanation of how to create a more stimulating environment.) I particularly recommend toys that you rotate in and out of use every day, climbing perches, window perches, food or treat puzzles, and tunnels. My cats really like battery-operated toys (see catwhispererproducts.com). Cats can spend a good hour on any of these toys. More playtime and mental exertion during the day can mean more sleep time during the night and wee hours of the morning.

Next, review your cat's environment for stressors. Can he easily get to all of his important resources? Is another cat blocking his access to a litter box or feeding area? Increasing and spreading out important resources throughout the home can be critical to decreasing the anxiety that may be leading to his excessive vocalizations. Pheromone products in spray and plug-in form can also help reduce anxiety-based meowing (see Chapter 5).

Destructive and Other Unwanted Behaviors

Now Chil the Kite brings home the night
That Mang the Bat sets free—
The herds are shut in byre and hut,
For loosed till dawn are we.
This is the hour of pride and power,
Talon and tush and claw.
Oh, hear the call!—Good hunting all
That keep the Jungle Law!
—"Night Song in the Jungle," *The Jungle Book*

IT'S IN THE NATURE OF ANIMALS, WHO HAVE A DISTRESSING disregard for sticker prices, sometimes to just tear things up. Cats will claw silk drapes into streamers, rugs into shreds, and couches into something that resembles the furniture you see at the most depressing yard sale you've ever been to. Or they do other things to annoy us, like jumping on the computer keyboard, plucking food off the dining room table while you're calling the guests in to eat, or licking the butter you left on the kitchen counter—even though you have sat them down many times and carefully explained how the cons of such behaviors outweigh the pros. Luckily, you can stop all of these behaviors—humanely.

SHREDDERS AND SNAGGERS: WHY CATS CLAW

Have you ever wondered why your cat runs to your sofa and claws when you enter the room or come home from work? Although clawing things is partly about removing old claw sheaths and is necessary to nail maintenance, cats also claw to mark territory, to exercise, and to relieve pent-up emotions. Cats are masters at destressing. They have many ways to release emotional energy even without a membership at a yoga studio.

Cats claw mark their territory with both a visual and a scent mark, the latter from the glands between their paw pads. In a single-cat household these marks give the cat a sense of familiarity and security. In multicat households, cats will, not surprisingly, scratch mark more often than single cats. Even cats whose toes have been amputated will paw to place their scent in certain locations around the home. The marks may also warn other cats and help all concerned to avoid physical confrontation. One study recently pointed out that cats have not been observed to actually smell claw marks left by other cats, so it may be that the visual marks are enough—as may be the ostentation of a dominant cat scratching in front of a subordinate cat.

Clawing also allows cats to stretch and exercise. Cats are digitigrade, meaning they walk on their toes instead of the soles of their feet or paws. Their ligaments, nerves, tendons, muscles, and leg and paw joints are all designed to distribute and support the cat's weight across its toes as it walks and runs. Cats use their claws for balance, for the climbing that's so important to their feelings of safety, and to stretch the muscles in their back, shoulders, legs, and paws. They stretch their muscles by digging their claws into a surface and then

pulling back in a form of isometric exercise. In fact, clawing is probably the *only* way they can exercise the muscles of their backs and
shoulders.

Clawing is a completely natural behavior that cats should be allowed to perform, but there's no reason to regard clawing on undesirable objects, such as couches, as inevitable—which most owners
do. For example, in one study of 122 cats whose owners viewed them
as having no behavior problems, 60 percent of the cats scratched furniture.[1] If you're one of these people, I can show you how to make
sure your cat claws only in desirable places. There are humane and
effective solutions. But first, a word about the inhumane practice and
Orwellian linguistic dodge called "declawing."

DECLAWING—UNNECESSARY AND INHUMANE

Before we get to real solutions for unwanted clawing, let me disabuse
you of an abusive "remedy" chosen by far too many cat owners and
their vets. Even the bland word we choose for it, *declawing*, is a
clinical-sounding effort to cover up plain cruelty. The procedure is
not a manicure or "a fancy claw trim."[2] Because a cat's claw is part of
the last bone in its toes (not like a human's fingernail), a de-"claw"
amputates the entire first joint of a cat's toes, akin to amputating the
first joint of every toe on your feet and every finger on your hands. In
both humans and cats that constitutes mutilation, but there the com-
parison ends, because the damage done to the cat is even more severe.
Cats walk on their toes. You do not—but imagine the pain and difficulty of walking if you did, and yet your toes had been amputated to
the first joint. Cats depend primarily on their claws for defense, and
their toes for balance. You do not need your toes for defense—but
imagine the feeling of helplessness if you did, yet all your toes were
mutilated.

Calling it declawing is dishonest. Toe amputation is not a mere
"declawing," just like sawing off your arm cannot be described as a de-
limbing: as if, like deicing, defrosting, or deodorizing, someone were
doing you a favor. The use of the bland prefix *de* hides the horror of
what is actually being done.

No veterinarian claims a medical purpose for declawing. It is a ten-fold mutilation that serves only the (imagined) convenience of the client. Some say that the ten amputations are necessary because otherwise clients will threaten to have their cats euthanized instead. I hope that my readers will not harm their cats in this way. When I was a vet assistant many years ago, at the beginning of my lifelong career working with cats, I was unlucky enough to see or assist in many of what I now understand were toe amputations. For a distressingly long time I thought we were merely removing claws, not parts of digits. And because I saw it being done so routinely—the vet ran frequent Spay-and-Declaw Specials—I didn't think to question it too much or to wonder what the other options might be. If you have previously de-clawed a cat because you also were unaware of the truth, I hope you'll reconsider in the future.

THE STORY OF CHARLIE CAT

When I worked as a veterinary assistant, I first saw the declaw surgery, and its aftermath, inflicted on a black-and-white tuxedo kitten named Charlie Cat.

Tiny Charlie Cat had bounded from his owner's arms into mine, and as I caressed him he mewled and pushed his forehead into mine. His purr was audible across the room. I felt his sandpaper-like tongue on my cheek. Carla, the vet performing the declaw, was a stout, cheerful woman who was working as a relief vet for the clinic that day. As she was anesthetizing Charlie Cat, she told me she didn't feel comfortable doing the surgery. "It's ridiculous and unnecessary," she said, but as the relief vet on duty it was her job. She said it had been a long time since she had done a declawing and at first she wasn't sure where to make the cut. Her hands shook as she picked up her surgeon's tool. You may have one in your own home: a dog's nail trimmer.

"I hate doing this." *Snap.* "I hate doing this." *Snap.* Carla's whole body trembled with each cut. I winced as the severed tips of each of Charlie Cat's toes spat onto the exam table. (Of course, it was only later that I understood that what I was seeing were the tips of Charlie Cat's toes. At the time, no one had ever uttered words like toe or digit

or even amputation, so I saw what I had been conditioned to believe by the language everyone used: What was being cut off, awful as it was, were merely the *claws at the end of the toes*.)

The owner wanted Charlie Cat to be able to climb so Carla did not remove the toe tips of his hind feet. After amputating the toe tips from each front paw, Carla held the toe holes open with a hemostat. I looked into the gaping, fleshy tubes where his claws (and, we now know, the attached toe bones) had been. Inside I could glimpse the glistening, pinkish white of the bones that remained. At Carla's instruction, I let fall into each hole a drop of tissue glue to seal the incision.

After the amputation was finished, Carla and I bandaged Charlie Cat's limbs from his paws to his elbows. They looked like two big drumsticks. Veterinary behaviorist Dr. Nicholas Dodman tells us what to expect next:

> The inhumanity of the procedure is clearly demonstrated by the nature of cats' recovery from anesthesia following the surgery. Unlike routine recoveries . . . declawing surgery results in cats bouncing off the walls of the recovery cage because of excruciating pain. Cats that are more stoic huddle in the corner of the recovery cage, immobilized in a state of helplessness . . . Declawing fits the dictionary definition of mutilation to a tee. Words such as deform,

disfigure, disjoint, and dismember all apply to this surgery. Partial digital amputation is so horrible that it has been employed for torture of prisoners of war, and in veterinary medicine, the clinical procedure serves as a model of severe pain for testing the efficacy of analgesic drugs. Even though analgesic drugs can be used postoperatively, they rarely are, and their effects are incomplete and transient anyway, so sooner or later the pain will emerge.[3]

When I arrived to open the clinic the next morning, I realized there actually *could* be something more horrific than what I'd seen the day before. Charlie Cat was no longer a black kitten with white markings. He was now a bloody ball of pain and fury. He'd come in with a black-and-white panda toy, which he loved to snuggle with and knead. The panda was now spotted with crimson. The kitten had pulled his bandages off during the night and thrashed around his small stainless-steel cage so much that blood streaked the walls, ceiling, floor, and even the grated door. There was no doubt he was in pain. He sat on his back legs, careful not to touch his front paws on the floor. He cried nonstop. I scooped him up to comfort him just as the vet walked in. We began to rebandage him and the vet noticed that one of his joints had popped through the glue-sealed incision. We had to anesthetize him again and reseal the incision, this time with sutures, and put his bandages back on.

If anthropomorphism could be advantageous in the fight against cruelty to animals, I would say that Charlie Cat was wondering what he could have possibly done to deserve such cruelty. I like having all my fingers and toes, and I think it's only fair not to put a beloved friend, my cat, through a pain I would not wish to endure myself, and a future disability I would not wish on anyone. Armed with the story of Charlie Cat, I would go on to covertly convince quite a few clients not to amputate their cats' claws and toes.

If the argument of excessive cruelty isn't enough to persuade you, let's look at some of the other disadvantages of toe mutilation in cats. Sometimes these surgeries are simply not performed well—all surgeries, including mutilations, have the potential for complications: In one study, 50 percent of toe amputation surgeries gave rise to complications immediately after surgery and almost 20 percent after the cat's release.[4] Some cats' nails will grow back, and badly, causing even more pain. Some cats may experience later discomfort or even phantom pain. I've seen cats who won't even groom their paws years after their amputation, or who are afraid to jump down from high surfaces or play with their once-favorite toy.

Toe pain can cause a cat to change his normal gait, causing stiffness and pain in his legs, hips, and spine of the kind you might experience if you were wearing ill-fitting shoes. A cat can lose the otherworldly balance synonymous with the word *feline*. An amputee cat has been robbed of its claws and the full functions of its toes, which are both oh-so-very-important to its physical and mental well-being. Many of the cat owners I've worked with over the last twenty years tell me if they had to do it over again, they would not amputate. Without claws, their once friendly and playful cat had become fearful, withdrawn, and introverted. Some cats also bite more after they no longer have their claws. Many are surrendered to shelters because of such behaviors.

Over the last two decades, amputation, along with tail docking and ear cropping of dogs, has been at the vortex of fevered ethical debate. The arguments for toe amputation are simple. Franny Syufy, an opponent of it and a writer at About.com, describes what happened when she proposed a "Disclose and Wait" bill to the California state legislature. A legislative aide took the proposed notification bill to the president of the California Veterinary Association, and "to the head of our local shelter for advice. Their consensus," Syufy writes, "was that 'if declawing were made illegal, more cats would either be "put down," or surrendered to shelters.' "[5] The no-nonsense Association of Veterinarians for Animal Rights rightly called this emotional blackmail, and questioned the suitability of such owners to act as feline guardians, "especially when there are millions of non-declawed cats living in harmony with people."

I have just one addition to make to this statement: Amputation is especially unethical because *unwanted clawing is such an easy problem to solve.*

Thankfully, declawing is becoming more and more unpopular. Declawing.com lists twenty-two enlightened countries in which declawing "is either illegal or considered extremely inhumane and only performed under extreme circumstances." Most are in Europe (Spain and Poland are large countries notably absent), along with Australia, New Zealand, Israel, and Brazil. The federalist system in the United States guarantees that there can be no nationwide solutions here.* Each state must, on its own, find legislators with the awareness and political will to prohibit toe amputation.

The American Veterinary Medical Association says amputation is appropriate only when a cat cannot be trained not to use its claws improperly. That's where I come in.

Case Study: Shanti the Feline Shredding Machine

Shanti was a two-year-old Tonkinese that, as her owner Rajeev put it, was "the best cat ever," but, with the caveat I hear so often, "except for just one small thing." Shanti's one small thing was a love of clawing Rajeev's stereo speakers and slicing up furniture in the house like confetti.

The Problem: Widespread Destruction

Extracted from owner's description:

> Besides my stereo speakers, the arms of my sofas and all my chairs are ripped to shreds. Sometimes she chews on the stuffing pieces or bats them around in the air. My house looks like it has been attacked by a lunatic with a machete.

The Consultation

When I entered Rajeev's living room, the first thing I saw was that the sofa's stuffing sprouted forth as if it had been frozen in midexplosion. Everywhere I looked there was visible damage to the furniture. Rajeev had certainly not overstated the level of Shanti's destructiveness.

---

* To be fair, the higher rate of toe amputation in the United States is probably related to the greater rate at which Americans (like Canadians) keep their cats indoors.

"What solutions have you tried so far?" I asked.

"I clap my hands and tell her *No!*"

"Hmm. That doesn't seem to be working so well."

"No, actually it's gotten worse. She now shreds the couches and speakers when I'm not around and I think she's finding some new places to start on."

"Exactly," I said. "You helped her develop something called owner-absent behavior. She has learned to perform the behavior only when you're not around so that she doesn't experience your reprimand." I added that any form of negative attention (even just clapping and yelling No!) could have caused her stress, and to reduce the stress, she may have clawed the fabric even more. He told me he had bought a cat scratcher pad to focus Shanti's clawing elsewhere. "But she just looked at the scratch pad, walked past it, and then walked over to the sofa and began clawing the side." He laughed. "But she does love to *sleep* on the cat scratcher."

You can't remove your cat's wild instincts, but you can orchestrate where they're acted out. You have to accept your cat for what she is— a cat—and accept that cats come equipped with claws and a drive to use them. It's easy to look at clawing as "bad" behavior, but it would be wiser to accept cats for the amazing creatures they are—claws and all. There are too many cat owners who want a "push button" cat— one with no claws, no fur, and no instincts.

PREVENTION

The best way to prevent future scratching problems may be to start your kitten out with scratching posts from the beginning and to get her used to having her nails trimmed. One reason older cats scratch is to remove the sheath from their claws. If you do this for them, by trimming their claws, they will feel less need to scratch. And of course with blunted nails, even when they do scratch, they will do much less damage to things.

Never trim a cat's claws immediately *after* she's been scratching;

she may view it as a punishment, and you want to avoid creating any negative associations with nail trimming (or with scratching appropriate objects, if that's what she was doing). Wait until your cat is calm and seeking your affection. While trimming, praise, pet, massage, and give food or treats. If your cat tends to exhibit status or other aggression, consider letting a professional do the trimming

C.A.T. Plan for Unwanted Scratching

CEASE the Unwanted Behavior

There's a behavior of your own that needs to cease: Stop all reprimanding. You know it doesn't work—as Rajeev agreed—and only causes your cat stress, so why do it? But following are some things you can do that will work.

Deter Unwanted Scratching

You have to remember that if a cat has been clawing the sofa for a while, she's developed a habit. That means you have to work on making the inappropriately clawed area unattractive to undo the habit.

To deter scratching in small areas, apply double-sided tape (or products made especially for cat clawing; see catwhisperer products.com) to the clawed areas. In large areas or on furniture, drape or secure plastic carpet runners with the pointy nubs facing up. Deterrence is the most effective method. Instead of yelling at your cat each time she scratches, you will help her learn on her own that her once-favorite scratching areas are now verboten.

At the same time (see the Attract section) you will be promoting the new areas where you *do* want her to scratch.

CONVENTIONAL ADVICE ALERT

Some people will tell you that if your cat tends to scratch only in certain areas of the home, you should try to prevent your cat from entering those areas because they encourage her to rehearse her habit. Whether you're home or not, they suggest, you can set up barriers like doors, baby gates, screens, or even (egad!) indoor electronic fences. Some suggest booby traps such as pull-string firecrackers that go off when pulled, or small balloons that pop.

As you might guess, I consider many of these deterrents inhumane; others, like baby gates, don't really address the problem. I wouldn't even bother to block off a room. Your cat will just learn to scratch *elsewhere* and ruin more furniture. I also don't recommend remote deterrents, like air cans, against scratching; you'd need several, and they'd go off continually as *anyone* — cats, dogs, or humans — passed within ten to twenty feet, and your cat's resulting stress could lead her to even more undesirable behaviors.

If covering your furniture with a deterrent doesn't sound appealing to you, you can experiment with plastic nail caps to cover your cat's nails, though caps require maintenance every six to twelve weeks as nails grow. You can also distract your cat when she's on the way to or even looking at the inappropriate scratching location. Lure her with a toy to a desirable scratching area (see the Attract section). Fitting your cat with a breakaway collar (the safest kind of collar because it snaps open when under stress, like a good ski binding, and therefore won't strangle her if it catches on something) and belling the collar is a good way to stay aware of where she is.

ATTRACT Your Cat to a New Behavior

Cat Scratchers — Positioning

Rajeev was on the right track, but he needed to experiment with different cat scratchers until he could find one that Shanti liked. He had purchased a horizontal scratcher that lay flat on the floor, but the quality and consistency of Shanti's handiwork on the chair, sofa, and stereo speakers made it clear she preferred to claw on the vertical. This is not uncommon, because vertical scratching gives a cat the added benefit of a good stretch. It's best to start with scratchers positioned like the objects your cat is drawn to. If it's the sofa, that's vertical. If it's the rug, that's horizontal. If you're not sure whether your cat likes horizontal or vertical — or both — experiment. Cat trees can be a good solution because most are basically vertical, scratchable structures and yet often have horizontal scratching areas on the bases and platforms.

Cat Scratchers — Location

You should place one or more scratchers on the way to and near to where your cat normally claws. Other scratchers should be located near the core areas of the home, because that's usually where cats instinctively do most of their scratching. They scratch somewhat less on the perimeter of their home range, so don't place scratchers in the far-off corners of the house (or a basement or garage) where the cat is less likely to use them. In thinking about where exactly to put the scratchers, try to replicate the feeling of space around the areas where your cat was doing its scratching, so that the scratchers are in areas that are as enclosed, or as open, as the previously favored scratching target.

Cat Scratcher Surfaces

You may be able to find a substance that is even more attractive to your cat than the surface she's inappropriately scratching.

Sisal rope, carpet, or corrugated cardboard are all great textures to experiment with. Some scratchers are made of hemp, logs, or even fabric. You may not like the idea of logs, but your cat may think he's a proper lumberjack. The researcher Benjamin Hart has found that cats like to scratch materials with long, straight fibers, and have less enthusiasm for tightly woven, nubby fibers.

Other Cat Scratcher Desirability Tips

Make sure the cat trees or scratchers have a stable base and won't wobble when your cat claws on them. If something threatens to tip over on her, or actually does, she may be afraid to use it again.

Because many cats will not use a cat scratcher that lacks their scent, add a little catnip or drag a wand toy across the new cat scratcher to lure her there so her scent will be added to it. Eventually, her claws will catch on the surface as she's playing with the toy and in the catnip and she'll get the idea. *Hey! This is great for scratching!* Never force your cat's paw toward or across the scratcher. Physically forcing a cat to do anything is counterproductive.

Do not ever use facial scent or pheromones on the scratchers. Cats tend not to claw mark where they facial mark, so you could be preventing the very behavior you are trying to encourage.

Pheromones as Scratch Guards

I warned you above about *not* using pheromones on anything you *do* want your cat to claw mark, like the cat scratchers. For the same reasons, you *should* apply them to the areas where you *don't* want your cat to claw mark, particularly the previously scratched areas and those similar to them (i.e., if your cat had scratched only the left side of the couch, it's wise to add pheromones to the right side, too). The pheromones will promote facial marking on all the areas to which it's applied. If you aren't able to find synthetic pheromones, use a cloth daily to transfer your cat's own facial scent to the objects you want to protect (see Chapter 4). You should also consider adding pheromone plug-ins near inappropriately scratched areas to reduce any stress-related claw marking.

Kind Words and Actions

Praise your cat when she scratches on her new scratching areas. Pet her, brush her (if she likes this), or bring out her favorite toy.

Clicker Training

See Appendix A on clicker training to promote desirable behaviors in your cat. When your cat scratches the scratcher, reward her with the clicker and treat her. This positive reward system can even help rebuild any bond that has been damaged between you and your cat as a result of your reprimanding.

POSITIVE REINFORCEMENT

It's important to show a cat what *to do* in the environment instead of just what *not* to do. If you're going to treat your pets like children, at least follow this basic principle!

After your cat is consistently using the new scratchers for a few weeks, you can remove the double-sided sticky tape or carpet runners from the previously scratched areas.

TRANSFORM the Territory

At the same time that you Cease the undesirable behavior and Attract more desirable behaviors, you will be transforming your cat's territory.

Toys, Trees, Tunnels, and Other Stress and Boredom Relievers

Take a good look at your cat's environment. Could he be bored and understimulated? Does he lack enough outlets to release pent-up emotion or stress? Create a stimulating environment for your cat. Use an interactive wand toy to play with your cat more often, at least once a day, give him toys and food puzzles he can play with on his own, and add a cat tree and cat tunnels. (See Chapter 5 for full details.)

Is he happy with his feeding and litter box situation? See Chapter 5 on how to create a litter box situation your cat will appreciate. How is he getting along with the other cats, dogs, or people in the home? Read Chapter 7 to deal with aggression and social conflict. Identifying and eliminating stressors can decrease extreme clawing behavior.

Follow-up with Shanti

After following the C.A.T. Plan for just a few days, Rajeev reported that Shanti would walk up to the couch, pause, and turn right around to go to one of her new cat scratchers. I asked him what he did next. "Praised her, of course, and sometimes gave her a treat!"

Rajeev's success happened fast. But be patient. It can sometimes take a week or more until you notice any decrease in the unwanted clawing behavior, and of course elimination of the behavior may require more time than that. Shanti was only two years old when I saw her. The older the cat and the longer the habituated behavior has been going on, the harder it can be to change it.

COUNTER CRAWLING AND TABLE HOPPING: WHY CATS LIKE HIGH PLACES

Clients also ask for my help in keeping their cats off various high surfaces—kitchen counters, stoves, dining tables, and chests of drawers. Perching and resting on high places are behaviors that, like claw marking, are innate. High places give cats vantage points from which to survey the territory and, very important, give them feelings of safety. And of course some high places have food and other attractive items on them, whether it's a piece of steak or something that looks like it might be fun to play with. You can channel your cat's desire to be above it all, but you can't stop it—or not humanely, anyway. As with excessive meowing, owners often inadvertently reinforce these behaviors, or fray the human-cat bond, with their negative reactions.

Many of my clients ask me, "How can I get my cat to obey me and stay off the counters?" If you've read this far, you already know the answer. You can get a cat to do what you want, but not by expecting her to obey a command in order to please you. This kind of obedience is for pack animals. But cats will usually avoid behavior that has a negative outcome—one rare exception being negative attention from *you*, which some cats actually crave—so the trick is to make the unwanted behavior unrewarding or even slightly unpleasant.

C.A.T. Plan for Counter Crawling and Table Hopping

CEASE the Unwanted Behavior

Make Food Inaccessible

First, if food is the draw attracting your cat to the kitchen counter, remove it! Whenever you're not in the area to keep an eye on any food you may be about to cook or serve, you should make sure that there's nothing your cat can get to. Keeping food on the counter or sink isn't really fair to the cat. And don't underestimate their ability to like any food. My cat Clawde has a fetish for bread, and until I followed my own advice he would find his way even to the top of the refrigerator to eat some. I'll never forget the client whose cat managed to wrestle an entire rotisserie chicken off the counter and drag it into the bedroom. The client followed the greasy trail and found the little scavenger under her bed. He had wrapped his body around the chicken and had sunk every claw he had into it. He hissed and growled and spat at anyone who tried to take away his prize or so much as peered under the bed.

In case your cat jumps on the counter because he's hungry, be sure you are feeding him frequently enough or, if he can self-regulate his food intake, free-feed him.

Stop Feeding in the Kitchen

If you normally feed your cat in the kitchen, you might also consider feeding him in a different location. Feeding in the kitchen can promote strong associations between that area and food, and more interest in the kitchen counters.

Avoid Sending Mixed Messages

Don't give your cat mixed messages when he's on the counter. Many, many people fall into the trap of only *sometimes* shooing the cat away when he jumps on the counter, while at other times petting him when he's there, conveniently located right at arm's height. For a cat who enjoys spending time around you— as most cats do—and who sometimes gets petted or talked to when he jumps on the counter while you're in the kitchen, hanging out on the kitchen counter may seem like the best way to get the attention he wants. So you need to choose: Allow the cat on the counter without shooing, or follow the advice here, while consistently keeping the cat off the counter.

Use Deterrents

Make being on the counter an unpleasant experience, albeit in a way that does not seem to be connected to anything you do, so that the bond between you and your cat will not be damaged. Place a remote deterrent, such as motion-sensing air-in-a-can, on your counter. (Of course you should be sure that you don't feed any of your cats in the vicinity of the air can.) Whenever your cat jumps on the counter, the can will emit a warning beep and then expel a gust of air with a sound that cats find unpleasant. Usually, after a few days of training, you can turn off the air so that the device emits only a warning beep. That alone may deter your cat from the area. Eventually, just the sight of the can on the counter, turned off, will remind your cat to stay off the counter. If your cat decides to test the boundaries and jump on the counter, turn the air back on for a few days. I've personally used this device with my cats and I will say it's very effective, yet humane. (You can also create decoy cans that look like the original can. These Potemkin cans are especially useful if you have a large kitchen and want to save money.)

However, if you have a multicat household with a timid cat in it, an air-blast remote deterrent may be too upsetting, even if it's a lot less distressing than a shouting owner.

In lieu of or in combination with a remote deterrent like the air-in-a-can, you can also place strips of double-sided sticky tape onto placemats and strategically locate them on the counters. You can also use baking trays with a little water in them, or set down plastic carpet runners with the sharp points facing up. Cut them to fit your counters and secure them with tape if needed. After a few weeks you can remove most of the carpet runners, except for a few pieces you leave to hang over the counter as a visual reminder to your cat of the unpleasant sensations he experienced there. If your cat starts jumping on the counter again, put the carpet runners back in place for a few days. These intermittent reminders can really make a difference in training cats. I do not recommend deterrents like upside-down mousetraps, shock mats, or foul-smelling chemicals.

Diversions—Snub of the Queen

If for some reason you don't use remote deterrents, then, if you see your cat eyeing the counter area, distract her with a toy and lure her out of the room before she has a chance to jump up. However, if your cat has already jumped on the counter (and especially if she typically does so to get your attention), stop giving her any form of attention. Don't pick her up and set her on the floor. Do not say a word, look at her, or move in her direction (unless of course there's something there that she is about to devour or break, or that could hurt her, such as a hot skillet). If you believe she jumped up to get attention from you (rather than, say, to investigate something), the best thing to do is to leave the room immediately. That's a connection she will start to make.

It's extremely important to use the least invasive, minimally aversive (LIMA) deterrent to produce the desired result. And this involves knowing your cat well enough to respect his sensitivity threshold and not go past it (and create new problems). For example, as noted earlier, for a very shy, nervous cat, a compressed-air deterrent might be too much.

It's also important that your chosen deterrent not result in owner-absent behavior. Squirt guns are often not effective in the long run. Some clients tell me they covertly squirt their cats with water every time they find them on the counter. But even if the cats don't see you squirt them, they may engage in some "thinking" of a higher order: *Funny—whenever I jump on the counter* and *she's around, I get wet. Oh, and look! Now that she's gone and I've jumped back up here, nothing happened!* The result can be a cat, now dry, who returns to the counter when you're not around. The only connection the cat made between getting soaked and being on the counter was that the soaking happened while you were hovering nearby, like a storm cloud. So you've got to take yourself out of the equation. The trick is to make the counter an undesirable place on its own merits, with or without you in the picture. That will also preserve your bond with your cat.

There may be other reasons your cat likes the counter. Perhaps he can see outside better while standing on it, or he feels safely out of the reach of the dog who barks or the two-year-old who loves to grab the cat's tail. The more you can find out about why your cat wants to be on the counter, the more likely you'll be able to make changes that will enable him to find satisfaction in other ways. If your cat is on the counter because he has a tense relationship with another cat, you may wish to read Chapters 4 and 7 on reintroducing cats and cat-to-cat tension, respectively.

ATTRACT the Cat to a New Behavior

While you are deterring your cat from inappropriate elevated areas, you *must* also give her alternative perching locations. It's possible to create an even more desirable area for her than the counters or tables. If your cat didn't already have enough vertical territory, your additions could make all the difference. Perhaps she was attracted to high places in order to get away from a dog, other cats, or small children? A cat tree, for example, could give your cat something of what she was looking for on the counter. If the counter offered a perch from which to watch birds out the window, set up alternative perches that safely allow bird watching. You can even strategically set up a bird feeder outside the window nearest the perch to which you want to attract your cat. If your cat really just wanted to be near you, as many of mine do, a new perch in the kitchen may be all you need to provide for some face-to-face or head-to-head bunting. In order to lure the cat to the alternative perching area that you want to promote, drag a wand toy over to it or place catnip or a treat on top of it.

Whatever you do, be sure to give your cat a lot of attention when she's in the desired area. If your cat is motivated by treats or food, clicker training is a great way to promote the behavior you want (see Appendix A). If you see your cat sitting in an approved perching area, click and reward her behavior. Soon she will be repeating it.

TRANSFORM the Territory

See Chapter 5 to learn all the ways that you can give your cats feelings of safety, desirable perching areas, and the right kind and amount of stimulation. You'll need ample cat trees and perches, hiding places, adequate litter box resources, dispersed food and water locations, food puzzles, and plenty of toys of all kinds. And of course you'll want to conduct frequent play/prey sequences with your cats.

TWELVE

The Compulsive Cat

None of the Jungle People like being disturbed.
— "Kaa's Hunting," The Jungle Book

FOR A VARIETY OF REASONS, SOME OF THEM SIMILAR TO THOSE that afflict people, cats and other animals can develop behaviors that we categorize as compulsive. The main cause of compulsive behaviors in cats is stress, especially the kind of stress that cats experience when they feel conflicted between two opposing courses of action. For example, your cat may simultaneously feel an urge to greet you and an urge to avoid you for fear of punishment. Or she may both want to run away from another cat *and* want to confront him. Similarly, if you call a dog and he wants to come but can't tell if you're angry, his brain may short-circuit and his response may be to start spinning around.

One form of compulsive behavior that results from these cognitive conflicts is what we call wool sucking or wool chewing—sucking or chewing on nonfood items, including not just wool but cotton, synthetics, paper, and even more surprising materials, as you will discover later in this chapter. Another more common compulsive behavior in cats is grooming excessively or even pulling out their own fur, which is called overgrooming (psychogenic alopecia). Or they may attack their own tails or paw at their own faces (as part of Rolling-Skin Syndrome, or feline hyperesthesia).

Besides cognitive conflict, other reasons for compulsive behaviors include genetic causes, in which the tendency appears to be passed on from parent to kitten. Compulsive behaviors may also develop because a cat was weaned too early, or because he's experiencing stress in the form of general anxiety, frustration, boredom, or separation anxiety—especially if these stressors recur frequently or persist over an extended period of time.

A cat gets frustrated for the same reasons you do. He wants to do or have something and he can't. Maybe he's indoors, looking out a window, and he wants to attack the cat walking across his territory. Maybe he wants to play, hunt, stalk, kill, or eat, but he has nobody to play with, no toys, or he's unable to get to the food. Cats with separation anxiety may grow upset when their owners leave home, and if left alone for too long may overgroom themselves.

In short, one cat may develop compulsive behaviors because she's been weaned too early, another because she's conflicted, anxious, bored, or frustrated, and another because of a genetic propensity for, say, chewing on nonfood items.

All animals have their characteristic ways of responding to boredom, frustration, conflict, and other forms of stress. In zoo environments, big cats pace; wolves, foxes, and polar bears may repetitively pace, crib (which consists of chewing wood or air as air is inhaled), and self-mutilate; while giraffes sway. Gus, the famously neurotic polar bear at the Central Park Zoo, compulsively swims back and forth. Horses may chew repeatedly or weave as they walk, and pigs will bite the bars of their pens.

Compulsive behaviors in cats, including overgrooming and wool sucking, are based on behaviors that are already part of the cat's natural repertoire, but have now become something abnormal because they're performed repetitively, out of context, with no apparent goal, and sometimes in ways that are destructive, not just to the environment they live in (yours!) but to the cats themselves. If you allow the stressor leading to the compulsive behavior to continue, then totally unrelated stressors may also end up triggering repeated episodes of the behavior. Over time, the compulsive behaviors may be performed even when no stress is present.

MEDICAL ALERT: COMPULSIVE BEHAVIORS AND ORAL FIXATIONS

Consulting a vet about compulsive behaviors can help determine whether the causes are medical or psychological. Original causes can include such health-related issues as dietary imbalances, organ dysfunction, neurological and metabolic diseases, serotonin depletion, hyperkinesis, cognitive dysfunction, and spinal and neurologic diseases.

Different skin conditions, food allergies, or allergies to pollen, mold, or (most commonly) flea bites can also cause a cat to chew, overlick, or just lose fur. Parasites or back pain can lead to compulsive behaviors. I have seen cats suffering from hyperthyroidism, impacted anal glands, bladder stones, or other urinary health issues who groom the fur off their stomachs either to try to relieve the localized pain or to soothe the anxiety that results from the pain. Cystitis, an inflammation of the bladder, can cause a cat not only to chew or lick its abdomen but to urinate inappropriately around the house. If a cat suffers an injury to its tail, it may begin to chase or chew it. Remember that even when the physical issues have been resolved, they can leave behind a residue of behaviors that become ingrained and must be behaviorally modified.

Some compulsive behaviors may be harmful to your cat, others may damage your property, while watching or listening to still others—*lick, lick, pause . . . lick, lick, pause*—may simply feel to you like Chinese water torture. All such behaviors should be dealt with, preferably sooner rather than later.

I'll discuss here the most common compulsive behaviors, which are the overgrooming that you saw in Nada in the Introduction, and wool sucking. But please keep in mind as you read my C.A.T. Plans for compulsive disorders that these are some of the most difficult behavior issues to diagnose and treat, because they can be or act like addictions. A veterinary visit and even medication may be a necessary addition to the behavior modifications I recommend. As you know if you've read this far, I don't believe in automatically resorting to drugging your cat for behavior problems, but if it's genuinely necessary, especially if you need to do it to prevent the cat from self-harm, then I'm all for it.

OVERGROOMING

Let's say your cat is outside, trying to decide whether to run away from the stray cat that's entered your yard or to stand his ground. He may momentarily groom himself as a way of displacing his anxiety elsewhere. Grooming is a perfectly normal self-soothing behavior in cats. You'll see them doing it on the way to the vet's office, or when meeting another cat, or after a tumble from a high place. But if the stressor is constant or repetitive, the cat may continue to lick himself beyond what would be considered normal, creating bald patches in his fur and abrading his own skin. Some cats will go as far as to chew at their fur, or pluck it out with their teeth, sometimes by the mouthful. In extreme cases, cats will excavate wounds so deeply that they can become infected.

Overgrooming is seen in cats with anxious temperaments, predominantly in purebred cats of oriental breeding. It affects females more than males. But I've seen it occur in virtually every breed and color of cat and in both sexes, and for a wide range of reasons. Let's look at a few.

First, look at the situation of Nada, whom you met in the Introduction. She'd been in conflict with a new cat in her territory, and they were maintaining a tense standoff, each cat from its respective floor of Susan's house. Nada's environment was also utterly barren, devoid of opportunities for play or stimuli of any kind. Sterile environments with no outlets for normal digging, play activities, or (in the case of unaltered animals) sexual expression can result not just in overgrooming but in masturbation, compulsive digging around the outside of the food bowl or litter box, and aggressive extremes in play behavior.[1]

Another cat I met who had an overgrooming problem was Caramello, an orange tabby whose owners originally came to me for a simple litter box issue. But as we talked, the owner, Patrice, mentioned to me that while the family was on vacation in Hawaii for three weeks, Caramello, who had not been invited to Hawaii and was being cared for by a pet sitter back home, had licked all the hair off his stomach. Patrice hadn't noticed right away. "He seemed fine when we got home," she told me.

But later that first night, Patrice was reading her newspaper in bed. "I remember hearing him lick, lick, lick. I'd put the paper down and the licking would stop. But as soon as I started reading again, he'd start up with the licking. Finally, my husband gathered him up in his arms like a baby—the way they both loved—and just gasped. All the thick fur on Mello's stomach was gone, and all he had left was peach fuzz."

I often uncover overgrooming during a behavior consultation for a completely different issue. When I ask a client if her cat is missing any fur on his body or has just a thin layer of fuzz on his stomach, I hear "Yes" more often than you might think, but often the owners are not concerned because they think grooming is just what cats do. They don't have a standard against which to compare what they see. Some owners have even told me they didn't realize that cats are supposed to have any fur at all on their tummies. Once I explain that the reason for the lack of fur is overgrooming, and that this is a sign of stress, many owners are shocked and find it hard to believe, since they have no idea that their cat is under any kind of stress.

Patrice, for example, was adamant that Caramello was not stressed now and had no reason to be when the family had been away. The pet sitter had stayed the night each night, she said, had played with him, and had given him everything he needed. As I probed more, however, I learned that the pet sitter had brought along her new puppy, a German shorthaired pointer who could well have been the source of stress for Caramello. The stress might have been exacerbated by feeling a *conflict* between two opposing urges—both to chase the puppy out of his favorite spot on the couch, and to avoid the spot himself out of fear of the puppy.

The plan I gave Patrice is the one I recommend for all overgrooming cats. For Caramello it worked very quickly, probably because his stress had been relatively short-lived and his overgrooming behavior had been going on for only a brief period of time, so the behavior hadn't become as fixed as it does in cases of longer duration. For other cats, however, it may take longer to go into effect.

C.A.T. Plan for Overgrooming (Psychogenic Alopecia)

CEASE the Unwanted Behavior

Act *Quickly*

Overgrooming is a serious matter. The longer you wait, the more difficult it can be to eliminate it. First, have your cat checked out by a vet to make sure it's not a medical issue.

Remove Stressors

Any kind of stresss can cause a cat to overgroom or chew at itself. Try to identify the stress triggers in your cat's life so that you can eliminate or at least reduce them. This can take a bit of investigative work, but it is very important. See Chapters 3, 4, and 5 for examples of stressors. Also make sure you're not reinforcing or aggravating the cat's behavior with reprimands (or any other form of attention) when the behavior is performed.

If the stressor remains unknown or cannot be removed, you may need to seek help from a professional cat behaviorist, who can help you identify the stressors causing your cat's anxiety, or show you how to use behavior modification techniques to help you deal with any stressors that can't be removed from the environment. She may also recommend that you speak to a veterinarian about drug therapy.

CONVENTIONAL ADVICE ALERT

You may be familiar with the advice to confine your cat to a cage or outfit her with an Elizabethan collar so that she can't overgroom. Neither one is a cure. Both confinement and collars simply prevent your cat from doing what it still badly wants to do. This may cause your cat even more stress. And when you eventually remove your cat from confinement or remove the collar, the behavior will immediately resume. Veterinary behaviorist Dr. Karen Overall dryly compares the logic of such collars with the devices used to restrain women who, in the nineteenth century, wanted divorces.[2]

Stop Reinforcing the Behavior

If you are giving your cat any form of attention, either positive or negative, when she is overgrooming, stop. Petting or talking to her to try to soothe her when she's overgrooming can positively reinforce the behavior and make her overgroom even more, while reprimanding her may just create more stress, which could also result in more overgrooming.

ATTRACT the Cat to a New Behavior

Offer Play Therapy

If you see signs that your cat is about to perform the compulsive behavior, distract him by giving him a toy, or play with him using an interactive wand toy. (See The Prey Sequence in Chapter 5.) Don't play with your cat once he's already begun the compulsive behavior, or you will likely reinforce it. Playing with your cat can reduce his pent-up tension and help increase his confidence, which can lower stress and anxiety. You should conduct a play session with your cat using an interactive toy twice a day.

Try Clicker Training

Rewarding him and teaching him tricks through clicker training is especially effective because it can give him enough stimulation to help keep his mind off overgrooming and reduce any stress or tension. (See clicker training in Appendix A.)

TRANSFORM the Territory

Minimize stress, reduce pent-up tension, and add a variety of stimuli in order to keep your cat's mind busy doing things other than overgrooming. Pheromones; free-feeding or food puzzles; a three-dimensional environment of climbing frames and cat tunnels; open boxes with catnip and toys inside; cat trees, window perches, or pieces of furniture arranged in a tiered configuration that allow cats to climb or see out of a window; fish tanks, DVDs made for a cat's viewing pleasure (and rated G of course!) and outside bird feeders—all of these can help entertain and de-stress your cat. I recommend frequent interactive play sessions. Battery-operated toys are also a good source of mental activity. Be sure to rotate toys and their location daily so there's always an element of novelty in the environment. (See Chapter 5 for full details on creating stimulating, stress-free environments.)

If your cat tends to perform her compulsive behavior in one or more specific locations, then you may want to try to keep her away from those places, if it's possible to do so *without causing her more stress*.

WOOL SUCKING AND WOOL CHEWING

It should come as no surprise that kittens develop a powerful drive to suck, since they nurse actively up to about the age of seven weeks. At that age their mother begins rebuffing their efforts during the gradual process of weaning. They may continue to seek out comfort nursing until they're as old as six months. Under normal circumstances the suckling drive should fade after that. But if the weaning is abrupt or occurs too early, the kitten may displace its nursing drive onto non-food surrogates that look or feel like her mother. A kitten without a queen's nipple to nurse is like a human infant lacking mom, bottle, *and* pacifier, and for a kitten, at least, various compulsive behaviors, mainly oral in nature, may be the result. Later, as an adult, she may try to chew or eat items similar to those she sucked on as a kitten, which, while not surprising, is not normal, either.

Undernourished kittens may also develop compulsive oral behaviors, including one called prolonged sucking, a maladaptive reaction to stress and lack of nutrition that redirects the kittens' innate need to suck onto such inappropriate targets as the bodies of their littermates, owners, dogs, or other animals—or even parts of their own bodies, such as their tails, the folds of skin on their flanks, or their vulvas or scrotums. Prolonged sucking may eventually turn into wool sucking, another compulsive and misdirected form of a kitten's natural nursing behavior.

As discussed above, both wool sucking and wool chewing in adult cats may be caused by stress, separation anxiety, boredom, internal conflict, or frustration. Wool sucking (as I'll now refer to both wool sucking and wool chewing) may also have a genetic component. A majority of the cats that develop this behavior issue are pure or mixed Oriental breeds like Siamese or Burmese.[3] However, I've seen it in almost every breed of cat.

Wool sucking behavior may not be a problem unless it results in damage to things you value, such as your clothing or your furniture; or involves sucking or teething on something that could be dangerous to the kitten or cat, such as plastics or electrical cords; or graduates to actual ingestion of nonfood items, which can result in intestinal obstructions, leading to surgery or death. When things get that bad, you have a problem. As Dr. Nicholas Dodman has put it, "Living with a wool sucker of this degree is like living with a ten-pound moth."[4]

POPULAR WISDOM ALERT

Contrary to popular belief, wool sucking doesn't just apply to wool! Cats will suckle or chew many fabrics, including wool (the material of choice among 93 percent of wool-sucking cats), cotton (64 percent), and carpet (53 percent); also synthetic materials such as rubber and plastic (22 percent); paper and cardboard (8 percent);[5] and even themselves, their owner's hair, or another animal's fur. (Because many cats direct their wool-sucking behavior to more than one kind of target, the percentages add up to much more than 100 percent.)

Wool-sucking behavior usually fades over time, but it may reappear in times of stress—just as oral fixations do in people. Next time you're stuck in rush hour traffic, observe the people in the cars next to you. Wanting to move forward, but frustrated that they can't, many of them will chew their fingernails and twirl their hair.

PICA

You'll be glad to hear that most wool-sucking kittens do not go on to chew and ingest nonfood items (but just in case, it's still a good idea to try to divert the kitten into other activities, by using elements of the plan described below). When wool sucking does progress to chewing and eating of nonfood items, it is known as pica, and the reasons for it are similar to those for the other oral fixations.

To remedy any of these oral fixation issues, it's important to try to isolate the reasons for your particular cat's problem. In addition to the many possible causes described earlier, some cats may just be hungry—hungry enough to feel an urge to eat holes in your sofa! Sometimes you may not be able to figure out the exact reasons, but the C.A.T. Plan in this chapter will still help you to manage the problem, even if you can't entirely eliminate it.

MEDICAL ALERT: WOOL SUCKING, CHEWING, PICA

Have your cat checked out thoroughly by your vet to make sure his behavior doesn't stem from a medical issue. Medical causes can include infectious and metabolic diseases such as distemper, liver problems, and diseases carried by ticks; neurological diseases such as psychomotor epilepsy; neoplastic disease of the central nervous system; and disk disease. Dietary imbalances can also cause oral fixations and are best treated by a vet.

Make sure your cat is getting a complete and adequate diet. Talk to your vet for recommendations, and see my recommendations for when to feed your cat in Chapter 5.

Under no circumstances should you resort to tooth removal. It's cruel and does nothing to address the underlying condition. And it may end up making the problem even worse since your cat might progress to ingesting nonfood substances whole without chewing, which could be very dangerous for him.

C.A.T. Plan for Wool Sucking, Chewing, and Pica

CEASE the Unwanted Behavior

Remove Stress Triggers

Take a good look at your cat's environment and eliminate or reduce any stress triggers. See Chapters 3, 4, and 7 for clues to triggers caused by conflict or frustration. Other stressors include fighting among resident cats, outside cats, separation anxiety, boredom, visitors whose presence causes fear or anxiety in the cat, and changes in the schedule—either yours or the cat's.

Add Dry Food to the Diet

If your chewer or eater is a kitten, she may be teething. If you are feeding her only wet food during her teething stage, you should be sure to give her some dry food, too, so that she has something to chew on to help with the teething process. Otherwise, she may chew on hard objects like the ends of books and the corners of laptops in order to soothe her gums. Ouch! Some adult cats may also crave the crunch of dry food, and its use has been proven to reduce or eliminate sucking, chewing, and ingestion of nonfood items.

Feeding your cats more frequently, or free-feeding them, may also help reduce their interest in nonfood items.

Make Nonfood Items Inaccessible—or Unappealing

If your kitten or cat is chewing on or ingesting nonfood items, the single most effective solution may be just to keep such items out of his reach. For pica, this can definitely be the most effective solution.

If that's not possible, you can try applying a bitter antichew product (see catwhispererproducts.com) to the items you want your cat to refrain from sucking, chewing, or eating. Be sure to apply enough, or you may not get the desired deterrence. For at least thirty days, leave the distasteful items strategically located in places where you know your cat will find them. You should monitor your cat to make sure the bitter antichew product is effective enough that it prevents him from ingesting the item; if one product or taste doesn't work, try using others until you find one that effectively deters your cat. Over time, your cat will learn to stop eating or chewing the forbidden items because they taste so bad.

ATTRACT the Cat to a New Behavior

Distract and Refocus

If you see your cat eyeing a potential target or getting in a position to chew, distract her by giving her a toy, or engaging her in a prey sequence.

Provide novel feeding opportunities to help your cat release pent-up energy or anxiety and replace the unwanted behaviors with other ways of soothing, diverting, stimulating, and comforting herself. You could hide several small bowls of cat food around the house, or tuck treats into hiding places that will be easy for her to find, or provide food puzzles to arouse her foraging and hunting instincts. (You may need to show her how the food puzzles work.)

Offer Substitutes

See the Plant Eaters sidebar, in Chapter 5, for types of greens to make available to your cat.

Make Adjustments to the Diet

Adding fiber to a cat's diet has been shown to reduce wool sucking, chewing, and ingesting behaviors, even if the behaviors are not necessarily *caused* by a diet lacking in fiber. Talk to your vet about giving your cat an extra source of fiber such as canned organic pumpkin (*not* the pie filling). If the vet approves, you could start by adding about one-quarter to one-half a teaspoon to your cat's wet food each day—or just put it on a plate by itself, as some cats like the taste and will eat it right up.

HIGH-FIBER DIET ALERT

Many clients have come to me about compulsive oral behaviors after their cats have been on a high-fiber weight-loss diet for a long time. Depending on the cat and the diet, the problem could be too much fiber and not enough nutrients, which can leave the cat feeling unsatisfied after eating and cause him to start to eat nonfood items.

Offer Free-Feeding

In case the cat is actually hungry, you could also try free-feeding (see Chapter 5) between scheduled meals, or provide your cat with more feedings throughout the day. You're increasing only the frequency of feedings, not the total calories, so weight gain is not really a concern. A timed feeder may be more convenient for some cat owners.

Try Clicker Training

Clicker training can help promote desirable behaviors and activities that stimulate, exercise, and divert your cat and make him feel more self-confident and relaxed—and less stressed.

TRANSFORM the Territory

To decrease stress and create a stimulating environment, follow the Territory suggestions in the C.A.T. Plan for overgrooming, and review Chapter 5.

If this C.A.T. Plan does not substantially reduce or eliminate the problem behavior within thirty days, your cat may have a disorder that requires medication. When in doubt, see your vet.

FELINE HYPERESTHESIA SYNDROME

Eek! Your cat may seem to see things you can't, dash around the room for no reason, and even morph from calm to fierce in an instant. Maybe the skin along his spine suddenly ripples, he starts pulling at his own tail, or biting his own leg. Is he possessed? Schizoid? It's more likely that he suffers from Feline Hyperesthesia Syndrome (FHS), also known as Rolling-Skin Disease. No one knows for sure what causes it, but it can manifest in seizurelike behaviors that may have a neurological basis, or in behaviors similar to the compulsive activities described earlier in this chapter, or in both. Hyperesthesia means, essentially, hypersensitivity—to any sensory stimuli. I've included a discussion of it in this chapter because it is often mistaken for compulsive behaviors, even though its causes, insofar as we understand them, are different.

Here's what hyperesthesia looks like: One moment a cat will be resting peacefully, when suddenly his skin starts to twitch or ripple. His eyes may become dilated, he may twist himself around to frantically groom or chew at his hindquarters or even attack a region of the lower half of his body, or he may suddenly take off running, as if to get away from himself. Because this condition involves a high degree of skin sensitivity, the excessive self-grooming and -chewing that some cats do in an attempt to find relief can cause hair loss, which is why FHS is sometimes mistaken for overgrooming. A cat with this disorder may appear restless and vocalize excessively or pace back and forth. These cats can also be very sensitive to touch along the back; FHS episodes may actually be triggered by petting a cat in this region. Another way this syndrome presents is as unprovoked aggression, which can disappear as quickly as it appeared. Any kind of stress or upset may trigger an episode of hyperesthesia in a cat who has a predisposition to it.

Treatment

If you think your cat may be exhibiting signs of FHS, please be sure to visit your vet for thorough diagnostic testing to rule out other health issues, and then get the help of a behavior specialist. This is one syndrome that's definitely too difficult for you to deal with on your own, which is why I'm not presenting a C.A.T. Plan for it. The one general piece of advice I *can* give you is that while FHS is not caused by stress, it can be triggered or exacerbated by it. It's important to remove stressors and tension from your cat's life, and to provide playtimes with wand toys and other interactive toys. Do adhere to the environmental guidelines in Chapter 5.

Of all the behavior problems for which medication is prescribed, compulsive behaviors like those described in this chapter are among those that will most benefit from it. In fact, medication may be not only useful but necessary. For serious cases of overgrooming, wool sucking and its variants, and for FHS, you should consult with a veterinarian about using psychoactive medication to help disrupt the psychological trigger for your cat's behavior cycle. But medication will be much more effective when used in conjunction with the behavioral plans outlined in this chapter.

Afterword

"I have no gift of words, but I speak the truth."
— *Mowgli's brothers*, The Jungle Book

IN SPITE OF MY EARLY IDEA OF MYSELF AS A KIND OF ALICE holding tea parties for my cats in a wonderland of my own devising, I suppose in the end I was at least as much Mowgli, from *The Jungle Book*. There was only one brief period in my late teens when I was not surrounded by a veritable menagerie of different species all at once, including but extending far beyond the feline kind. My friends were onto something when they said that I was raised by animals.

I'm very grateful for the unself-conscious time I spent among the animals in my childhood. When you learn about animals at a young age, as I did, you realize that you can't really *tell* them to do anything—not by shouting and not even by "whispering." And of no animal is this more true than of cats. The secret to being a "cat whisperer," as it were, is to be a cat listener—to learn to *listen* to what they are telling you about their needs and desires, and to *see* the world through their eyes.

Cats have taught me much, including a lot about the human species and, especially, myself. I hope this book brings you at least a fraction of what cats and other animals have given me. I really don't think I could ever be completely happy without having them around me. They have always been my truest friends.

I know it is possible for you to live in complete harmony with your cats, in a state of mutual calm and contentment. Practice looking at your world through their eyes, and the rest will come.

APPENDIX A

Clicker Training for Cats

CLICKER TRAINING, A FORM OF OPERANT CONDITIONING, IS A reward-based training system that can train your cat to repeat desirable behaviors in only a few minutes a day. Instead of ineffectively reprimanding your cat when he does something you don't like, you will use positive reinforcement to promote behaviors that you *do* like. If you want to discourage him from jumping on the counter, you'll reward him when he's on the floor or his cat perch. If two cats who often feud with each other are in the room together minding their own business, you will use clicker training to reward that behavior. If your cat often attacks you in the hallway, you will click and reward him whenever he doesn't. Cats learn by experience. They will more frequently perform behaviors, or manage to end up in locations, that bring rewards. They will tend to stay away from behaviors or locations that do not (or that are actively unpleasant, such as a counter with sticky tape on it).

Here, very briefly, is how clicker training works: When your cat has performed a certain behavior, or has refrained from an undesirable behavior (such as swatting you as you pass in the hallway), you will click the clicker and immediately give him a treat. When you give your cat a treat at the same time he hears the clicker, he will begin to connect the dots and realize that the clicker means something positive and that it only goes off when he performs a certain behavior. The great thing about clicker training is that you can mark a behavior very accurately, at the exact moment it's performed, and from all the way across the room. Very efficient!

There is only one prerequisite: Your cat must be motivated by treats or food for clicker training to work. Later, after the initial training, you can experiment with the effectiveness of other rewards, like petting, brushing, or playtime.

Clicker training will stimulate your cat's mind and help prevent the wide array of behavioral problems that can be caused by a mundane, unstimulating environment. It's also a great way to build a cat's confidence, play with him, rebuild damaged bonds with him, and help him release pent-up physical and mental energy (this last is especially useful in eliminating compulsive behaviors). Clicker training can increase your chances of success in introducing and reintroducing cats (see Chapter 4), and can be very helpful in helping feral cats become more relaxed and behave more predictably and pleasingly. If you're introducing a new person to the household, having that person do the clicker training can provide the resident cat with an experience that's predictable and positive, so that she views the presence of the newcomer—the click-and-treater—as welcome, a source of good things. So get those husbands and boyfriends, wives and girlfriends on board to do clicker training!

After a few lessons you can gradually ask more from your cat. He will usually experiment with his behaviors to find out which ones receive the click and treat. If your cat loves to roll around and stretch on the floor, you can train him to perform that behavior more, or even to roll over.

I once trained one of my cats, Jasper Moo Foo, to high-five my hand. My cats tend to use their paws a lot so I just used clicker training to shape that common behavior into the high-five. Because he *loves* to be combed (so much that he prefers combing even to his beloved treats), I would click and reward him with a brief combing every time he took an incremental step toward the high-five, such as when he lifted his paw off the ground toward me. Jasper Moo Foo had been high-fiving for years when one day a new kitten, Farsi, watched him doing it and imitated it. Because I made sure to click and treat her that first time, and afterward saw to it that any time she touched her paw to my hand a click and treat were immediately sent her way, she caught on quickly and is now as good a high-fiver as Jasper Moo Foo.

You might think of these behaviors as just tricks having no real value. However, when you clicker train your cat, you're not only teaching him to perform specific desirable behaviors (ideally while using other methods in this book to eliminate unwanted behaviors), but you're setting up a valuable foundation for modifying any problem behavior that arises later. I have a very quiet, problem-free, high-fiving cat household!

Here is what you'll need.

- A clicker, which can be purchased at most pet stores. For cats, I recommend the softest-sounding clicker you can find. Your average small plastic clicker usually works well with cats. If your cat doesn't like the click sound, you can wrap the clicker with tape and a cotton ball to muffle the sound.
- Treats or food that are *immediately* available, highly desirable, and about pea-sized. You'll want to break a larger treat into smaller pieces. For the purpose of clicker training, it's extremely important that your cat desire this food or treat more than any other. The more your cat wants the food reward, the more quickly the training will go. If your cat isn't a big fan of treats, you will need to experiment with different foods. Canned food usually works very well, as do select brand-name treats (see catwhispererproducts.com). But as always, ask your vet before introducing anything new into your cat's diet. If you have food out all the time for your cat, you may have to remove it about three hours before a training session so that he will be more interested in eating. Special note: Some cat owners think that their cat doesn't like treats, but many of these owners expect the cat to take the treat out of their hand. Cats may prefer to take

food off a plate or the floor. I have found that if I drop the treat on the floor, and bat it around for them a bit so that it looks like prey, even the most particular cats will usually eat it.

- Especially in the beginning, you will need a quiet room where your cat has no distractions from noise or from any other animals. Sometimes a small bathroom works best.

STEP 1: CLICK MARKS THE SPOT
(OR THE ACTION)

You first need to teach your cat what the sound of the clicker means, because at first that sound will be just a sound, lacking any positive connotations or associations. But if the sound (the secondary reinforcer) is *immediately* followed by a reward (the primary reinforcer), you will be teaching the cat that the click does indeed have some value.

Once you have the cat in a quiet, enclosed space, press the clicker one time (push in and release—this will produce a double click) and immediately give your cat the food morsel or treat—whatever your cat goes crazy for. When I say immediately, I mean it. Timing is everything! You don't have time to dig the treat out of a bag or your pocket; it has to be instantly available so that the click and the treat occur within one second of each other. Click, treat, click, treat—just like you're reading this now. The more valuable the reward, the more success you will have with clicker training. Again, make sure the treats are small—one piece of his dry kibble, one treat, or a very small morsel of wet food, each about the size of a pea. If you feed your cat too much too quickly, your training sessions will end too soon, so keep food or treats small. Do this activity with your cat several times. Your clicker training sessions will always last only a few minutes, though you may wish to, and can, conduct them several times a day.

Eventually, when your cat hears the click he will look for the food or treat. When he starts doing this, it means he's starting to associate the sound of the clicker with food. With my cats it took only four click-and-treats for them to connect the dots. With other cats, it may take a few clicker sessions over the course of a few days. Every cat is different. Be patient. Do not punish or reprimand your cat if he doesn't catch on right away. Never punish or reprimand your cat!

Once your cat is responding to the sound of the clicker (expecting the food reward to be produced), you can move on to the next step.

STEP 2: PROMOTE DESIRABLE BEHAVIORS

You can now begin clicking and treating any behavior you would like your cat to repeat. If he sits, click and treat this behavior. If he is walking toward his cat tree or scratching post, even taking just a step or two, click and treat these incremental steps that are leading to the behavior you want him to perform — scratching on the post, or climbing on his cat tree. Any behavior that is a step toward the behavior you want to promote is worthy of a click and treat. In other words, the cat doesn't have to perform the entire behavior all at one time in order to receive a click and treat.

Clicker training is multifaceted and can become much more elaborate and quite specialized. I recommend a book by Karen Pryor called *Getting Started: Clicker Training for Cats*. So go ahead and start this very rewarding activity with your cat.

Checklist for Curing Outside-the-Box Elimination

THIS CHECKLIST WILL BE A HANDY RESOURCE THAT YOU CAN come back to again and again to remind yourself of how to keep your cat litter-box happy.

CEASE

- Identify the cat with the problem.
- Make sure he's not urine marking (see Chapter 9).
- See a vet about possible medical causes.
- Clean the soiled areas with enzyme cleaners.
- Check your cat's backside hair length and RSVP with a firm "No" to the Fecal Ball.
- Interrupt and address aggression or threats from any dominant cat deterring your cat from the box (see Chapter 7).
- For stool-related behaviors, rule out middening.
- Associate the soiled areas with a competing drive.
  - Complete prey sequences in the soiled areas.
  - Leave food in the soiled areas (after prey sequence if your cat plays).
- If there are many soiled areas, temporarily make some unattractive by using barriers.

- If you don't mind keeping a litter box permanently in the soiled area, you can put one there.

ATTRACT

- Box number and placement
  - Provide at least one more box than the number of cats or floors, and in challenging cases up to *double* that number during the retraining process.
  - Place boxes where your cat has a good view of the territory.
  - Place boxes on the way to the areas of former soiling.
  - In multicat households, distribute boxes throughout the territory to increase the number of critical pathways to the boxes, decrease feelings of competition for important resources, and minimize the chances of one cat deterring another from using an available box.
  - Avoid:
    - putting more than one box in a laundry room, bathroom, or other crowded or noisy areas
    - putting boxes under windows where outside cats could see your cat
    - putting boxes in locations not easily accessible or hidden, or a long walk away from the main area of the household
    - putting boxes in high-traffic areas
    - putting boxes near nest items (food, water, bed, perching areas)
    - wedging boxes against walls or other objects that decrease the number of entrances and exits to and from the boxes
- Type of box (see Chapter 5)
  - If you're using an automated, self-cleaning box, make sure you have some manual boxes available.
  - If you're using a covered box, take off the cover *now*.
  - Make sure the box is roomy—at least sixteen by twenty inches—but low-sided (i.e., no more than five to seven inches high).
  - Don't use plastic liners.

- Box hygiene
  - During retraining, clean at least twice a day for thirty days, then at an absolute *minimum* once a day (though twice is still best), or as needed for frequency of use and preference of your cat.
  - Get a new box if the box you have is so old (usually six months or older) that the plastic has absorbed stool, urine, or cleaning-solution odors.
- Type of litter
  - Check that the litter is not too hard, too soft, too small, or too large for your cat. Your cat will have his own preferences, so you may have to experiment.
  - Use retraining litter for thirty days and then a maintenance litter.
  - Litter levels, generally two to three inches high, should not be too high or too low, and once the right level has been achieved, you should maintain that level, replacing the discarded litter with equal amounts of fresh litter when you clean the box.
  - Unless you are willing to scoop out pellets twice a day or entirely replace them often generally try to avoid pellet litters.
  - Avoid paper-based litters. Most cats dislike soggy litter.
  - Litter should not have a smell that is unappealing to the cat, as pine-scented and perfumed litters often do.
  - I do not recommend corn litters or wheat litters, which are food substances that conflict with cats' urine and stooling drives.

TRANSFORM

- Keep the area well lit, night and day
- Minimize stress.
  - Plan ahead to reduce the stress caused by changes inside the home (e.g., introducing a new spouse, see Chapter 7), the addition of new furniture (make it attractive by using the cat's own and synthetic pheromones), or the arrival of a

new baby (have a friend come over with an infant to get your cat used to babies).
- Avoid sudden changes to important resources (change of food brands, litters, or location of food or water, just to name a few).

APPENDIX C

Behavior Tools

THE MANUSCRIPT OF THIS BOOK WAS FINALIZED IN EARLY JUNE 2012. To be sure that you have the most up-to-date recommendations on products, be sure to consult www.catwhispererproducts.com. Products reviewed and recommended there include:

- pheromones (spray, plug-in, and collars)
- holistic remedies such as essential oils and flower essences
- remote deterrents (including outdoor deterrents)
- interactive wanded toys
- battery-operated toys
- litter boxes
- maintenance litters
- retraining litters
- litter attractants
- cat trees
- cat perches
- cat beds
- scratching posts and pads
- cat food
- timed feeders

- automatic litter boxes (if you must)
- treats
- food puzzles
- cat tunnels
- cat videos
- bitter antichew products
- walking jackets, harnesses, and leashes
- water fountains

Also provided are links to:
- vets who don't perform toe amputations
- vets who donate their time to sterilization

Acknowledgments

I am forever grateful to my literary agent, Michelle Brower of Folio Literary Management, and my editors at Random House Publishing Group, Beth Rashbaum, Caitlyn Alexander, Kelli Fillingim, and Hannah Elnan for believing in my cause and dealing with my severe lack of organization. For additional editing, John Babbitt also deserves a big thanks. I want to thank my son, Joel, for putting up with all the cat hair on his clothes and backpack each day, and for being understanding of the time I've had to put into this book. You are a true animal lover and have a big heart, and I'm proud of who you are.

I want to thank artists Tamara Hess and Maya Wolf for their concerted efforts with the cat drawings in this book. I am grateful to kindred spirit, friend, and cat aficionado Holly M. Sorensen and family, including her Russian Blue, Puck, as well as to young Daphne Sorensen for allowing Puck to contribute to the book. Thanks to Leo Lam, my photographer, and his cat, Spotty Dotty (most beloved cat in the fashion industry), for all the beauty you create toward a greater love of cats.

I want to thank all the clients and compassionate, hardworking veterinarians I've helped and learned from over the last twenty years. I am in your debt, and continually grateful for your trusting me to help your clients with their cat behavior issues. I would also like to thank and gratefully acknowledge Dr. Jim Shultz, DVM, for his enthusiastic involvement and contribution to this book.

To Ua, my heart thanks you for your love and support that, in the end, made this book possible.

I will always be grateful to Inge Cheatham, true animal lover and my biggest fan and supporter. Thank you for believing in me and for your love. I will never forget you.

And the last, and certainly the biggest, thanks to Cameron Powell, without whom this book would not be as good as it is. Thank you, too, for your dedication and belief in me and my dreams.

Notes

Introduction

1. Bonnie Beaver, *Feline Behavior: A Guide for Veterinarians,* 2nd edition, p. 20 (Elsevier Science, St. Louis, MO, 2003).

2. Beaver, p. 5 (4 to 9 million are euthanized every year), p. 131 (70 percent of the 10 million in shelters are euthanized). Borchelt, 1991; Sung and Crowell-Davis, 2006, Patronek et al., 1996 (cited in Aileen Wong, *Management of Cats with Inappropriate Elimination*).

3. news.nationalgeographic.com/news/2004/09/0907_040907_feralcats.html. In metro L.A. alone, estimates suggest that there are more than 2 *million* feral cats, as compared to only 45,000 dogs. See www.spay4la.org/pages/facts.html.

4. www.hsus.org/pets/issues_affecting_our_pets/pet_overpopulation_and_owner ship_statistics/us_pet_ownership_statistics.html.

5. Karen Overall, *Clinical Behavioral Medicine for Small Animals,* p. 11 (St. Louis, Missouri: Mosby Inc., 1997). Note that cats also have extensive vocal and nonvocal communication, and reach sexual maturity before they reach social maturity.

6. Of the top ten reasons for pet relinquishment of dogs to shelters in the United States, only one is related to behavior (biting), and it is a relatively rare problem ranking ninth among reasons given. By contrast, cat behavior problems are not only more common numerically, but are more likely to be cited as the reason for cats being sent to shelters. Problems ranked first (too many cats and the problems they cause), seventh (soiling), and tenth (aggression) are among the most common reasons for relinquishment of cats, all of which are related to *preventable behavior.* Source: www.petpopulation.org/topten.html.

ONE

1. Louis Liebenberg, *The Art of Tracking: The Origin of Science* (Sterling, VA: International Publishers Marketing Inc., 1990).

2. Richard Rudgley, *The Lost Civilizations of the Stone Age*, p. 109 (New York: Touchstone, 2000).

3. Rudgley, p. 109.

4. Liebenberg, p. 4.

5. Carlo Ginzburg, "Clues: Roots of an Evidential Paradigm," in *Myths, Emblems and Clues*, trans. John and Anne C. Tedeschi pp. 96–125 (London: Hutchinson Radius, 1990).

6. Beaver, p. 139.

7. Jeffrey Moussaieff Masson, *The Nine Emotional Lives of Cats: A Journey into the Feline Heart*, p. xv (New York: Random House, 2002).

TWO

1. "If You're Aggressive, Your Dog Will Be Too, Says Veterinary Study," *ScienceDaily*, University of Pennsylvania (February 18, 2009). Retrieved August 2, 2009, from www.sciencedaily.com/releases/2009/02/090217141540.htm. The study also examined the results gotten by dog owners who, often violently, played alpha with their dogs, as popularized by "TV, books and punishment-based training advocates." They often elicited "an aggressive response from at least 25 percent of the dogs on which they were attempted."

Dr. Overall states that "in the case of the dominantly aggressive dog, it is known that such dogs dislike being stared at, dislike being physically reprimanded, and become more aggressive if they are reprimanded or physically forced to do something (such as lie down or move from a piece of furniture)." Karen Overall, *Clinical Behavioral Medicine in Small Animals* p. 3 (St. Louis, MO: Mosby Inc., 1997).

THREE

1. Stephen Budiansky, *The Character of Cats*, p. 16 (New York: Penguin Group, 2002) (emphasis in original).

2. Beaver, p. 4.

3. Dennis C. Turner and Patrick Bateson, *The Domestic Cat: The Biology of Its Behaviour*, 2nd ed., p. 230 (Cambridge, U.K.: Cambridge University Press, 2000).

4. "Extinct Sabertooth Cats Were Social, Found Strength in Numbers, Study Shows," *ScienceDaily*, University of California–Los Angeles (October 31, 2008). Retrieved August 1, 2009, from www.sciencedaily.com/releases/2008/10/081031102304.htm.

5. Miklósi Á., Polgárdi R., Topál J., and Csányi V., "Use of Experimenter-given Cues in Dogs," *Animal Cognition*, 1998;1:113–121; Gacsi M., Miklósi À., Varga O., Topál J., Csányi V., "Are Readers of Our Face Readers of Our Minds? Dogs

(*Canis familiaris*) Show Situation-Dependent Recognition of Humans' Attention." *Animal Cognition*, 2004; 7:144–153.

6. James A. Serpell, "Domestication and History of the Cat," in Turner and Bateson, p. 180.

7. Serpell quoting Reay Smithers in Turner and Bateson, p. 180.

8. MacDonald, Yamaguchi, and Kerby, "Group-living in the Domestic Cat: Its Sociobiology and Epidemiology," in Bateson, p. 105.

9. Beaver, p. 219.

10. Beaver, p. 11.

11. Overall, p. 52.

12. Dennis C. Turner, "The Human-cat Relationship" in Turner and Bateson, p. 196.

13. Beaver, p. 67.

14. Beaver, p. 5.

FOUR

1. Jon Bowen and Sarah Heath, *Behaviour Problems in Small Animals: Practical Advice for the Veterinary Team*, p. 30 (St. Louis, MO: Elsevier/Saunders, 2005).

2. Bowen and Heath, *Behaviour Problems*, pp. 29–30, 198.

FIVE

1. Beaver, p. 219.

2. Beaver, p. 220.

3. Nicole Cottam and Nicholas Dodman, "Effect of an Odor Eliminator on Feline Litter Box Behavior," *J. Feline Med Surg.*, 2007; 9(1): 44–50. Cottman and Dodman (2007).

SIX

1. Overall, p. 174.

2. Overall, p. 175. However, medication can be useful in getting the spraying to stop while the owner has a chance to make the critical changes to the cat's environment and get all the urine cleaned up once and for all.

SEVEN

1. Budiansky, p. 186.

2. Claude Beata, "Understanding Feline Behavior," World Small Animal Veterinary Association World Congress, 2001, available at http://www.vin.com/VINDBPub/SearchPB/Proceedings/PR05000/PR00025.htm.

3. Beaver, p. 4.

4. Overall, p. 5.

5. Budiansky, p. 75.

6. Some studies suggest, unpersuasively to my mind, that play in cats has no evolutionary adaptation or maturational purpose.

7. Plataforma SINC (May 1, 2009), "Dogs Are Aggressive if They Are Trained Badly," *ScienceDaily*. Retrieved August 2, 2009, from www.sciencedaily .com./releases/2009/04/090424114315.htm.

8. Stefanie Schwartz, "Cat Fights: Aggression Between Housemates," January 1, 2002, www.iKnowledgenow.com.

9. I'm grateful to Sarah Hartwell for her lucid description of the defensive postures in her article "Cat Communication and Language," at www.petpeoples place.com/resources/articles/cats/27-cat-communication-language.htm.

EIGHT

1. Beaver, p. 251.

2. Beaver, p. 259.

3. Beaver, p. 11.

4. Stefanie Schwartz, "Litter Training Your Kitten or Cat," January 1, 2002, www.iknowledgenow.com.

NINE

1. Beaver, p. 255.

2. Beaver, pp. 251, 118; Overall, p. 74.

3. Bradshaw and Cameron-Beaumont, "The Signalling Repertoire of the Domestic Cat and Its Undomesticated Relatives," in Turner and Bateson, p. 85.

4. Curtis, citing Hart and Barrett, 1973; *Paws and Claws*, February 10, 2009.

5. Gary Landsberg, "Why Practitioners Should Feel Comfortable with Pheromones—the Evidence to Support Pheromone Use," p. 2 (paper presented at the North American Veterinary Conference, January 7, 2006), accessible at www.iknowledge.com.

ELEVEN

1. See Beaver, p. 234; Overall, p. 251 (citing Morgan and Houpt [1990]).

2. Overall, p. 253.

3. Nicholas Dodman, *The Cat Who Cried for Help* (New York: Bantam Books, 1999).

4. Karen Swalec Tobias, "Feline Onychectomy at a Teaching Institution: A Retrospective Study of 163 Cases," *Veterinary Surgery*, July–August 1994, 23(4):274–80.

5. See cats.about.com/od/declawing/f/uslaws.htm, accessed September 23, 2009.

TWELVE

1. Beaver, p. 75.

2. Overall, p. 225.

3. Beaver, p. 229.

4. Nicholas Dodman, "Wool Sucking," www.petplace.com/cats/wool-sucking/page1.aspx, accessed August 29, 2008.

5. Beaver, p. 229.

Index

About the Author

MIESHELLE NAGELSCHNEIDER is one of the nation's most renowned and sought-after cat behaviorists. In addition to working with thousands of cat owners in person, by phone, and online, she has consulted with vets to help them deal with the problem behaviors that their clients complain about and that they themselves have with their own cats. The Cat Behavior Clinic, which she founded, opened in 1999 and serves clients all over the world. She has been featured in *USA Today, Cat Fancy, Real Simple,* and *Feline Wellness,* and on Animal Planet's *Must Love Cats,* Martha Stewart Living Radio, Salon.com, Pawnation.com, and NBC's Petside.com, and she serves on the advisory council for Pet360 .com. She lives in Portland, Oregon, with her family and nine animals: six cats, two dogs, and one monitor lizard.

www.thecatbehaviorclinic.com